# IMPERIAL DEMOCRACY

## The United States since 1945

**MELVYN DUBOFSKY**
*State University of New York at Binghamton*

**ATHAN THEOHARIS**
*Marquette University*

Prentice-Hall, Inc., Englewood Cliffs, New Jersey 07632

*Library of Congress Cataloging in Publication Data*

DUBOFSKY, MELVYN, [date]
   Imperial democracy.

   Bibliography
   Includes index.
   1. United States—History—1945–present.  I. Theoharis,
Athan G.  II. Title.
E741.D82  1983      973.92      82-12342
ISBN 0-13-451740-7

*Chapters 2–3 of* Imperial Democracy *incorporate parts of Chapters 22–23 of Dubofsky, Theoharis, and Smith,* The United States in the Twentieth Century: *Chapter 4 incorporates parts of Chapters 24–25; Chapter 5 incorporates parts of Chapter 27; Chapter 6 incorporates Chapter 27, pp. 435–437; Chapter 7 incorporates parts of Chapter 28; Chapter 8 incorporates parts of Chapters 26 and 30; Chapter 9 incorporates parts of Chapters 29–30; Chapter 10 incorporates parts of Chapters 31–32; and Chapter 12 incorporates parts of Chapter 33.*

PRINTED IN THE UNITED STATES OF AMERICA

10  9  8  7  6  5  4  3  2  1

ISBN 0-13-451740-7

PRENTICE-HALL INTERNATIONAL, INC., *London*
PRENTICE-HALL OF AUSTRALIA PTY. LIMITED, *Sydney*
PRENTICE-HALL CANADA INC., *Toronto*
PRENTICE-HALL OF INDIA PRIVATE LIMITED, *New Delhi*
PRENTICE-HALL OF JAPAN, INC., *Tokyo*
PRENTICE-HALL OF SOUTHEAST ASIA PTE. LTD., *Singapore*
WHITEHALL BOOKS LIMITED, *Wellington, New Zealand*

# CONTENTS

## CHAPTER THREE
# FROM FAIR DEAL TO HOT WAR, 1948–1952        **33**

## CHAPTER FOUR
# THE GENERAL AS PRESIDENT:
## *The Politics and Diplomacy of Stability, 1953–1960*        **57**

## CHAPTER FIVE
# ECONOMIC GROWTH AND A CONSUMER SOCIETY, 1950–1970        **85**

# PREFACE

Two firm beliefs governed the writing of this book. First, we do not believe that facts speak for themselves. Nor that the truth can be found simply in accurate transcription of the historical record. Quite the contrary. Rendering the past into meaningful patterns requires the intervention of human intelligence. Thus we, as historians, seek to make sense of the "blooming, buzzing confusion" that is the past. In the words of the historian William H. McNeil, "only by acting *as if* the world made sense can society persist and individuals survive."

Second, we believe along with George Orwell that "Who controls the past controls the future. Who controls the present controls the past." This book tries to help students understand better their recent past in order to enable them to deal with present perplexities and shape future tendencies.

Writing about the recent past (what some call contemporary history), however, is fraught with perils. On the one hand, we are deluged with details. Facts and "news" bombard us from every side. On the other hand, we lack the perspective that chronological distance alone provides. When all seems so fresh and vital, the trees dominate the forest, the gilt appears as good as the gold. How does one decide what is ephemeral, merely a passing fad, and what will prove durable? How does one separate that which will seem insignificant about our time from that which will appear of great importance to historians a century or more from now? How can we know that public decisions represented the central objectives of political leaders? Will the declassification of documents suggest a far different reality?

Frankly, we have no simple solutions to the dilemma of writing contemporary history. Like all of us, we, too, are partially prisoners of our heritage and times. We lay no claim to sole possession of the truth. Nor do we pretend that our view of recent American history is the only one, or necessarily even the best one.

What we do suggest is that our history of the last thirty-five years brings some order out of confusion, weaves patterns out of diversity. It also strives to make students think seriously about the late twentieth-century world in which they find themselves. Our title, "Imperial Democracy," captures what we see as the dominant theme or pattern of the recent American past, the tension between the imperatives of empire and democracy.

The United States came out of World War II as the most powerful nation-state on the globe. Moreover, after the war, United States leaders, unlike their predecessors of the World War I generation, accepted and acted on the responsibilities of global power. But they did so in a divided world, one in which the Soviet Union organized a competing bloc of "socialist" nations with a different vision of the future. The ensuing contest between the forces of liberal democracy and socialist collectivism shaped all aspects of American politics, economics, society, and culture. The battle seemed to imperil not just American values but also the nation's basic security. Technological developments permitted instant communications and broke down a traditional sense of isolation. Oceans provided no impenetrable barriers against modern nuclear weapons, at the same time as the third world was swept by forces that upset the existing balance of power. After almost two centuries of "free security," the United States could no longer take its future safety for granted.

This new reality generated much of the tension between the impulse to empire and that to democracy. An imperial nation required a large professional military and a worldwide intelligence capability—new phenomena in the American experience. This necessitated a more powerful and centralized national state bureaucracy. In order to implement America's global responsibilities and to protect vital national interests, Washington policymakers expanded the size and scope of the domestic and foreign intelligence agencies. Secrecy, spying, and covert activities became a normal part of the national government's imperial design. Inevitably, then, the openness, decency, and humaneness associated with democracy conflicted with the imperatives of world power.

Thus the stress on national security developments and intelligence agencies in the book's diplomatic-political chapters is by design, not accident. The history of the intelligence and national security communities both at home and abroad explains much about the behavior of an "imperial democracy." Believing that the clash between imperial responsibilities and democratic desires is at the heart of the contemporary American experience, we focus much of Chapters 2-3 and 8-11 on the national security state and its significance. This may seem strange and even unwarranted in a general text. We think that it will make the recent past more intelligible to students.

Domestically a somewhat different tension made itself felt, that between equality of opportunity and equality of condition. In practice, equality of opportunity produced gross inequality of condition. Moreover, full equal opportunity rarely existed. The factors of class, race, and gender handicapped many in the American opportunity derby. Yet as long as the domestic economy grew rapidly (the reality from 1945 to 1970), the tension between the two forms of equality remained submerged. For those who lacked even equality of opportunity—mostly nonwhites and women—economic growth alone provided slight succor. And in the mid-1970s, as economic growth slowed, Americans faced a "zero-sum" society in which some could gain only as others lost. This intensified the tension between equality of opportunity and equality of condition. Thus Chapters 5, 7, and 12 seek to inform students about the realities of class, race, and gender as well as the role of workers and the labor movement in contemporary America. For citizens in today's world, the relationship between the two forms of equality remains an inescapable presence.

A final word about the book's contents and themes. Why, many will ask, is there so much about politics, diplomacy, and economics, and so little about art, literature, and ideas (culture)? In answer we can only confess that neither of us pretends to be a cultural or intellectual historian. Nor are we expert in any way about contemporary art, literature, music, or film. We might also say that, difficult as it is to distinguish the forest from the trees in the jungle of contemporary history, it is harder yet to separate cultural silk from dross, lasting patterns from passing fancies. People's basic beliefs, traditions, and mores (what French historians call *mentalite*) change only slowly and incrementally. To differentiate a long-term shift in values from short-term popular trends requires a grasp of long periods of time that a history of the last thirty-five years alone forecloses. Political, diplomatic, economic, and some forms of social history at least provide precise dates and firm benchmarks, which enable the historian to weave perceptible patterns on the loom of the recent past.

We offer this book, then, not as gospel or truth. Rather we write it in gratitude to those among our students during the past two decades who made us ponder more thoughtfully and wisely about what it means to be a citizen of the United States and the world in the last quarter of the twentieth century. We hope that the students who read this book will ponder similar questions and, perhaps, find answers. It is for them to create a nation and world in which people can live decent, humane lives, and most important, *survive*.

*Melvyn Dubofsky*
*Athan Theoharis*

# CHAPTER ONE
# THE UNITED STATES IN 1945

The spring and summer of 1945 was a time of joy and sadness for the American people. Joy in the fall of Hitler's Germany and its unconditional surrender to the Allies in May. Greater joy three months later on August 14, when the Japanese, too, surrendered. The war was over. Church bells pealed, men, women, and children filled the streets to celebrate raucously, and automobile horns tooted the sounds of victory—peace, at last, no more killing—the GI's would soon be home.

Yet sadness blemished the elation. On April 12, 1945, Franklin Delano Roosevelt died. For millions of Americans who had chosen him president four times, a beloved leader had fallen. The man who had revived spirits during the depths of the Great Depression and led the World War II Grand Alliance to the brink of victory was gone. The torrent of tears shed by Roosevelt's mourners suggested his irreplaceability.

No sooner had Americans recovered from the trauma of Roosevelt's death than more horrible revelations stunned them. Throughout the war years rumors and news spread of a Hitler-inspired campaign to exterminate all Jews and lesser breeds of people. Such stories seemed too horrible to believe. Then, as the Allied armies swept across Poland and Germany in April and May 1945, the unimaginable became real. At Bergen-Belsen, Buchenwald, Dachau, and most horribly at Auschwitz, the conquering troops saw the remnants of a people annihilated. Corpselike concentration camp survivors greeted their liberators as did the even more numerous dead bodies piled in mass graves or scattered about the campgrounds. Everywhere was the stench of death and also its apparatus: the gas chambers and crematoria. The victors thus bore witness to the greatest crime of the twentieth century—the Holocaust. And a new word entered the everyday vocabulary, genocide!

The Allies too had used a new and terrible weapon to compel Japan to sue for peace. Not once but twice in 1945, on August 6 and 9, the United States dropped atomic bombs on Japan. The new president, Harry S. Truman, when he had learned from his advisers about the successful test of an atomic weapon in the desert of New Mexico, wrote in his diary: "We have discovered the most terrible bomb in the history of the world. It may be the fire destruction prophesied in the Euphrates Valley Era, after Noah and his fabulous Ark."

Aware of the new weapon's destructiveness, Truman ordered its use "so that military objectives and soldiers and sailors are the target and not women and children." But the bombs were not dropped on isolated military bases. Instead they fell first on the city of Hiroshima and then Nagasaki.

Mass graves at the Belsen Concentration Camp, c. 1945 (U.S. Office of War Information/National Archives)

A new age dawns (Official U.S. Airforce Photo)

Civilian men as well as women and children were indiscriminately incinerated or irradiated in two dense urban centers. Yet Truman had few qualms about his use of the new weapon. "Let there be no mistake about it," he wrote in his *Memoirs*, "I regarded the bomb as a military weapon and never had any doubt that it should be used." Insisting that he never lost sleep over his decision and would do it again if he had to, Truman observed, "It was merely another powerful weapon in the arsenal of righteousness."

Thus did World War II end in the shadows of the Holocaust and the mushroom cloud. Thus did its close produce joyous celebrations yet also expose the full dimensions of man's inhumanity to man.

## POSTWAR DILEMMAS

The end of the war also stirred doubts about the future of America. Recall that for nearly all Americans, the most recent peacetime experience was the Great Depression. For those whose memories of the 1930s were still fresh, peace could very well mean a stagnant economy, mass unemployment, domestic discontent, and class struggle.

The war had changed all that and much more. For almost five years, a war economy boomed, jobs chased workers, and Americans earned more than they could spend. If during the Great Depression women worked only at the least-skilled, lowest-paid jobs, and nonwhites were fortunate even to find jobs, the war economy opened new opportunities for both women and nonwhite workers.

But what would peace bring? When twelve million men and women were discharged from military service, how would the economy absorb them? With factories no longer producing tanks, planes, jeeps, guns, and munitions, how would workers find jobs? How would an economy and a society that for five years had tolerated government-set prices and wages, the planned allocation of materials and peoples, and the commanding presence of national authority adjust to the elimination of wartime controls and the diminution of federal power?

The past offered no solace and few hopeful guidelines. When peace last came to America in 1918, it had brought surging inflation, violent class conflict, racial violence, and the infamous "red scare." Would 1945-1946 repeat that experience? Or would the new peace only restore the status quo ante, that is, a semiparalyzed capitalist system whose most notable feature was mass unemployment?

Even deeper fears underlay war's end. Would the United States "lose" the peace as it had in 1919? The "war to end all wars" had proved an illusion. Only a generation after Woodrow Wilson's great crusade, the world erupted into an even more global and costly struggle. Would the peace of 1945 prove any more durable? If not, what future awaited a world cursed with nuclear weapons?

Such were the dilemmas and questions which faced the American people at the end of World War II. The future of the nation and also the world depended on how the United States, in 1945 unquestionably the globe's wealthiest and most powerful nation-state, responded to the reality of peace.

## WAR'S DOMESTIC LEGACY: PERSISTENCE AND CHANGE

Global war had left few aspects of domestic politics, economics, and society untouched. Yet beneath the surface the more things changed in the United States, the more they had remained the same.

Americans had always been a people on the move. War accelerated mobility. White Americans moved increasingly from the Northeast and Midwest to the Southwest and especially the West Coast, where the airplane and shipbuilding industries boomed. Black Americans, however, migrated most heavily to the older industrial heartland in the mid-Atlantic and Great Lake states. Between 1940 and 1950 every state in those two regions gained in black population, while every former Confederate state, except Forida, lost blacks (the net loss totaled almost thirteen million, the largest proportion of whom left Alabama and Mississippi). And now, more rapidly than ever, people deserted the nation's farms. Between 1942 and 1944, nearly six million people left agriculture. Perhaps more remarkable, migrants, who traditionally had been overwhelmingly male, were now increasingly female. Indeed, three out of every five civilian migrants were women.

People, whether they stayed put or moved, also lived differently during the war. More women, especially married ones, worked for wages. The rate of female labor force participation rose by 24 percent, reaching in 1944 a peak of 19,370,000 women workers. Women not only took jobs customarily allocated to them but also worked at positions hitherto reserved for men. Former waitresses, clerks, and hairdressers left poorly paid service employment for higher wages in coke plants, steel mills, shipyards, airplane factories, and on the railroads.

The economic necessities of war also benefited black Americans. By 1943 the number of skilled black workers had doubled and the proportion of semiskilled had risen more steeply. And nearly two-thirds of the one million blacks who took war jobs were women.

Despite the changes in female and black employment patterns wrought by the war, much remained the same. Divorce rates did not rise and, more important, birth rates reversed a long decline—in 1943 reaching the highest level since 1927. But for married women wage work brought added burdens. Most female workers not only toiled a full day; they still ran the household, which was made more onerous by wartime rationing, long food lines, and the lack of daycare centers for young children. Also implicit at the time was the notion that when the war ended and the "boys" came home, single women would surrender skilled industrial employment and married women would return to the home. The sanctification of the family during the 1950s and the postwar baby boom had their roots in the years 1941 to 1945.

Afro-Americans also experienced reminders of oppression as well as opportunities. Despite a presidential proclamation (Executive Order 8802) banning discrimination in employment on all federal defense-contract related work and establishing a Fair Employment Practices Commission (FEPC), employers remained loath to upgrade black workers. North American Aviation, for example, stated: "The Negro will be considered only as janitors and in other similar capacities." The absolute shortage of workers, not federal orders or awakened consciences, led many employers to alter racist hiring practices.

Afro-Americans, moreover, found it hard to obtain decent housing and recreational facilities. When they sought better off-the-job living conditions, blacks frequently fought with local whites. Such black-white friction could explode into open confrontation, as happened during the summer of 1943 "race riots" in Detroit and Harlem. Indeed, the Detroit "riot" was so violent that in the midst of a global war, federal troops were sent to the Motor City to maintain domestic peace.

If nonwhite Americans benefited economically from the imperatives of war, they remained socially more vulnerable than others. The 1943 "race riots," which included attacks on young Chicanos in Los Angeles and the Southwest as well, proved the explosiveness of racial divisions, even in a time of national peril.

Wartime prosperity may have saved many small businessmen from failure and opened fresh opportunities for aspiring entrepreneurs. But its greatest rewards went to large corporations. Executives from the largest corporations served as the administrators of federal war-production efforts. They saw to it that their own firms and other giant corporations received the bulk of prime federal contracts—thirty-three corporations receiving over one-half of the $175 billion in prime contracts allocated between June 1940 and September 1944. Small business received proportionately less, principally as subcontractors to the corporate giants. A war economy had, if anything, functioned to further the concentration of corporate power in the United States and to increase the assets of firms on the list of *Fortune*'s 500. Indeed, corporate profits after taxes increased from $6.4 billion in 1940 to $10.8 billion in 1944.

Organized labor, too, made substantial gains during the war. Yet union successes did not prove to be an unalloyed triumph for workers. Federal policies and rulings enabled labor to overcome the resistance of the last major antiunion corporations, mostly Ford and Republic Steel, and to achieve a level of inplant organizational security previously unimaginable. By 1944 more than twelve million workers, almost 30 percent of the civilian nonagricultural labor force, belonged to unions. In return, labor leaders had to surrender much. They were no longer free to bargain with employers as unimpeded private parties. Federal agencies and administrators set basic employment conditions, which corporations and unions were then to implement. As a result, labor leaders often served not as the advocates of rank-and-file unionists but as agents who disciplined workers in the interest of greater efficiency and productivity. In the words of one student of wartime labor relations, federal policies bequeathed trade unionism an "ambiguous legacy." More secure and powerful in 1945 than ever before, organized labor was less militant in its relations with corporations and the federal government.

All the changes occasioned by war minimally affected the general distribution of wealth and income. In 1946 the top fifth of the population received 46.1 percent of personal income compared to the 5.0 percent received by the bottom fifth. Wealth holding was more concentrated, with 50 percent or more of the population possessing no economic resources other than small amounts of war bonds or savings accounts. Wartime prosperity and full employment notwithstanding, a Senate committee reported in January 1944 that twenty million Americans "dwell constantly in a borderland between subsistence and privation, where even the utmost thrift and caution do not suffice to make ends meet."

## NEW DEAL, GLOBAL WAR, AND A TRANSFORMED PRESIDENCY

Surprisingly, war had not altered the traditional American pattern of politics as usual. The 1942 congressional elections occurred as if all was normal, and Republicans built on their gains of 1938 and 1940, capturing 44 additional seats in the House (222–208) and 9 in the Senate (57–38). Two years later, the presidential election followed an equally conventional pattern. Renominated for an unprecedented fourth term, Roosevelt stressed economic themes. He reminded voters that the Republicans were the party of Hoovervilles and bread lines. While Republican nominee Thomas E. Dewey endorsed the New Deal, he sought to exploit antilabor and anti-Communist themes. Republicans warned: "You don't have to 'Clear Everything with [CIO President] Sidney [Hillman].' Vote Republican and keep the Communists, Hillman and [Communist leader Earl] Browder, from running your country and your life." The candidates, Roosevelt and Thomas E.

Dewey stressed personalities over principles, rhetoric over issues, slander above truth. In the event, the New Deal coalition proved invincible for a fourth time with Roosevelt winning 3.6 million popular majority (25,606,000 total votes—53.4%) and 432 electoral votes. Democrats lost strength among farmers, rural folk, and middle-class city dwellers. But Roosevelt's support held firm in larger cities among union members, Catholics, Jews, most ethnics, Afro-Americans, and also the white "solid South." The New Deal coalition remained in 1945, as it had been at its acme in 1936, a contradictory amalgam of non-Protestant, urban, working-class ethnics and rural, evangelical Southern Protestants, most nonwhites, and those most commited to "white supremacy."

War, however, speeded the transformation of the presidency and the reach of federal power which had started with the New Deal. From 1941 through 1945 federal authority became extended to what had formally been exclusively private areas. All men had to register with their draft boards and more than twelve million were conscripted. Federal labor policies compelled workers to join unions. Federal agencies set prices and wages, and rationed the amount of meat, sugar, coffee, and gas Americans could consume. And, for the first time in their lives, most ordinary working Americans felt the impact of the federal income tax, as their higher earnings placed them in taxable brackets and the withholding system, a wartime innovation, reduced their weekly take-home pay.

The insinuation of federal power into the everyday lives of citizens paralleled an enormous expansion of presidential authority. The president appointed the administrators who set prices and wages, allocated materials to manufacturers and consumers, and managed the domestic war effort. These officials were solely responsible to him. It was the president who issued proclamations creating fair employment practices and interning Japanese-Americans in concentration camps. As commander-in-chief, the president made basic military decisions, whether to pursue a particular strategy against the Japanese in the Pacific or when and where to open a second front in Europe. He also committed the nation to numerous diplomatic undertakings through executive agreements and wartime conferences not subject to congressional approval. And he used the FBI, as a presidential police agency, to engage in forms of domestic political surveillance hitherto considered improper—including investigating prominent conservative critics of his administration's foreign policy such as Former Republican President Herbert Hoover. All these manifestations of an imperial presidency were either overlooked by Congress and the judiciary or sanctioned by the Supreme Court in *Hirabayashi* v. *U.S.* and *Korematso* v. *U.S.* (1944) in cases involving Japanese internment.

It was unlikely that federal power and presidential prerogatives would shrink back to pre–New Deal levels. Postwar Americans would have to come to terms with the federal leviathan and the imperial presidency.

## FROM GRAND ALLIANCE
## TO COLD WAR

Victory in the war had depended on cooperation among the Big Three: the United States, Great Britain, and Soviet Russia. So, too, did a stable and peaceful postwar world.

It was no easy matter to establish good feelings among the Big Three. Since the 1917 Bolshevik Revolution Americans had been encouraged to distrust the Soviet government and its international objectives. Now they had to be reeducated. Roosevelt, the Office of War Information, and Hollywood began the process. Soviet resistance against the Nazis and Russian victories at Stalingrad and elsewhere in 1942 furthered the course of reeducation.

Complicating this relationship, the Soviets suspected the intentions of their Western allies. Every Anglo-American delay in opening a second front on the European continent intensified such Soviet fears as did the later apparent United States moves toward a separate peace with Italy and Germany.

While he lived Roosevelt proved a master at allaying Soviet fears and calming the American public. Big Three conferences, first at Teheran (1943) and then Yalta (1945), cemented Allied cooperation. In June 1944, the second front was established when the Anglo-American forces invaded France. At Yalta Stalin won Roosevelt's acceptance for Soviet security interests in Eastern Europe. In return, Stalin pledged Soviet intervention in the war against Japan, democratic elections in liberated Poland, and compromises with the United States concept of a postwar United Nations to preserve the peace.

Beneath the surface, however, differences divided the allies. Roosevelt, like Woodrow Wilson a generation before, believed that the United States stood above power politics and harbored *no* territorial designs of its own. When Churchill and Stalin discussed the postwar order in terms of spheres of influence, Roosevelt accused them of practicing imperialism. To which an exasperated Churchill retorted in Parliament in January 1945: "What are power politics? . . . Is having a Navy twice as big as any other Navy in the world power politics? Is having the largest Air Force in the world, with bases in every part of the world power politics? Is having all the gold in the world power politics?"

Roosevelt's death in April 1945 complicated relations among the already uneasy allies. His successor, Harry S. Truman, was ill-prepared for the delicacies of global diplomacy. Truman and his advisers, on the one hand, sought amity and continued cooperation with the Soviets. Yet, on the other hand, they pursued policies fated to poison Soviet-United States relations. Because the Russians refused to allow liberated Poland to reestablish its own government, as the Americans and British rightly claimed the Yalta agreements required, Truman protested Soviet behavior in Eastern Europe. And while the United States demanded a voice in regions on the Soviet Union's western frontier, it denied the Soviets a coequal voice in liberated Italy and France. In May, Truman had cut lend-lease aid to Russia, further irritating Stalin.

When the Big Three finally met at Potsdam, near Berlin, from July 17 to August 2 to make final arrangements for the restoration of postwar Europe, tensions among the allies proved stronger than cordiality. They quibbled over occupation zones in Germany, reparations payments, and the future of Poland. Truman and his advisers complained to each other about Soviet intransigence and Stalin's determination to establish Eastern Europe as an exclusive Soviet sphere. The president refused to be open with Stalin about the successful development of the atomic bomb. Aware of the United States breakthrough in nuclear weaponry, Stalin might have suspected that Americans intended to use their atomic monopoly as a diplomatic club. If only six months earlier Yalta had represented the high tide of Big Three amity, Potsdam symbolized its ebb.

A week after the Potsdam conference closed, the United States dropped its atomic bombs on Hiroshima and Nagasaki. Not only did the nuclear weapons lead Japan to sue for peace, they served as an American warning to Russia, a clear reminder of the real balance of military power in the summer of 1945.

The mushroom clouds that rose over Japan presaged man's inability to build as well for peace as for war. The post–World War II generations were to endure under the perpetual shadow of nuclear extinction. Peace was to become as perilous as war for the duration of what quickly came to be called the Cold War.

## THE PROSPECT AHEAD

In the late summer of 1945 nothing could outweigh relief at the end of war. It was time to rejoice in the blessings of peace, not to bewail an uncertain future. It was a time to welcome the victorious troops home, not to worry about battles yet to come.

Americans had much to be thankful for in 1945. Despite a rapid reconversion from war to peace, the quick elimination of many wartime economic controls, and the demobilization of millions of servicemen and women, the United States prospered. Federal power did not atrophy to prewar or pre–New Deal levels. Instead, Congress in 1946 passed a law—the Employment Act—which mandated that the federal government accept the responsibility for guaranteeing full employment through national economic planning for prosperity. Subsequent federal decisions to rebuild war-torn

Europe and extend New Deal income security measures, combined with the release of wartime savings, fueled an economic boom.

Not even the most severe strike wave in United States history (1945-1946), involving more than 4.5 million workers in almost 6000 strikes, retarded economic expansion. In 1945 to 1946, unlike 1919 to 1920, employers did not seek to operate plants with strikebreakers or attempt to smash trade unions. Instead, sometimes with federal intervention and sometimes without, corporations and unions engaged in hard collective bargaining. The major industrial unions won substantial wage gains for their members and the corporations gained the right to pass on added costs in the form of price increases. In return for raising wages and bargaining constructively, corporations also compelled labor leaders to respect managerial prerogatives and to promise to discipline unruly workers.

By 1946 Americans had come to terms with the type of modern industrial society that John Kenneth Galbraith made famous in his 1952 book, *American Capitalism*. Galbraith asserted that the United States had achieved stable prosperity under a system in which three primary power centers—big business (including agriculture), big labor, and big government—countervailed each other to the benefit of the consumer. The outcome of the 1945-1946 strike wave apparently confirmed Galbraith's description of social reality. The New Deal followed by the wartime planning experience had seemingly taught Americans how to make capitalism stable and beneficent. People thus decided to enjoy postwar prosperity, as they prepared to embark on the greatest consumption spree in American history.

# CHAPTER TWO
# BUILDING THE POSTWAR GLOBAL-DOMESTIC ORDER, 1945–1948

The cracks in the Grand Alliance that opened at the Potsdam conference of July 1945 foretold the tenor of relations among the victorious allies in the postwar world. With Germany and Japan defeated, the two surviving world powers—the United States and the Soviet Union—eyed each other warily. Their cooperation during World War II had broken a tradition of U.S.-Soviet hostility dating back to the 1917 Bolshevik Revolution. No longer compelled by wartime needs to collaborate, United States and Soviet policy makers soon began to challenge each other's postwar aims. United States officials saw Soviet efforts to secure Russia's western flank by control of the Baltic, East European, and Balkan nations as a part of a Kremlin plot to advance communism everywhere. Soviet leaders viewed the emergence of the United States as the world's preeminent power as a threat to Russian security. Mutual suspicions insured tense relations between the former wartime allies. Both sides opposed each other's objectives but without resorting to military action—a situation soon aptly described as "Cold War."

From our present perspective it can be seen that neither side alone bears the onus for the Cold War. After the end of World War II, Stalin pursued traditional Russian national security goals in Eastern and Southern Europe while solidifying his personal power domestically. To the new American president, Harry S Truman and British Prime Minister Winston

Churchill, however, the Soviet ruler's actions violated wartime agreements. To them, the Soviet Union sought to seize control of Poland and other Eastern European countries. Previously, Churchill, and less so Roosevelt, had conceded the Soviet Union's need for "friendly governments" along her frontiers. Truman balked at what he characterized in 1946 as enforced "sovietization." Given the deep-seated fears of Soviet expansions held by prominent conservatives and ethnics, open acceptance of Soviet policy in Eastern Europe by the administration was politically risky even though a milder opposition might have moderated Soviet behavior and lessened the intensity of the ensuing Cold War. The United States, to be sure, had its own, if more benevolent "sphere," in Japan and Latin America.

U.S. policy makers had traditionally not been principally concerned about Eastern Europe, nor had the area been a target for U.S. overseas investments. Regardless, the prospect of Soviet political expansion in Eastern Europe after the war created anxiety among U.S. policy makers who feared the further spread of Soviet influence into the heart of Western Europe. The war, moreover, had badly shattered the economic and social systems of Western Europe. Truman's advisers were worried that communism, feeding on disorder and decay, could make serious inroads in such countries as Italy and France and might even come to power by parliamentary means. In 1946 and 1947, U.S. policy makers began to devise measures to contain Soviet influence and hold Western Europe for democracy and liberal capitalism. In the process, they did not sharply distinguish between Soviet influence and indigenous radicalism, and defined the problem in Western Europe in terms of Soviet military power and expansionist designs. Despite demobilization in 1945 and 1946, however, the United States possessed the world's second largest army, largest navy, an atomic monopoly, and an economy unharmed by war's destruction.

Each side felt threatened as fears fed upon fears, insecurities upon insecurities. The postwar period thus shattered the wartime hopes of most Americans for a peaceful, democratic, and free trade world, based upon great power cooperation and the United Nations. Once again, as had happened in 1918 and 1919, American desires for a democratic and liberal capitalistic world order seemed threatened by communism.


## THE BREAKDOWN OF
## BIG THREE COOPERATION

Even as World War II ended, Big Three amity collapsed. The first diplomatic attempt to implement the general principles agreed to at Yalta and Potsdam, the London Foreign Ministers Conference of September 1945, ended in deadlock when Soviet Foreign Minister V.M. Molotov rejected western complaints about Soviet-imposed governments in Rumania and

Bulgaria. Responding to the American objection to a closed Soviet "sphere" in Eastern Europe, Molotov protested Soviet exclusion from an equal voice in Japanese occupation policy. The greatest stumbling block to amity between the Soviet Union and the West throughout 1946, nonetheless, remained Poland. Despite promises to hold "free and democratic" elections, the Soviets in 1947 established a Communist satellite government in Poland. Soviet troops also continued to occupy northern Iran, despite a wartime agreement for the prompt withdrawal of British and Soviet forces. These troops were withdrawn only in early 1946, in response to western pressure. The Soviet Union meantime menaced Turkey, demanding a new treaty that would permit the Soviets to establish bases within the strategic Dardanelles. Civil war raged in Greece between the western-backed conservative government and Communist-led rebels.

Simultaneously, the Soviet press denounced the West and reemphasized the ideological theme of hostile capitalist versus Communist worlds. In a February 1946 address, Stalin reaffirmed the validity of the Marxist-Leninist thesis of permanent rivalry between the two competing systems. A new Soviet five-year plan was launched to prepare the Soviet Union for possible attack by the hostile capitalist powers.

Strangely, Stalin's militant language contrasted strikingly to his cautious behavior. In 1945 and 1946, he neither supported the Greek rebels nor urged French and Italian Communists to seize power. Whatever his reasons, Stalin recognized Western spheres of influence, as he expected the Anglo-Americans to tolerate Soviet spheres. Stalin became more threatening in late 1947. Soviet leaders established the Cominform in September, demanded among Communists everywhere a "hard line" recognizing the division of the world into two opposing camps, and denounced Western European socialists as "social fascists" or "social traitors."

Despite the initial limits of Soviet expansion, which were consistent with the "spheres of influence" agreement Churchill had first suggested to Stalin in October 1944, the former British Prime Minister[1] in a speech at Fulton, Missouri, on March 5, 1946, denounced Soviet policy. He called for an Anglo-American alliance to lift the "iron curtain" which Stalin had dropped across the center of Europe "from Stettin in the Baltic to Trieste in the Adriatic." Delivered in President Truman's home state with the American president a silent witness on the platform (Truman had read the speech in advance and U.S. officials had coaxed Churchill to adopt a hard line), Churchill's Fulton speech signalled the formal beginning of the Cold War.

This was clearly highlighted by the strained relationship among the former allies over the question of postwar policy toward Germany. The deterioration in U.S.-Soviet relations since 1945 rendered it impossible to manage Germany through the Four Power Control Commission. Eager for

[1] His government had been defeated in the 1945 British general election.

compensation and unconcerned about German feelings, the Soviet Union stripped her zone of industrial equipment and even current production. Food and raw materials were also not shipped to the western zones as agreed upon at Potsdam in exchange for reparations. The British and the Americans—France initially was uncooperative as she had her own designs upon Germany—believed that they would be required to export food to their zones indefinitely to prevent mass starvation. They were also convinced that Germany must reindustrialize more fully and rapidly than previously planned in order to bolster the economic revival of Western Europe. Consequently, in May 1946 Great Britain and the United States halted the dismantling and shipping of industrial equipment from their zones to the Soviets. Soviet officials in turn treated their zone as virtually a closed area, placing German Communists or subservient Germans in positions of power, prohibiting independent political parties, confiscating all large estates, closing all banks and accounts, and nationalizing most industries.

President Harry S Truman, inexperienced in statecraft but resolute, decisive, and loyal to his advisers, soon tired of what in February 1946 he called "babying the Soviets." Even then, Truman and Secretary of State James F. Byrnes sought to allay Soviet fears of a German military revival. In April 1946, Brynes offered the Soviet Union a four-power treaty guarantee for twenty-five years against German rearmament. When the Soviets responded coolly, Byrnes at Stuttgart, on September 6, 1946, clarified the administration's "policy of firmness and patience." The United States, he declared, would not retreat from Germany. Instead it would keep troops there as long as necessary. Germany would not become a pawn between East and West, its living standard would not be reduced further, and Germany would pay no more reparations until it had become economically self-sufficient. Subsequently, on December 2, 1946, the British and Americans formally merged their zones into Bizonia. France joined in 1949, thus laying the basis for the Federal Republic of Germany (West Germany). Soviet leaders responded with a Communist-ruled government in East Germany.

Not all Americans were pleased by the Truman administration's firmer foreign policies. Until 1948 some influential spokesmen still believed in the possibility of cooperation with the Soviets. Henry A. Wallace, formerly FDR's secretary of agriculture (1933-1944) and vice president (1941-1945), and in 1946 secretary of commerce, regarded himself as the heir to the New Deal policies at home and abroad. Wallace publicly challenged Byrnes's policy in an address in New York City on September 12, 1946, six days after the secretary of state's Stuttgart speech. The Soviet Union naturally would socialize her spheres of influence as the West democratized its spheres. Still, he argued, the Soviet Union did not threaten Western Europe. A hard-line policy, he noted, would merely sharpen world tensions: "The tougher we get, the tougher the Russians will get." Wallace called instead for mutual trust and cooperation.

Areas annexed by USSR
Areas controlled by Poland
Allies of U.S., 1955
Allies of USSR, 1955
Independent communist states, 1955

**Division of Europe, 1945–1955**

Byrnes responded to Wallace's challenge by threatening to resign unless President Truman repudiated the commerce secretary. Truman promptly dismissed Wallace. Seeking to wrap himself in the mantle of the New Deal, Wallace denounced the evolving Truman policy of containment and in 1948 became the presidential candidate of the Progressive party. He was decisively defeated as many liberals rallied behind Truman's program of anti-Communism abroad and domestic reform at home.

## A RADICALLY TRANSFORMED PRESIDENCY

The impact of the emerging Cold War was not confined exclusively to international politics. Even more profoundly, the Cold War contributed to a substantial expansion of presidential powers and to the evolution of a more secretive and globalist foreign policy.

Pearl Harbor and World War II had seemingly confirmed the need for greater coordination across the military services and for improved intelligence gathering and dissemination capabilities. Reacting to these lessons, Congress enacted the National Security Act of July 26, 1947. Debate over this act centered on its provisions to unify the armed services. Yet, the measure's most far-reaching changes involved the creation of the National Security Council (NSC) and the Central Intelligence Agency (CIA). In effect, this act centralized executive control over foreign policy by creating institutions for planning foreign policy, and estimating resources and capabilities, totally under presidential control. Because the personnel appointed to these agencies would not be confirmed by Congress, they were protected against congressional scrutiny. In time, Truman also established by executive order an elaborate classification system restricting congressional and public access to intelligence information, planning papers, and policy decisions.

Of equal consequence, the presidency grew bureaucratically as Executive Office staff employees expanded from 600 to 1200. No longer simply preparing the federal budget, the Bureau of the Budget also acted as the clearing house for departmental legislative proposals. The bureau's legislative reference service and the requirement that all departmental recommendations receive bureau clearance permitted the president to exercise tighter control over the budgetary and legislative requests of federal agencies. Simultaneously, Truman reorganized his White House staff. The legal counsel to the president (Clark Clifford until 1949, thereafter Charles Murphy) assumed responsibility for coordinating the staff's activities, and met daily with the president and weekly with key White House personnel. Additional administrative innovations enabled specialized staff members to use their knowledge best and to concentrate their lobbying efforts. Administrative expansion and reorganization enhanced Truman's ability to shape national policy. These changes did not, however, insure that Truman could achieve his full foreign policy and legislative programs.

These institutional changes coincided with an increasing presidential resort to so-called executive privilege claims. First enunciated by President

Truman on March 13, 1948, to justify his refusal to honor a subpoena from the House Committee on Un-American Activities for the loyalty file of Bureau of Standards director Edward Condon, executive privilege claims were employed six times during Truman's presidency to reject a variety of congressional demands for information. Because they insulated presidential planning from congressional scrutiny, executive privilege claims altered executive-legislative relations. Moreover, on September 24, 1951, President Truman issued an executive order (10290) extending classification restrictions to include civilian agencies.

When enacting the National Security Act of 1947, the Congress intended to rationalize decision making—in the language of the measure to "provide for the establishment of integrated policies and procedures for the departments, agencies, and functions of the Government relating to the national security." Concerns about Soviet power and objectives soon altered the function of both the CIA and the NSC. Foreign-policy decision making became even more centralized in the executive branch. Congress's decision, in the Central Intelligence Act of June 20, 1949, to exempt the CIA from normal budgetary accounting requirements furthered such executive centralization.

Alarmed by the political appeal of Western European Communist parties and Communist control of the French trade union movement, Truman administration officials reacted quickly. An overseas "psychological warfare" capability was needed as well as non-Communist European trade union movements. The State Department, however, refused to assume responsibility for financing and directing such programs. It contended that intervention in the internal affairs of Western European states would compromise the department's integrity and ability to operate diplomatically. Accordingly, relying on a vague provision of the National Security Act of 1947—empowering the CIA to "perform such other duties and functions related to intelligence affecting the national security as the National Security Council may from time to time direct"—the NSC issued two directives, NSC 4A on December 19, 1947, and NSC 10/2 on June 18, 1948. The CIA was directed in December 1947 to undertake covert psychological operations to counter Soviet subversion in Western Europe—including subsidizing French and Italian trade unions and publications. In June 1948 a special CIA division was created, the Office of Policy Coordination, to execute covert operations. A special review board, the 10/2 panel, was created with limited authority to evaluate all proposals to initiate covert action proposals.

The initial decision to assign covert operations to the CIA—despite the language of the 1947 act confining its functions to intelligence coordination—derived from the CIA's having agents in the field and unvouchered funds. As covert operations became more common, a formal review mechanism was needed—thus the 10/2 panel. By 1951, covert operations had become a central element in the Truman administration's Cold War arsenal. Accordingly, on October 23, 1951, NSC 10/5 authorized the expansion of the CIA's worldwide covert operations ("subversion against hostile states, including assistance to guerilla and refugee groups, and support of indigenous anti-Communist elements in the countries of the free world") and vested planning for covert operations exclusively within the CIA in the newly created Office of Policy Coordination. The CIA now subsidized anti-Communist publications, political parties, and trade unions, and further sought to support guerilla movements within Soviet-dominated Eastern Europe. Moreover, a special branch within the Office of Policy Coordination, Program Branch 7, created in 1949, assumed planning responsibilities for such covert actions as assassination, kidnapping, sabotage, and countersabotage.

This expansion of the CIA's responsibility from intelligence gathering to covert operations had been unplanned. Nonetheless, U.S. foreign policy was thereby revolutionized: Decisions to launch covert operations were executed without being known or subject to congressional control. In theory, Congress might still retain exclusive power to declare war and to fund executive agencies. In practice, highly sensitive executive decisions had become insulated from congressional scrutiny. Such freedom as well as real concern over Soviet activities encouraged Truman and his successors to turn to the NSC and the CIA for the formulation and execution of foreign policy—thereby relegating the State Department to a secondary role.

Motivated by Cold War concerns, the Truman administration also authorized a recognizably illegal international communications interception program, Operation SHAMROCK. During World War II, officials of the international telegraph companies (RCA Global, ITT World Communications, and Western Union International) had allowed military censors to screen all messages passing through their terminals. After 1945, U.S. military officials sought continuance of this practice, by targeting messages of the Soviet Union and her satellites. Unwilling to assume the legal risks intrinsic to the program, in 1947 and again in 1949, company officials secured assurances from Truman administration officials that they would neither be prosecuted nor exposed for violating provisions of the Federal Communications Act of 1934. And, in November 1952, with a similar desire to widen U.S. international intelligence capabilities, President Truman established by a secret executive order the National Security Agency (NSA) to which he assigned control over communications intelligence.

The expansion of the CIA's role, the creation of NSA, and the authorization of Operation SHAMROCK had major policy consequences. In effect, they symbolized the institutional impact of the Cold War: High public officials now consciously authorized illegal intelligence activities by secret executive actions and shielded them from congressional or public scrutiny.

## THE TRUMAN DOCTRINE
## AND CONTAINMENT

The Truman Doctrine signaled the final abandonment of official hopes for cooperation with the Soviet Union and the formal resort to measures to contain Communist expansion in Europe. On February 21, 1947, the British government advised the Truman administration that it could no longer finance Greek and Turkish resistance to Communist penetration. Truman and his advisers seized this opportunity to launch a new policy to contain Soviet power and influence in the eastern Mediterranean. Heeding the advice of Republican Senator Arthur H. Vandenberg to "scare hell out of the country," Truman on March 12, 1947, addressed a joint session of Congress and requested $400 million for military and economic aid to bolster Greece and Turkey. After starkly describing the Communist threat to Greece and Turkey, the president warned the American people that a peaceful and free world could never be realized "unless we are willing to help free people to maintain their free institutions and their national integrity against aggressive movements that seek to impose upon them totalitarian regimes." Having unsuccessfully protested Soviet violations of the Yalta agreements that imposed Communism on Poland, Rumania, and Bulgaria, the United States must now prepare to aid others to resist enslavement: "I believe that it must be the policy of the United States to support free peoples who are resisting attempted subversion by armed minorities or by outside pressures."

Most Americans responded positively to the president's address. A few conservatives feared that an open-ended commitment to containment might bankrupt the United States; some liberals contended that the administration was weakening the United Nations by bypassing it. Still others, such as the columnist Walter Lippmann, warned against an ideological holy crusade against Communism. A Republican-controlled Congress, however, in a display of bipartisanship under Senator Vandenberg's guidance, approved the Greek and Turkish aid bill in July. It was an epochal step. The Truman Doctrine signified the United States' assumption in a time of nominal peace of long-range commitments and obligations to contain Communism. Initially focused upon Europe, the doctrine rejected a diplomacy of accommodation for one aimed at limiting most revolutionary change. In time, its premises were extended to East Asia, the Middle East, and Africa, containment becoming in effect a global policy. Finally, despite the president's rhetorical reference to "free peoples," containment did not represent a doctrinaire support of democracy. American aid subsidized governments who resisted Moscow, whatever their character, as exemplified by U.S. support in 1950 of the Communist regime of Tito in Yugoslavia and of such right-wing authoritarians as Syngman Rhee in Korea, Chiang Kai-Shek in Taiwan, Francisco Franco in Spain, and Antonio Salazar in Portugal.

The philosophy of containment, publicly enunciated by "Mr. X," the

State Department adviser George F. Kennan, in *Foreign Affairs* in July 1947, placed the Truman Doctrine in a broadened global setting. Carefully analyzing Communist ideology and the nature of the Soviet state, Kennan concluded that Soviet leaders were impervious to argument. Relying upon the Marxist "science" of history, the Soviets continuously pressed forward probing for weak spots, confident of their ultimate triumph. Lasting cooperation and amity therefore were unlikely. Only a counterforce strategy could make any impression upon an ideologically blinded opponent: "The main element of any United States policy toward Soviet Russia must be that of a long-term, patient but firm and vigilant containment of Russian expansionist tendencies." The contest was a test of American maturity as a great power; if a containment policy were followed, Kennan predicted the Soviet Union would either collapse under the pressure of its own internal weaknesses or gradually mellow as a regime. Although in his memoirs, Kennan later wrote that the administration had misconceived the Soviet threat as primarily military, in fact, as dramatized in the CIA's evolving covert operations role, Truman administration officials had viewed it also in political terms and had adopted both economic and military measures to bolster anti-Communist governments in Western Europe.

## THE MARSHALL PLAN

The Marshall Plan further underscored the fact that the objectives of containment were economic and political as well as military. In April 1947, Secretary of State George C. Marshall, the retired wartime chief of staff appointed by Truman to that post in January 1947, returned from a futile Foreign Ministers' Conference in Moscow. At that conference Molotov had refused to cooperate in an economic policy for all Germany unless the Soviet Union obtained a share in control of the Ruhr. Marshall instead proposed a western role in controlling Upper Silesia, which the Soviets had already turned over to Poland. Molotov in turn charged that the Anglo-American Bizonia of July 1946 violated the Potsdam Agreement, though he was silent about Soviet violations in seizing current production as reparations and isolating East Germany from the West. Marshall was distressed less over these disagreements than the multiplying signs that Communist parties all across Europe were successfully exploiting growing economic and social disorder.

Despite U.S. aid to Western Europe and Japan of around $14 billion since the end of the war, by 1947 Europe seemed on the verge of collapse. U.S. loans of $3.7 billion to Great Britain and $1.4 billion to France did not repair the damages of war and restore the accustomed British and French trading roles. Germany still lay in ruins and its people endured semistarvation. Europe suffered another blow during the severe winter of 1946-1947, with its freezing weather followed by disastrous spring floods. Mines flooded, factories closed for lack of fuel, and homes went heatless for days. In Great Britain production fell by 50 percent while other countries suffered as severely. As unemployment and misery spread, American policy makers worried that Communism might well triumph by democratic means. Indeed, the Communist polled around one-fourth the popular vote in France and one-third in Italy during the postwar elections of 1945 to 1947.

This concern prompted Marshall to direct State Department officials to formulate a plan to cope with Europe's economic and political crisis. To these advisers, the crisis was primarily one of economic misery upon which Communism fed. They decided that the best program required a cooperative approach whereby Europe would plan its economic needs collectively and the United States would promise to finance a long-term recovery program. To minimize potential Western European opposition to an anti-Soviet policy, the plan as drafted included Soviet participation—but U.S. policy makers were confident that Soviet leaders would refuse to accept the proposal. The Russians would never promote capitalism or release information about Soviet productivity. Western European unity would be encouraged while the United States would be less vulnerable either to charges of anti-Communism or of trying to dominate Europe.

Secretary Marshall announced the new policy in a commencement address at Harvard on June 5, 1947. The European response was immediate and favorable. Britain and France invited the Soviet Union to a meeting in Paris to draft a reply to Marshall. Apparently, Stalin at first viewed the offer as a source of economic aid, for he sent Molotov and a large delegation to the Paris meeting. Subsequently, denouncing the whole proposal as a scheme by Yankee imperialists to dominate Europe, on July 3, 1947, Molotov walked out of the conference. There were several reasons for this Soviet rejection. First, the Soviet Union wanted aid to be given to each state individually and opposed any cooperative planning or controls. Second, Stalin apparently became apprehensive when Czechoslovakia wanted to participate. The Marshall Plan might weaken Soviet control over Eastern Europe. Finally, Stalin feared anything that increased American influence in Europe.

By July 1947 sixteen nations had met to establish the Committee on European Economic Cooperation and to draft plans for a systematic recovery over the next four years. Franco's Spain was excluded, while the Soviet Union and the eastern bloc absented themselves. Although some American conservatives criticized the Marshall Plan as a global giveaway that would bankrupt the United States, most citizens agreed that it was a wise measure to shore up Western Europe against Communism and to prevent American isolation within its hemisphere. Senator Vandenberg again led a bipartisan effort to obtain congressional approval.

An unexpected Communist coup in Czechoslovakia in February 1948 also reduced congressional opposition to a costly aid program. With a coalition cabinet containing nine Communists, Czechoslovakia had sought to serve as a half socialist-half capitalist bridge between East and West, retaining democratic institutions and ties with the Western world while existing within the Soviet sphere of influence. Until the Western powers began to integrate West Germany more firmly into their sphere, Stalin had tolerated an ambiguous status for Czechoslovakia. This ended in February 1948 with the seizure of power by Czech Communist Party leader Klement Gottwald, and the death (whether a suicide or assassination) of Jan Masaryk, the Czech foreign minister and son of the founder of the Czech republic.

In April 1948, Congress appropriated $5.3 billion to implement the Marshall Plan. Over the next five years, the United States expended $13.6 billion for European economic recovery. The Marshall Plan was an immense success as Western Europe's industrial production increased by 200 percent in four years. Communist political influence diminished in the West, and Communists were excluded from the ministries governing France and Italy. The aid worked so effectively because of its planned long-term approach and because Western Europe, unlike many other recipients of American aid, possessed the basic industries, skills, and resources to use it effectively. The Marshall Plan clearly served the enlightened self-interest of the United States, strengthening an area vital to the United States strategically, economically, and culturally.

## THE COLD WAR HEATS UP

Stalin responded to the Marshall Plan by tightening Soviet controls over Eastern Europe and by seeking to discredit the United States and thereby reduce its influence on the continent. In September 1947 the Soviets created the Cominform (Communist Information Agency) to perfect their control over the countries within the eastern sphere. The Czech coup followed, and Communist activists and labor unions precipitated a wave of strikes and protests across Europe to challenge American influence. The pro-Communist artist Pablo Picasso even designed a "peace dove" for this massive anti-American campaign. The United States, Soviet propaganda implied, might wage a preventive war while it still possessed a monopoly of atomic weapons.

The Berlin blockade precipitated widespread fear of war within Europe and America. On June 24, 1948, the Soviets blockaded Western access routes to their zones in Berlin in reaction to Anglo-American attempts to build the German economy. Early in 1948, the British and the Americans established a transitional government for Bizonia and launched a currency reform, foreshadowing creation of the West German state. Stalking out of the Four Power Control Commission (permanently, as it turned out), the Soviets soon imposed a blockade of Berlin.

The Soviet interdiction of the road, rail, and water routes linking the western zones in Germany with western zones over a hundred miles away in Berlin posed a crucial challenge for American leadership. The president was immediately beset by conflicting advice as to how the United States should respond. Some of his advisers saw no choice but to abandon Berlin, arguing that the United States faced vastly superior Soviet armies in Europe and the atomic bomb seemed an inappropriate weapon. Others claimed that the Soviets were bluffing and advised running an armed convoy through East Germany to Berlin. The president chose a middle way between capitulation and force. Without consulting Congress and on his own initiative, Truman ordered an airlift of food and supplies to the western garrisons and the 2.5 million people in West Berlin. Unprepared for Truman's action and recoiling from the prospects of war, Soviet leaders tolerated the airlift. By flying in planes around the clock, the airlift brought in 13,000 tons of supplies, including coal, to Berlin daily. (This far exceeded the estimated daily minimum requirements of 4,000 tons.) After 324 days of blockade, in May 1949 Soviet leaders quietly acknowledged failure and lifted it.

## COLD WAR AT HOME:
## THE POLITICS OF
## DOMESTIC ANTI-COMMUNISM
## AND THE EXPANSION
## OF THE FBI, 1945–1948

If Truman acted boldly and decisively in the foreign arena, his domestic policy role was less dominant. Continually throughout Truman's tenure, leaders of the conservative political and journalistic communities accused his administration of "softness toward Communism" and of being infiltrated by Communists. Senator Joseph R. McCarthy might have ridden charges of "Communists in Government" to national prominence during the early 1950s; he neither invented the tactic nor was he its sole practitioner. The phenomenon of anti-Communist politics was popularly labeled as "McCarthyism" in the 1950s; yet, all the senator from Wisconsin did was to dramatize an issue that had first emerged in 1938.

Conservative critics of the New Deal had consistently attempted to exploit the subversion issue since the 1930s. As part of this effort they supported the formation in 1938 of the House Committee on Un-American Activities (HUAC) and the subsequent annual extension of the committee's authority and appropriations until it was made a permanent committee in 1945. For such House conservatives as John Rankin of Mississippi and J. Parnell Thomas of New Jersey, HUAC served as a forum from which to challenge the loyalty and policies of New Deal personnel. For FBI officials J. Edgar Hoover and Louis Nichols, HUAC was in addition a useful conduit for the dissemination of derogatory information about American radicals and leaks of unsubstantiated bureau charges concerning subversion.

Beginning in February 1946 with a decision by the FBI Executive Conference, the bureau initiated through "available channels" an "educational" campaign about the basically "Russian nature of the Communist party in this country." As part of this "educational" campaign, FBI officials leaked derogatory information from their files to conservative congressmen (Karl Mundt, Richard Nixon, and Joseph McCarthy) and journalists (Don Whitehead, Jim Bishop, Fulton Lewis, Jr., Frederick Woltman, and Walter Trohan). FBI Director Hoover aptly described the positive advantages of leaks to HUAC in 1947: "Committees of Congress have served a useful purpose in exposing some of these [subversive] activities which no Federal agency is in a position to do, because the information we obtain is either for intelligence purposes or for use in prosecution, and committees of Congress have a wider latitude."

HUAC became a serious political threat to the Truman administration only in 1949 in the aftermath of the Alger Hiss-Whittaker Chambers confrontation. A professed ex-Communist, in 1948 Chambers was a senior editor of *Time* magazine. In testimony before HUAC in August 1948, he accused Hiss, then president of the Carnegie Endowment for International Peace and a former employee of the Agricultural Administration Agency (AAA) and the State Department, of having been a member of a Communist cell during the 1930s. At first denying that Hiss or other members of his alleged Communist cell had engaged in espionage, on December 2, 1948, Chambers dramatically changed his accusations. Leading HUAC staff members to a pumpkin patch on his Westminster, Maryland, farm, Chambers produced three rolls of microfilm of classified State Department documents, the so-called Pumpkin Papers, which he claimed to have received from Hiss in 1938. These classified documents were to have been transmitted to the Soviet Union.

Exploiting Chambers's December 1948 testimony, HUAC shifted to focus on internal security. Thereafter, HUAC and its Senate counterpart, the Internal Security Subcommittee of the Committee on the Judiciary, publicized the gravity of the Communist threat to national security. In 1949, HUAC initiated an investigation into espionage in the atomic bomb project. In July 1951, the Internal Security Subcommittee investigated the role of Communists and fellow travelers in the Institute for Pacific Relations, an academic institute specializing in the study of Far Eastern history. The institute, the committee concluded, had shaped U.S. policy toward China thereby contributing to the defeat of the Chinese Nationalists.

Well before then, anti-Communism had become a central issue in national politics. The events precipitating this phenomenon were a June 6, 1945, FBI raid of the offices and private residences of the editors of an obscure Far Eastern periodical, *Amerasia*, and the release in the spring of

1946 of a Canadian Royal Commission report on wartime Soviet espionage. Both events apparently confirmed the existence of a serious internal security problem. The FBI raid had uncovered that the *Amerasia* editors had in their possession 1,700 classified State and Navy department documents. Members of the Canadian Communist party in collaboration with military and scientific personnel, the Canadian Royal Commission's investigation concluded, had sought to transmit secrets involving wartime military installations and technology to the Soviet Union.

Responding to these disclosures, in the spring of 1946, various conservative congressmen demanded the tightening of security procedures for federal employees. In July 1946 a subcommittee of the House Committee on Civil Service recommended legislation requiring that all federal employees be fingerprinted and the establishment of a special committee to ascertain the need for additional internal security legislation. In a companion action, on July 5, 1946, conservative Democratic Senator Pat McCarran introduced a rider to a State Department appropriations bill authorizing the secretary of state to dismiss summarily all individuals whose continued employment he deemed dangerous to the national security. This rider was approved on August 16, 1946.

Republican candidates stressed the loyalty issue during the 1946 congressional campaign. The choice facing the electorate, Republican National Committee Chairman B. Carroll Reece maintained, was "Between communism and republicanism . . . no taint of communism attaches to the Republican party. The same cannot be said of our opposition." Republican candidates denounced continued federal wartime controls, housing and food shortages, postwar inflation, and "monopolistic" labor unions. Republican campaign slogans suggested: "Had Enough? Vote Republican"; "To Err is Truman"; and "Under Truman: Two Families in Every Garage." Truman's unpopularity was so great that pundits affirmed that the president's smartest move was not to campaign for Democratic candidates; in an effort to capture the magic of Truman's predecessor, the demoralized Democrats played recordings of Roosevelt's voice.

This strategy paid off handsomely—Republicans won 25 governorships and for the first time since 1930 gained control of both houses of Congress: 245-188 in the House (with 1 American Laborite) and 51-45 in the Senate. Because of the seniority principle, conservative Republicans became chairmen of important congressional committees. For these Republicans, the 1946 election results and their party's steady gains since 1938 were a mandate to repudiate the New Deal. And their control of committees like HUAC, Judiciary, and Appropriations pushed their assault on the New Deal toward investigations into federal employee loyalty and administration security procedures.

The 1946 election results influenced an administration already concerned about internal security matters. Citing the House civil service subcommittee's recommendation to tighten loyalty procedures, in July 1946, Attorney General Tom Clark urged Truman to institute a federal loyalty program. Truman at first did nothing; the 1946 congressional elections changed all this.

In late November 1946, President Truman appointed the Temporary Commission on Employee Loyalty to study existing loyalty procedures. Eager to retain the initiative, Truman directed the commission to report back to him by February 1, 1947. Political realities virtually insured the establishment of a loyalty program, announced by the president on March 22, 1947. The objective of this program was absolute security: As Truman emphasized, the existence of "even one" disloyal employee would constitute a serious threat to national security.

Truman's loyalty program required all incumbent and prospective federal employees to pass an intensive loyalty investigation administered by specially created departmental loyalty boards. All federal employees were to be covered, janitors as well as atomic scientists. Federal employees were to be dismissed if it were proven that "reasonable grounds exist for the belief that the individual is disloyal to the Government of the United States." "Reasonable grounds" included past or present membership in alleged subversive organizations. Despite having the right to appeal a dismissal ruling, the accused employee was not guaranteed the right to question directly those who challenged his loyalty. To compound matters, in December 1947 the attorney general publicly released a list of alleged subversive organizations. Private, state, and local employers soon used the list to determine the loyalty of their employees.

The administration's haste to thwart congressional conservatives resulted in a faulty yet far-reaching loyalty program. The same hesitancy to resist anti-communist political pressures rendered the Truman administration vulnerable to FBI efforts to expand the bureau's investigative authority. Thus, in July 1946, President Truman approved a recommendation by Attorney General Tom Clark (actually drafted by the FBI) to authorize FBI wiretapping of "subversive" activities. Truman had unknowingly expanded the FBI's wiretapping authority—unknowingly because Clark's recommendation had been proffered as an affirmation of President Roosevelt's May 1940 wiretapping directive. In fact, by deleting a key sentence from that directive, the Clark/Hoover recommendation expanded FBI wiretapping authority to include "subversive activities."

Furthermore, FBI officials secured Attorney General Clark's approval for a "Security Index" program to list "dangerous" persons to be detained in the event of war or "national emergency." Although the FBI had earlier initiated a preventive detention program in 1939, in 1943 Attorney General Francis Biddle had ordered its termination. Technically complying with Biddle's order to end a "Custodial Detention" program, Hoover circumspectly directed FBI officials to continue the program but under a different title, Security Index. FBI officials encountered a more sympathetic attorney general with Clark's appointment in September 1945. Stressing need for such a program (but not advising him of the FBI's ongoing program in violation of Biddle's order), FBI officials in August 1948 obtained Clark's formal authorization.

Ironically, Truman's loyalty program did not disarm congressional conservatives. Almost immediately they challenged the adequacy of the president's program. Responding again to political pressure, the administration appointed individuals holding conservative anti-Communist views to administer the loyalty program. In 1951, moreover, the president revised the standard for dismissal from proof of "disloyalty" to "reasonable doubt as to loyalty." Not accidentally, then, the program was often arbitrary, and some employees were denied a loyalty clearance simply because they opposed racial segregation or subscribed to such left-liberal periodicals as *The Nation* or the *New Republic*.

The institution of a loyalty program soon led to a confrontation between HUAC and the executive branch. In response to a HUAC request for the loyalty file of the director of the Bureau of Standards, Edward Condon, on March 13, 1948, President Truman prohibited department heads from turning loyalty files over to congressional committees unless specifically authorized by the president. Truman's executive order changed the emerging congressional-executive debate from one centering on the adequacy of the administration's loyalty program to one involving congressional prerogatives and the executive's refusal to cooperate with an ongoing congressional investigation. In 1948 and thereafter, Truman's bold assertion of the claim to executive privilege intensified congressional protest from members who charged the president with a desire to "cover up."

## LEGISLATIVE-EXECUTIVE CONFLICT: REBUILDING THE NEW DEAL COALITION AND THE ELECTION OF 1948

A conflict between the president and the Congress had been building over executive powers and the wisdom of New Deal policies. Indeed, HUAC's hearings of 1947 and 1948 coincided with a broader congressional effort to reverse New Deal programs. Congressional conservatives attempted to reverse New Deal reforms by reducing corporate and individual income taxes, and enactment of restrictive labor legislation. In 1947, Congress also approved the Twenty-Second Amendment (ratified in 1951), limiting the president to two terms, delayed reaction to Roosevelt's four-term presidency.

Popular support for legislation to curb the powers of labor unions had increased in reaction to the flurry of strikes in 1945 and 1946. Capitalizing on this sentiment and convinced that the Wagner Act of 1935 was a partisan labor bill, congressional conservatives enacted the Taft-Hartley Act to outlaw "unfair labor practices." This bill specifically prohibited secondary boycotts, jurisdictional strikes, and direct union political contributions; made unions liable for breach of contracts with management; authorized employers to petition the National Labor Relations Board (NLRB) for new representation elections which might decertify unions; denied NLRB rights to unions having Communist officers; and (through the controversial section 14b) permitted individual states to enact laws banning the closed and union shops (so-called right-to-work laws).

Reacting to the plight of almost two million homeless refugees in postwar Europe, many of whom wanted to emigrate to the United States, the 80th Congress enacted the Displaced Persons Act of 1948. The act permitted the admission of only 200,000 displaced persons over a two-year period; its eligibility standards reserved 30 percent for those employed as agricultural workers and 40 percent for former residents of the Protestant Baltic states (thereby discriminating against Catholics and Jews). Furthermore, only those were admissible who had entered Western-occupied zones before December 22, 1945 (eliminating approximately 100,000 more Jews). Condemning the Displaced Persons Bill's "callous discrimination" against Catholics and Jews, Truman nonetheless signed the measure into law on June 25, 1948.

Earlier on June 20, 1947, Truman had vetoed the Taft-Hartley Bill, denouncing it as a "slave labor bill" which would increase labor strife. Although Congress overrode his veto, Truman's action enabled the president to pose as a friend of the workingman. The veto also diminished union hostility to his administration which followed his attempt in 1946 to break a railroad workers' strike.

Unable to shape congressional policy, Truman frequently resorted to the veto, which brightened his liberal image and identified the Republican Congress with reaction. In 1947, the president successfully vetoed a tax-reduction bill, claiming that it granted savings of only $30 to those having annual incomes under $2,000, but $5,000 to those in the $50,000 bracket. Truman also vetoed a protectionist wool bill, pocket-vetoed a bill establishing the National Science Foundation, pocket-vetoed a bill that would have excluded newspaper vendors from social security coverage, and unsuccessfully vetoed a measure exempting motor carrier associations from antitrust prosecutions.

Truman's relations with Congress had changed from accommodation in early 1947 to conflict by late 1947; the switch in tactics also reflected wise politics. Truman would have to acquire a more liberal image, White House Counsel Clark Clifford emphasized in late 1947. Only then could he circumscribe former Vice President Henry A. Wallace's appeal to New Deal liberals who had grown disenchanted with Truman's foreign and domestic policies. Indeed in 1948, the obstacles to Truman's renomination and reelection appeared overwhelming. The Roosevelt Democratic coalition was tottering. The left wing of the party had rallied behind Wallace. Many conservative southern Democrats threatened to defect over the administration's civil rights program. In addition, many labor leaders, particularly in the left-wing CIO unions, opposed the administration's foreign policy, its loyalty program, and its actions in 1946 against railroad and coal miners' unions.

Truman followed Clifford's advice. To retain the support of liberals, labor, and southerners, Truman exploited their fears of the Republican-controlled 80th Congress. Truman wooed liberals (many of them Jewish-Americans) by extending diplomatic recognition to Israel on May 14, 1948, the same day the independent state was created. For Afro-Americans he proposed a bold civil rights program. Finally the president and his supporters sought to "red-bait" the Wallace campaign.

Truman's revival of the New Deal as a Fair Deal, however, almost immediately complicated the president's relationship with the conservative southern wing of the Democratic party. When more liberal party members led by Minneapolis mayor, Hubert Humphrey (then a candidate for the U.S. Senate), compelled the Democratic National Convention to adopt a strong civil rights plank by a narrow vote, 300 infuriated southern delegates walked out. One week later, on July 17, delegates from thirteen southern states convened in Birmingham, Alabama, and nominated a States Rights (Dixiecrat) ticket of Governors Strom Thurmond (South Carolina) and Fielding Wright (Mississippi). That same month, Truman issued two executive orders desegregating the federal civil service and the armed services.

Confronted by divisions and apathy in his own party, Truman developed an aggressive strategy. He revealed its essence in an electrifying acceptance speech delivered at the Democratic convention, in which he announced that he was calling Congress back into special session on July 26 to vote on a series of needed measures, reminding the delegates in a nationwide radio address that the Republican platform of 1948 pledged to enact such proposals. Truman thus sought to dramatize Republican duplicity and make the "reactionary" record of the 80th Congress (Truman's specific phrasing) *the* issue of the presidential campaign. The 80th Congress, Truman subsequently charged, had passed a labor bill that could "enslave totally the workingman," had "stuck a pitchfork in the backs of farmers," and had passed an "anti-Semitic, anti-Catholic" immigration bill. If the Republicans came to power, he warned the voters, America would become "an economic colony of Wall Street."

The Republican convention had been held in July. Their proceedings were harmonious, the Republican delegates having concluded that they were selecting the next president of the United States. New York Governor Thomas Dewey's efficient organization and skillful efforts at projecting an image of statesmanship secured him the nomination on the third ballot. As the Republican nominee, Dewey emphasized the need for unity and for responsible, moderate leadership; he sharply critized Truman's appeals to diverse special interest groups—blacks, ethnics, Catholics, organized labor, farmers. Acting as if he had already won the presidency, Dewey's campaign statements consisted of glittering generalities. Rather than concentrate on key states, Dewey dispersed his campaign appearances in an effort to promote Republican candidacies in closely contested senatorial and gubernatorial races. The Dewey campaign staff, moreover, profited from covert assistance from the FBI—in the forms of derogatory information on Truman's former associations with the corrupt Pendergast machine in Kansas City and the actual preparation of position papers on the Communist issue.

Dewey's optimism flowed from splits in the Democratic party, Truman's unpopularity, and the predictions of professional pollsters and commentators. Sixty-five percent of the nation's dailies editorially supported Dewey, to Truman's 15 percent. In its election eve coverage the *New York Times*, for example, estimated that Dewey would win 345 electoral votes to Truman's 105 and Thurmond's 38. And a *Chicago Tribune* banner headline in an edition that went to press before the election results were in proclaimed: DEWEY DEFEATS TRUMAN.

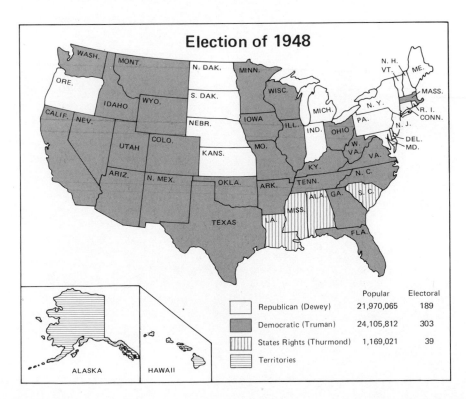

**Election of 1948**

| | | Popular | Electoral |
|---|---|---|---|
| | Republican (Dewey) | 21,970,065 | 189 |
| | Democratic (Truman) | 24,105,812 | 303 |
| | States Rights (Thurmond) | 1,169,021 | 39 |
| | Territories | | |

There was a low voter turn-out in 1948—less than 55 percent of eligible voters. Truman won, polling 24,179,349 popular votes (49.5%) and winning 28 states with 303 electoral votes to Dewey's 21,991,291 popular votes (45.1%) and 189 electoral votes (carrying only 16 states). Thurmond received 1,176,125 popular and 39 electoral votes, carrying the Deep South states of South Carolina, Mississippi, Alabama, and Louisiana. Wallace's candidacy had failed to dent northern urban and industrial support for the Democratic ticket. He polled just 1,157,326 popular votes. The defection of southern conservatives and northern liberals, then, had not cost Truman reelection. By invoking the legacy of Roosevelt and the sins of the Republicans, Truman retained the support of most liberals, blacks, and workers, and also enough middle-income groups, small businessmen, and farmers who feared that a Democratic defeat would mean a reversal of the New Deal. This strategy further enabled the Democrats to regain control of Congress: 263-171 in the House and 54-42 in the Senate.

# CHAPTER THREE
# FROM FAIR DEAL
# TO HOT WAR,
# 1948-1952

Elected president in his own right in 1948, Harry Truman inherited the ambiguous legacies of his first term in office. His successful campaign strategy had not garnered a popular mandate for his so-called Fair Deal program of medical care; agricultural, housing, and labor law reform; or civil rights legislation. For one, southern Democrats, who controlled key committee chairmanships, held more conservative views on national policy while conservative Republicans opposed Truman's Fair Deal in principle. Truman's effective and bitter campaign attacks on the Republican 80th Congress, moreover, had intensified partisan and antipresidential sentiments. At the same time, Truman's success led many Republicans to reassess their strategy of directly challenging the accomplishments of the New Deal. National security issues were an easier, more effective tactic for political success.

If the years 1948 to 1952 were marked by a bitter, often rancorous debate over presidential powers and over the loyalty of administration personnel, Truman's second term nonetheless witnessed a further expansion of executive powers. Truman unilaterally committed the nation to war and he radically expanded the power of the federal intelligence agencies.

## THE LIMITS OF DOMESTIC REFORM:
## REALITIES OF THE
## REPUBLICAN-SOUTHERN
## DEMOCRATIC COALITION

In coining the phrase *Fair Deal* during his January 1949 inaugural address, Truman intended in part to convey the distinctiveness of his administration's reform program. Truman's Fair Deal incorporated goals neglected during the Roosevelt New Deal such as strong civil rights legislation and national medical insurance. But the principle behind the new programs remained decidedly New Deal—federal responsibility to redress social and economic injustice and to assist the disadvantaged.

Truman faced major obstacles to the implementation of the Fair Deal. Despite his victory in 1948 and Democratic success in regaining control of the Congress, the public had not voted to extend the New Deal. During the campaign, Truman had failed to articulate specific principles, outlined no precise programs, and hence rallied no popular enthusiasm for a Fair Deal. His appeal derived largely from the effectiveness of his attacks on the Republican 80th Congress and successful exploitation of popular fears about a Republican victory. The manifest target of Truman's ire in 1948 might have been the "do nothing," "reactionary" 80th Congress; the latent theme was Herbert Hoover's and the Republicans' responsibility for the Great Depression.

Furthermore, despite Democratic majorities in both houses of Congress, southern Democrats controlled the key committee chairmanships. As early as 1938 even Roosevelt found himself stymied politically by an informal southern Democratic-Republican coalition which resisted further domestic reforms. In 1949 the conservative congressional coalition remained a powerful obstacle to the Fair Deal. Led by the patrician Georgia Senator Richard Russell, southern Democrats were unenthusiastic about the Fair Deal and bitterly opposed the administration's civil rights recommendations.

The ensuing stalemate between a liberal president and a more conservative Congress surfaced dramatically in 1949 over civil rights legislation. Calling in 1949 for enactment of legislation outlawing the poll tax, making lynching a federal crime, prohibiting segregation and discrimination in interstate transportation, and creating a permanent federal fair employment practices commission (FEPC), Truman and the Democratic liberals pressed for a federal assault on southern segregationist practices. In the House, liberals succeeded in weakening southern control of the Rules Committee—long the impediment to floor consideration of civil rights. But in the Senate, the Republican-southern Democratic coalition withstood a liberal effort to restrict the right to filibuster, that is to debate an issue without limit. The victory for unlimited Senate debate buried Truman's civil rights program.

Southerners were less hostile to other Fair Deal proposals. Nonetheless, with the exception of the National Housing Act of 1949, none of Truman's major legislation recommendations were enacted into law. The Brannan Plan, the administration's proposal for resolving the perennial problems of farm surpluses while insuring fair agricultural prices, never even came to a vote. Proposals to provide for national health insurance, federal aid to education, the creation of a permanent FEPC, and repeal or modification of Taft-Hartley also never came to a vote. The Congress did extend social security coverage to an additional ten million workers, doubled social security benefits, and raised the minimum wage from 40 cents to 75 cents an hour, all victories for established New Deal principles. The only notable victory for Truman's Fair Deal involved congressional approval of a public housing and mortgage assistance bill. Even this bill was gutted by the conservative coalition and funded the construction of only 810,000 low-income housing units. Ironically, the National Housing Act's provisions for slum clearance combined with its provisions authorizing federal mortgage assistance to middle-income groups abetted the "white flight" to the suburbs which intensified the race, housing, and urban desegregation crises of the 1960s and 1970s.

## RELATIVE PRESIDENTIAL FREEDOM ABROAD: CONTINUED CONFLICT WITH THE SOVIETS AND NATO

The exigencies of the early Cold War had seemingly necessitated a more secretive foreign policy and the resultant expansion of the CIA's role; the further deterioration of U.S.-Soviet relations after 1949 intensified these tendencies. The NSC soon evolved into the central policy-making institution in foreign policy, in the process undermining both the role of the Department of State and Congress's traditional oversight powers. The Truman administration's quest for secrecy, as part of its efforts to contain Soviet expansion, effectively transformed U.S. diplomatic priorities and decision-making procedures.

The Soviet explosion of an atomic bomb in August 1949 (publicly announced by President Truman on September 23, 1949) and the outbreak of the Korean War on June 25, 1950, constituted the specific catalysts to the evolution of a more centralized secretive diplomacy. In the interim between these shocks, the Truman administration initiated a major policy reassessment which culminated in two momentous decisions of 1950. First, as announced by President Truman in January, the United States embarked on an accelerated program to develop thermonuclear weapons. Second, as suggested in National Security Council Directive 68 of April 14, 1950, the nation substantially expanded defense spending, redefined the national interest and international responsibilities globally, and expanded the CIA's covert operation personnel and capabilities.

The language of NSC 68 outlined how the administration defined the Soviet threat and its proposed response. "The [Soviet] design," the writers of NSC 68 concluded, "calls for the complete subversion or forcible destruction of the machinery or government and structure of society in the countries of the non-Soviet world and their replacement by an apparatus and structure subservient to and controlled from the Kremlin."

To meet this threat to U.S. security and world order, NSC 68 recommended a "bold and massive program of rebuilding the West's defensive potential to surpass that of the Soviet world." U.S. defense spending which had averaged $12 to $13 billion annually for the years 1945 to 1950, in the 1950s rose to an annual level of $50 billion. By November 1952 the United States successfully tested a hydrogen bomb, the first in a new generation of deadly thermonuclear weapons. Between 1949 and 1952, the CIA's Office of Policy Coordination (the covert operations division) increased from personnel of 302 and budget of $4.7 billion to 2,812, and $82 billion.

Because secretively and unilaterally initiated, neither the public nor the Congress learned the scope of these changes which diminished Congress's role in foreign affairs. Truman, however, still had to turn to Congress whenever treaties had been negotiated and to fund programs. This was especially true of his decision in April 1949 to conclude with the Western European states the first peacetime military alliance in U.S. history, the North Atlantic Treaty Organization (NATO).

On March 17, 1948, reflecting their fear of Soviet intentions, five Western European states (Great Britain, France, Belgium, the Netherlands, and Luxemburg) formed the Brussels Pact. The signatories empowered French Premier George Bidault and British Prime Minister Ernest Bevin to approach Secretary of State George Marshall to secure U.S. participation. On June 11, 1948, by an overwhelming 64-4 vote the Senate adopted the Vandenberg Resolution (proposed by the Republican chairman of the Foreign Relations Committee) authorizing the president to conclude peacetime alliances outside the western hemisphere. Two years of Cold War had effectively neutralized once-traditional American opposition to binding foreign entanglements.

The 1948 U.S. presidential election delayed formal negotiations between the United States and the Brussels Pact states although a preliminary treaty was drafted by December 28, 1948, and was completed on March 18, 1949. On April 4, 1949, the treaty was formally signed (by the United States, Great Britain, France, Holland, Belgium, Luxemburg, Italy, Portugal, Iceland, Norway, Canada, and Denmark) in Washington. Subject to denunciation or alteration after twenty years, it provided for consultation among the signatories in the event of threatened or actual aggression and for collective military assistance. The key clauses defined an attack upon one member as an attack upon all and pledged mutual cooperation in planning the common defense. The commitment to war was partially qualified—in the event of aggression in the North Atlantic region each signatory state agreed to undertake "immediately, individually and in accord with the other parties, whatever action it shall judge necessary, including the use of armed force."

Senate debate over the NATO treaty revealed the impact of the Cold War on American diplomatic traditions. Despite an unprecedented break from the historic policy of nonalignment, few senators directly opposed the concept of NATO. The treaty's few critics endorsed a United States commitment to Western Europe, opposing only open-ended defense expenditures. To disarm the congressional opposition, Secretary of State Dean Acheson (Marshall's successor) unreservedly assured the Senate that under the treaty the United States had assumed no commitment to station troops in Western Europe or to provide military assistance. On July 12, 1949, the Senate formally approved the treaty by a vote of 82 to 13.

Their fears of encirclement, which had led Soviet leaders to tighten their control over Eastern Europe in 1947 and 1948, thus unwittingly stimulated the encirclement the Soviets dreaded. Claiming that the pact was aimed solely at them, the Soviets also charged that it violated the spirit and letter of the United Nations Charter. It did, to be sure, reflect Western disillusionment with the veto-ridden UN as a peace-preserving agency. In effect, then, the North Atlantic Treaty froze East-West differences into a permanent mold; eventually in 1955 the Soviet Union forged a counteralliance with Albania, Czechoslovakia, Bulgaria, Hungary, Poland, Rumania and East Germany—the Warsaw Pact. In time, Greece and Turkey (in 1952) and West Germany (in 1955) joined the NATO alliance.

The North Atlantic Treaty had not been initially planned as an actual military alliance. Intended to deter war, NATO was formed to counter any neutralist tendencies within Western Europe stemming from concerns about the desirability of alignment with the United States at a time of worsening U.S.-Soviet relations. The Soviet Union's successful testing of an atomic device, obviously ending the American nuclear monopoly, along with Western European fears of their vulnerability to Soviet nuclear blackmail, called for an altered U.S. commitment.

Accordingly, in January 1950, President Truman announced his administration's decision to develop the hydrogen fusion or "super-bomb." Concurrently pressuring the NATO allies to increase their military expenditures, the administration acted to forge NATO into an effective military alliance. By May 1950, NATO had been established with a council and secretariat; and by December 19, 1950, a supreme headquarters (SHAPE) and regional commands of military, aerial, and naval forces were formally established. General Eisenhower resigned the presidency of Columbia University to serve as NATO's first supreme commander. Given its limited force levels, this revised strategy called for NATO troops to provide a "tripwire" in case of a Soviet armed aggression anywhere in Europe, unleashing the U.S. Strategic Air Command to strike directly at the Soviet Union with nuclear bombs. Later, as tactical nuclear weapons became available, U.S. policy makers adopted a new strategy, "flexible response," which presumably allowed a choice ranging from conventional to tactical weapons in case of an overt Soviet attack.

As 1949 drew to an end, U.S.-Soviet relations had reached a bitter and frightening denouement. The early verbal protests against Soviet aims in Eastern Europe and the Middle East had given way to stronger action. U.S. military strength and covert operation capabilities had been increased while Western defenses on Soviet frontiers had been bolstered. The Truman Doctrine only hinted at a global policy of containment; such a policy was formally adopted by NSC 68. Not even the implementation of NATO insured a globalist policy of containment, since the U.S. military commitment to NATO was confined to the European continent. But the Soviet rupture of the U.S. atomic monopoly and the accelerating militarization of the Cold War threatened global annihilation. The bright dreams of 1945 had turned into a dreadful nightmare.

## DEBACLE IN THE FAR EAST

The Truman administration had met the crises of the early postwar years without resort to direct military force. By both overt and covert means, the administration had provided economic, technical, and military assistance to anti-Communist governments and parties. Nonetheless, the Truman administration had succeeded in containing Soviet influence at minimum cost. Events in the Far East in 1949 and 1950, however, dramatically underlined the fragility of public support for what soon became a costly policy of global containment.

The final collapse of Nationalist China in 1949, the frustrations of the Korean War, which began in June 1950, and the domestic spy exposes of 1948 to 1950 precipitated conservative charges of extensive Communist infiltration in government. The intensification of fear of Communism at home and abroad also touched off the "great debates" of 1950 and 1951 about the soundness of the Truman administration's foreign policy. In these debates the nation's basic policies were reexamined in an atmosphere of hysteria amidst often irresponsible charges either of blundering or treason in high places.

# THE "FALL" OF CHINA

In December 1941 the Japanese had attacked Pearl Harbor in part because the Roosevelt administration had refused to abandon Nationalist China to Japan's "New Order" for East Asia. Consistent with these priorities, during World War II the Roosevelt administration provided limited military and economic aid to the Nationalist Chinese to fight Japan and to strengthen Chiang Kai-shek's government. Yet, China never was considered an area requiring a major U.S. military and economic commitment. Japan's control of most of the Pacific throughout 1942 allowed only a trickle of military supplies to Chiang's armies. In addition, Japanese forces held China's seacoast and drove the Nationalists into the remote interior of China. In China itself, the Nationalists and the Chinese Communists, led by Mao Tse-tung, were at each other's throats. Having priorities distinctively different than those of his American ally, Chiang tied down huge Nationalist forces in containing the Chinese Communists, rather than in fighting the Japanese. His regime, moreover, was thoroughly corrupt and inefficient. Despite U.S. economic aid, China suffered a raging inflation, which devastated the Chinese middle class and which created a politicoeconomic situation ripe for revolution. Finally, the success of General Douglas MacArthur's island-hopping drive from the South Pacific and Admiral Chester Nimitz's naval aircraft carrier raids westward into the Japanese ring of island bases promised the most direct and speediest means of terminating the war. China, therefore, was pushed into the background as a theater of war.

Nevertheless, the Roosevelt administration sent several military and political missions to China to strengthen Chiang's war effort against Japan and also to soften conflict between the Nationalists and the Communists. In short, American policy favored a unified China strong enough to protect her own interests and to play a constructive role in the postwar world. President Roosevelt frequently referred to China as one of the great powers, much to the annoyance of British Prime Minister Churchill, who realized that she did not merit so exalted a rank.

In 1942, Roosevelt sent General Joseph W. "Vinegar Joe" Stilwell to China to control American aid and to serve as Chiang's chief of staff. Stilwell found his mission a series of frustrations. Chiang refused to overhaul his army to eliminate corrupt and inefficient officers, and was reluctant to commit sizable forces to any large-scale and risky campaigns against the Japanese. The crux of the difficulty lay in the American desire to concentrate all allied forces against the Japanese versus Chiang's determination to crush the Chinese Communists. From Chiang's point of view, the United States should take care of Japan, so that he could concentrate upon the Chinese Communists.

Such divergent interests insured the failure of all American attempts during and after World War II to arrange a truce between the Nationalists and the Communist Chinese. The Chinese Communists originally had comprised the left wing within the Nationalist movement of Sun Yat-sen, but the latter's death and his succession by Chiang Kai-shek had caused civil war between the right and left wings. In the Long March of 1934 to 1935, the Chinese Communists retreated to remote North China, where they dug in and emphasized peasant reforms. The war thrust both sides into an uneasy and fragile truce. The truce of 1937 to wage a common war against the Japanese invaders soon broke down and both fractions warily watched and maneuvered against each other. By exploiting the power vacuum created by Japanese occupation, the Chinese Communists steadily enlarged the areas under their control and strengthened their army, until by 1945 they controlled an estimated 116 million people, one-fourth of China's population, and had over a million troops under arms.

From the perspective of the Roosevelt and Truman administrations, compromise alone offered hope of averting a ruinous Chinese civil war. All efforts, such as Vice President Henry A. Wallace's 1944 trip to China, failed. Neither the Nationalists nor the Communists trusted each other; both felt confident of ultimate victory, and so refused to make the compromises essential to forging a workable coalition. The Americans persisted in their efforts to mediate China's internal conflict, and at the Yalta Conference of February 1945, the Roosevelt administration attempted to protect China against either a Soviet seizure of Manchuria or Soviet recognition and aid to the Communists. In return for specifically defined territorial concessions (joint Sino-Soviet ownership of the Chinese Eastern and Manchurian railroads and naval base and port rights to Port Arthur and Dairen), Stalin agreed at Yalta to Chinese sovereignty over Manchuria and to conclude a mutual defense treaty with the Chinese Nationalist government. Apparently Stalin had no great affection for Mao Tse-tung and his followers[1], perhaps because they were too independent for his taste, and, like his Western counterparts, Stalin also overrated the strength of Chiang's regime.

The Pacific War ended in August 1945 before the United States could build up the Nationalists' power via newly opened sea routes to China. More important, as soon became evident, Chiang's regime was morally bankrupt and had alienated vast numbers of Chinese. Driven inland by the Japanese during the war, Chiang had been compelled to rely upon the conservative landlord class. Consequently, it proved impossible for his regime to undertake needed rural reforms as his Communist rivals were doing. Runaway wartime inflation, heavy taxation, discriminatory military conscription (often exempting sons of the wealthy), and corrupt officials further alienated the peasant class from the Nationalists. After the war, the Nationalists lost

[1]Stalinist policy and advice had been partly responsible for Communist setbacks during the 1920s in China.

support among intellectuals and students, who were repelled by the corrupt and undemocratic nature of the regime. Business and financial groups were irked by inflation and the nepotism of the ruling Chiang Kai-shek family and its friends. Drastic police controls and looting and raping by the "liberating" Nationalist armies completed the popular disaffection. In contrast, Communist behavior seemed impeccably honest. Under these circumstances the Nationalists lost the "Mandate of Heaven," or popular consensus to govern, as more and more Chinese either became apathetic or defected to the Communists. Nonetheless, in 1945 and 1946 the Truman administration provided whatever economic and military aid it could to Chiang, supplying and helping the Nationalists to move their armies to key areas where they could disarm the Japanese and take control before the Communists arrived. In 1946, moreover, President Truman sent General George C. Marshall to China as a special envoy to try to achieve a truce between the warring Nationalist and Communist factions in some form of coalition government. His mediation effort, however, failed.

Instead, in 1947 a confident Chiang Kai-shek launched a major campaign to crush his enemies. Chiang's government commanded nearly three million troops against slightly over one million Communist regulars and guerrillas. Ignoring American advice, Chiang employed his forces to capture and hold cities, and not pursue the Communists. Having thereby spread his forces thin, Chiang left them virtually besieged in cities while the Communists controlled the countryside. With growing strength and confidence, beginning in 1948 the Chinese Communist forces assumed the offensive against the Nationalist armies. Nationalist forces met a series of devastating disasters. By November 1948 Chiang's army had lost Manchuria and 400,000 troops; by early 1949, Peking and North China fell; in May, Shanghai; and in October, Canton and the south. Demoralized, Chiang's armies had lost the will to fight, as during 1948 and 1949, 75 to 80 percent of the arms and military goods supplied by the Americans (over $2 billion worth) fell into Communist hands. By the end of 1949 the Chinese Communists reigned supreme on the mainland, while Chiang and a remnant of the Nationalists sought refuge on the island of Taiwan (Formosa).

The Truman administration finally publicly repudiated the Nationalist cause in the famed China White Paper of August 1949. As the State Department contended in this document, the United States could do no more to save the Nationalists. It had supplied generous aid and sound military and political advice, which had been wasted or ignored. In 1948 and 1949, the United States lacked the troops to intervene on the China mainland, and most Americans probably would have opposed any such entanglement so soon after the end of the bloody Second World War. The Truman administration's chief political mistake, in the event, lay not in allowing Chiang to fall, but in failing earlier to present Congress and the public squarely with the painful alternatives in China.

Following the resumption of military conflict between the Nationalists and the Communists, the Truman administration in 1947 had dispatched General Albert Wedemeyer to China to assess the situation. In a starkly brutal report, Wedemeyer emphasized the need for U.S. military and economic aid if the Nationalists were to prevail. Without far-reaching political and economic reforms, Wedemeyer further cautioned no amount of military aid could save Chiang. Wedemeyer also recommended the creation of a UN trusteeship in North China and Manchuria (allowing Chiang to concentrate his forces in the south). Wedemeyer's report was not publicly released. Its brutal comments on Nationalist corruption would have compromised U.S.-Nationalist Chinese relations while his call for substantial economic assistance might have threatened congressional approval of the Truman Doctrine's commitment to the Mediterranean and Western Europe. Had the Wedemeyer Report been issued in 1947, Congress and conservative political leaders would have been required to debate the wisdom of large-scale aid to China and also the desirability of a U.S. troop commitment. Ironically, Truman's failure to be frank with Congress, by releasing the Wedemeyer Report, left his administration open to subsequent charges that it had betrayed Chiang Kai-shek and abandoned China to Communist rule.

The collapse of Nationalist China, long regarded by most articulate Americans as a friendly ally and the principal hope for a stable Far East, and its replacement by an alien and hostile Communist regime, proved to be a traumatic event. Many Americans simply refused to realize that China was not theirs to lose.

## THE FRUSTRATING KOREAN WAR

Soviet and U.S. forces had jointly occupied Korea after Japan's surrender in 1945. Soviet troops had disarmed Japanese forces north of the 38th parallel, U.S. troops south of that line. This division had been designed only to effect a quick Japanese surrender and had not been intended as a permanent political boundary. The United States remained committed to the unification of Korea. In 1948, despite the deterioration of U.S.-Soviet relations, the United States persuaded the United Nations to supervise elections in all of Korea. The Soviet Union, however, refused to permit the UN elections to be held in the north but withdrew its troops that year after first installing a Communist regime in its sector. Following elections held only in the southern zone, the United States recognized the Republic of Korea in the south and withdrew its occupying forces in 1949, leaving behind a revanchist, authoritarian government headed by Syngman Rhee. The Truman administration continued to supply economic and military aid to the Rhee government. U.S. military assistance, however, was essentially defensive and was intended to discourage Rhee from an attempt to unify his country by force. Nonetheless, as Secretary of State Dean Acheson's famous "defense perimeter" press statement of January 12, 1950, made clear, South Korea was considered of marginal strategic importance to American security in the Pacific.

Suddenly, on June 25, 1950, a heavily armed North Korean army invaded the south and threatened to overrun South Korea. The cause of the attack remains obscure, but, at the time, American leaders believed that North Korea acted at Stalin's orders. Stalin's role in the invasion, however, seems ambiguous, considering that the Soviet delegate to the Security Council had just "walked out" over the Western refusal to admit Communist China to the UN. Much like their southern counterparts, the North Koreans were not resigned to the permanent division of Korea and in view of Rhee's unpopularity (dramatized in recently held elections of May 30, 1950) apparently concluded that the time for achieving unification by force was opportune.

The Truman administration found itself in a painful dilemma. As NSC 68 confirmed, by 1950 the Truman administration interpreted radical insurgent movements as Soviet-directed and thus a threat to American security. But the United States was ill-prepared to fight a ground war in Asia—having only 542,000 troops in service, the vast majority of which were committed to the German and Japanese occupation. Since 1945, the administration had relied upon atomic weapons and air power to deter a Soviet military attack against Western Europe. In keeping with that deterrent strategy, but also reflecting domestic political realities, the defense budget had not provided for substantial contingents of ground troops.

In June 1950, President Truman decided that the North Korean aggression must be resisted. At America's behest and with Russia absent, on June 27 the UN Security Council first demanded a North Korean withdrawal and then requested member states to "render such assistance to [South Korea] as may be necessary to repel the armed attack and to restore international peace and security in the area." Asserting his executive authority to protect American occupation forces in Japan and to uphold treaty commitments (the UN Charter), on June 27 the president unilaterally ordered naval and air forces to aid South Korea. On June 30 Truman sent U.S. ground forces into battle in Korea and directed the Seventh Fleet to neutralize the Formosa Straits. Without congressional authorization, a Cold War president had for the first, but not the last, time involved the United States in a foreign war.

The Korean War oscillated wildly in 1950. General Douglas MacArthur was immediately appointed UN supreme commander in Korea (fifteen other nations sent troops to serve under the UN flag, but the overwhelming burden fell upon the United States and South Korea). MacArthur first rallied allied forces around Pusan at the southern end of the peninsula.

RUSSIA

*Amur R.*

MONGOLIA

*Sungari R.*

CHINA

Vladivostok

Farthest penetration
by UN northward,
Nov. 24, 1950

*Yalu R.*

Peking o

o Pyongyang    *Sea of Japan*

KOREA

o Seoul    JAPAN    o Tokyo

*Yellow R.*

Armistice Line,
July 27, 1953

38th Parallel

*East
China
Sea*

*R.*

*Yangtze*

Shanghai o

Pusan perimeter,
farthest penetration
by North Korea
Sept. 15, 1950

*PACIFIC   OCEAN*

**The Korean War
1950–1953**

Adopting bold tactics, in September he coordinated an offensive from Pusan with an amphibious landing behind North Korean lines at Inchon. Caught in a nutcracker, North Korean armies were almost annihilated, and the remnants fled north of the 38th parallel. With Truman's approval, on September 11 the Joint Chiefs of Staff authorized MacArthur to advance beyond the 38th parallel provided "there was no indication or threat of entry of Soviet or Chinese Communist elements in force." Despite Communist warnings, relayed through the Indian ambassador, in October the United States decided, with UN Assembly backing, to cross the 38th parallel, the prewar border separating North and South Korea, and unify Korea into one republic. The CIA then uncovered intelligence suggesting the likelihood of Chinese Communist involvement in the event the United States attempted to unify Korea militarily (but erroneously estimated that there were less than 150,000 Chinese troops massed along the Yalu). At an October 14 conference on Wake Island, however, General MacArthur assured President Truman that there was little danger of Chinese intervention; if China intervened, he confidently declared, American air power would prevail.

MacArthur's forces drove northward, on October 19 capturing the North Korean capital at Pyongyang. Although by November it was known that Chinese troops had entered Korea, MacArthur grossly underestimated their number. On November 24 he ordered a final offensive to liberate all Korea and end the war before Christmas. With his troops approaching the Yalu River, the border between Korea and Manchuria, and spread thin along a 300-mile front, MacArthur was surprised on November 26 by a massive Communist Chinese counteroffensive. Extricating themselves with great difficulty, MacArthur's forces fell back rapidly. Once more the Communists drove into South Korea and recaptured Seoul before the allies rallied and retook that battered capital. By spring 1951, the UN forces had fought their way back to approximately the old 38th parallel line. Heavy casualties were inflicted upon the Communists in an operation known as "Meat-Grinder" which utilized American air supremacy and superiority in artillery and mechanized warfare.

## THE GREAT DEBATES

In the wake of the military reverses in Korea, a shrill debate erupted within the United States. The twin shocks of the fall of Nationalist China in 1949 and of President Truman's September 1949 announcement that the Soviet Union had exploded an atomic bomb weakened the credibility of the Truman administration. Since 1947, administration spokesmen had confidently predicted the painless success of containment. While emphasizing the magnitude of the Soviet subversive threat, the administration had not counseled the public about either the risks or costs of an effort to contain revolutionary change. Korea dramatized those risks and costs at a time when the American nuclear monopoly had ended.

Because the administration fought the Korean War as a limited conflict, a frustrating and costly strategy all the more incomprehensible to most Americans accustomed to thinking in terms of decisive military victory, this strategy lacked popular support. Congressional investigations and concurrent "espionage" trials created a decidedly different context for appraising the wisdom of containment. By late 1950 many Americans had become convinced that a major cause of Cold War difficulties stemmed from extensive Communist infiltration of the Federal bureaucracy.

The Republican congressional leadership sought to exploit and intensify such popular concerns. The source of the crisis, conservatives raged, stemmed not from Soviet power but domestic subversion. Succinctly summarizing this appeal, one Republic senator sputtered, "How much more are we going to have to take? Fuchs [a British scientist who admitted having committed atomic espionage for the Soviet Union during World War II] and Acheson [by 1950 a frequent target of witch-hunters] and Hiss and hydrogen bombs threatening outside and New Dealism eating away the vitals of the nation. In the name of Heaven is this the best the nation can do?" This outlook plunged the United States into a search for domestic Communists and traitors known as "McCarthyism." More crudely than his conservative associates, the Wisconsin senator accused the Truman administration of wittingly or unwittingly engaging in treason: "We know that since Yalta the leaders of this Government by design or ignorance have continued to betray us. . . . We also know that the same men who betrayed America are still leading America. The traitors must no longer lead the betrayed." The State Department, headed by the suave, arrogant, and highly intelligent Dean Acheson, became the principle target of conservative Republican attacks. By 1950 the Department had become the symbol of unwanted responsibilities and foreign frustrations.

Former President Herbert Hoover's late 1950 condemnation of America's allies as unreliable and his call for a defensive strategy, Fortress America, to make the Western hemisphere an impervious Gibraltar precipitated the so-called Great Debate of 1951. Others followed the opposition crystallized around Republican Senate leader Robert A. Taft. This debate about the wisdom and costs of postwar foreign policies received new vigor when President Truman in late 1950, claiming authority as "commander in chief," ordered four U.S. troop divisions to Europe to strengthen NATO against a possible Soviet attack. In the wake of the Korean War, wherein the U.S. military commitment had been taken by the president without a formal congressional declaration of war, congressional opponents railed against this presidential "usurpation." Led by Republican Senators Taft and Kenneth Wherry, who felt that the executive branch acted too unilaterally in foreign affairs, conservatives demanded restrictions on presidential powers. Articulating themes which he developed further during his 1952 campaign for the Republican presidential nomination, Taft genuinely feared that costly foreign aid projects and defense commitments, plus extensions of the New Deal at home, would produce bankruptcy and socialism. Hence he advocated what his critics called "bargain-basement" containment, reliance upon less costly sea and air power to deter the Communists and reduction in expensive foreign economic aid. Although this debate was often couched in constitutional terms—executive usurpation of congressional prerogatives—Truman's critics were mainly criticizing the wisdom of a policy relying on ground troops and not air power.

The last and most important of the great debates grew directly out of the frustrating Korean War, the "Asia First versus Europe" debate touched off with President Truman's abrupt dismissal of General MacArthur from the Far Eastern command in April 1951. An able but histrionic general who found reverses difficult to tolerate, MacArthur's concept of the international

Communist threat caused him to advocate bold measures to win total victory in Korea. For the general, the threat of world Communism focused upon Asia rather than Europe and time was on the Communists' side. Therefore, he urged the administration to widen the Korean conflict: Manchuria should be bombed to cut off supplies and troop movements to Korea; China's coast should be blockaded; Chiang should be unleashed to threaten a diversionary invasion of the mainland; and the bombing of China proper should be considered.

After a brief internal discussion, and in response to British and other allied pressures, the Truman administration rejected MacArthur's recommendations. In its view, the chief danger of Communist expansion still lay in Europe. The administration further feared that MacArthur's strategy might culminate in Soviet intervention and World War III, or, at the least, bog down American forces in an interminable war in Asia. A prolonged war in Asia would "bleed us dry," Truman and his advisers concluded, and divert attention from the main task of defending Western Europe against Soviet power. In contrast to MacArthur's "Asia First" approach, the Truman administration adhered to an Europe-first strategy and decided to limit the Korean War until it could be ended by negotiations.

MacArthur refused to accept his superior's decision. Instead, he tried to force Truman's hand by public appeal. Contrary to military discipline and in violation of direct orders, in letters and telegrams to various Americans MacArthur urged an Asia-first policy. For the Truman administration the hardest blow came when the general's letter to Republican Congressman Joseph W. Martin, Jr., was read on the floor of the House of Representatives: "If we lose the war to communism in Asia the fall of Europe is inevitable; win it and Europe most probably would avoid war and yet preserve freedom. There is no substitute for victory."

For many conservative Republicans searching for a viable political issue, MacArthur's criticisms of the Truman administration's Asian policies were cogent and timely. MacArthur's confident assurances of victory over Communism also appealed to many Americans accustomed to victory in war and weary of the Korean stalemate. Fearful of the resultant political storm, President Truman still decided that he had to remove his insubordinate commander and thereby uphold the president's constitutional authority as commander-in-chief and the principle of military subordination to civilian authority. On April 11, 1951, Truman announced his decision to recall MacArthur from his Far Eastern command. As Truman's critics later lamented bitterly, the ex-haberdasher in the White House had fired the great war hero of the Pacific.

The storm broke upon the administration with unbelievable fury. Condemnatory letters and telegrams flooded the White House, Truman was publicly booed, and several Republicans in Congress even muttered darkly about impeachment. "This country today is in the hands of a secret inner coterie which is directed by the agents of the Soviet Union," Republican

Senator William Jenner charged. "We must cut this whole cancerous conspiracy out of our Government at once. Our only choice is to impeach President Truman." A Gallup poll revealed that among those contacted, 69 percent supported MacArthur and only 29 percent Truman. MacArthur returned to the United States to receive a hero's welcome and to address a joint session of Congress. His popular appeal waned as rapidly as it had waxed, and the unsuccessful aspirant for the Republican presidential nomination in 1952 soon accepted a post with the Remington Rand Corporation.

The MacArthur dismissal unleashed the last of the great debates amidst shrill charges of blundering and betrayal. Critics of the administration apparently supported all-out war in Korea regardless of the consequences. During congressional hearings, conducted from May 3 to June 25, 1951, Republicans charged that China had been lost by blunders or worse, and that the same processes were at work in Korea. Even Senator Taft suggested "treason in high places," arguing that, "The Korean War and the problems which arise from it are the final result of the continuous sympathy toward communism which inspired American policy." Calling for the repudiation of the policies and personnel which they claimed had insured Soviet expansion in Europe and Asia, Taft and other Republican conservatives demanded a housecleaning of the State Department, adoption of a policy of liberation, a more dynamic strategy insuring victory in the Cold War, and an end to executive secrecy and unilateralism. Such arguments were immensely appealing to many Americans because they promised victory at minimal cost and seemed ideally suited to protect vital U.S. interests against Soviet challenges.

## THE FREEZING OF
## AMERICA'S CHINA POLICY

The great debates did not change the Truman administration's policy toward Korea. Despite the war's unpopularity, the Truman administration continued its limited war strategy and the president made policy on his own. Upon second thought, many Americans apparently were persuaded by General Omar Bradley's 1951 congressional testimony that MacArthur's approach would lead to "the wrong war at the wrong place, at the wrong time, and with the wrong enemy." In the final analysis, the Truman administration's critics did not advocate increasing U.S. military commitments nor were they committed to a policy of overseas retrenchment. Wedded to a strategy of containing Communism, conservatives differed from the Truman administration over methods, not goals. For them, as for the Truman administration, the Soviet Union, and not China, posed the principal threat to western security. Europe thus remained the focal point of the Cold War struggle.

In July 1951, moreover, the Communists agreed to Korean truce negotiations. These talks at Panmunjom dragged on for two years during small-scale fighting until an armistice was ultimately signed in July 1953. Total American casualties numbered 33,629 dead and another 115,000 wounded. Expenses mounted to $22 billion. Despite these costs, Korea delineated the delicate boundaries of Communist-Western conflict in a nuclear age in which both sides increasingly feared mutual destruction. More important, it precipitated an intraadministration debate which led to increasing reliance on the CIA's covert operations capabilities and, in the process, to an increase in executive authority. For executive branch officials Korea's most important political lesson was the need for a preventive counterinsurgency capability.

The Korean War and the ensuing domestic debate paralyzed American Far Eastern policy. Prior to Korea, the Truman administration had been feeling its way toward eventual recognition of the People's Republic of China. Taiwan had not been deemed vital to American security in the Pacific, and its fall to the Chinese Communists appeared inevitable. Then came the fateful Korean War, Truman's order to the Seventh Fleet to patrol the Formosa Straits, and Communist China's intervention in Korea. The People's Republic of China had become a military adversary. American reactions to the Korean War and to Chinese Communist intervention froze U.S. policy into rigid nonrecognition and hostility toward the Mao government. For the next two decades nonrecognition and containment of the People's Republic became fixed dogmas in American foreign relations. In 1951 a peace treaty was unilaterally negotiated with Japan; in 1954 a defensive alliance was concluded with the Nationalist regime on Taiwan; and in 1954 SEATO (Southeast Asia Treaty Organization) was formed to bar Communist expansion southward. Twice—in the off-shore islands clashes of 1954 and 1955 and again in 1958—American entanglement with Taiwan threatened to involve the nation in a large-scale war with China. Long after the People's Republic of China began to drift apart from the Soviet Union, American policy still regarded the People's Republic as a Soviet client and a menace to U.S. interests in Southeast Asia and the Pacific. It awaited the Nixon administration in 1971 and 1972 to take the first steps toward dissolving this rigid policy in East Asia.


## THE POLITICS OF McCARTHYISM,
## THE EXPANSION OF FBI POWERS,
## AND THE ELECTION OF 1952

Truman's successful campaign strategy of 1948 attacking the "reactionary" 80th Congress and accusing his Republican opponents of selfish motives had exacerbated already tense executive-legislative relations. This sharpened conflict dominated the politics of Truman's second term. To Republican strategists, Truman's victory had demonstrated the popularity of the New Deal and thus the need for a revised political strategy. Beginning in 1949, moderate and conservative Republican congressmen rather than simply attacking domestic reform began to condemn the Roosevelt and Truman administrations' past foreign policy decisions, to question the adequacy of presidential internal security procedures, and to accuse executive personnel of "appeasement" or "disloyalty." National security appeals replaced domestic conservatism as Republican gospel. Senator Robert Taft, known as Mr. Republican, pointedly counseled fellow Republicans, "We cannot possibly win the next election unless we point out the utter failure and incapacity of the Truman administration to conduct foreign policy. We cannot possibly win on domestic policy, because every domestic policy depends entirely on foreign policy." In another speech, the Republican senator attributed foreign failures to internal subversion: "The greatest Kremlin asset in our history has been the pro-Communist group in the State Department who succumbed to every demand of Russia at Yalta and Potsdam and promoted at every opportunity the communist cause in China until today [1950] Communism threatens to take over all of Asia."

The new Republican strategy proved timely; Americans had become frightened over the Chinese Communist defeat of the Chinese Nationalists and the Soviet explosion of an atomic bomb. The public rationale for the security procedures instituted under the Atomic Energy Act of 1946 had been the need to preserve the American atomic monopoly. Key military officials promised that the United States would retain its monopoly for twenty years. Reacting to President Truman's September 1949 announcement of the Soviet's atomic success, conservatives attributed it less to Soviet science and technology than subversion.

A number of events which dominated the news in 1949 and 1950 apparently confirmed the seriousness of Soviet subversion and the inadequacy of administration internal security efforts. On July 20, 1948, the twelve leaders of the U.S. Communist party were indicated under the Smith Act, and their trial lasted through 1949 and dominated news coverage. Simultaneously, on December 15, 1948, Alger Hiss was indicted and in 1949 was tried on two counts of perjury. His first trial ended in a hung jury; in the second trial, Hiss was found guilty and sentenced to prison. On March 6, 1949, Judith Coplon, a Justice Department employee, was indicted and tried on the change of having given departmental secrets to a Soviet UN employee. Then, on February 3, 1950, Klaus Fuchs was arrested in Great Britain, where he confessed that while employed at the Los Alamos, New Mexico, atomic bomb project during 1943 to 1945, he had passed atomic secrets to Soviet agents. His confession led to the arrest of American Communist party members Julius and Ethel Rosenberg and to widely publicized FBI charges of an atomic espionage ring. Capitalizing on these events, conservative journalists and congressmen (relying in some cases on informa-

tion leaked by FBI officials) consciously linked Communist party membership or popular front activities with disloyalty and treason. More important,
these conservatives succeeded in fostering the belief that subversion (and not
Soviet power or resources) had brought about the postwar extension of
Soviet international influence.

In the midst of this charged atmosphere Senator Joseph R. McCarthy
burst into national prominence. In a February 9, 1950, speech in Wheeling,
West Virginia, the Wisconsin senator attributed the Soviet Union's postwar
expansion and the origins of the Cold War directly to Communist infiltration of the State Department. McCarthy's listing of "known Communists" in
the State Department (the figures he cited were variously 205 in the Wheeling speech, 57 in February speeches in Reno, Nevada, and Salt Lake City,
Utah, and 81 in a February 20 speech on the Senate floor) provided the
Republicans with a convincing explanation for why the United States was
"losing" the Cold War: Communist infiltration had resulted in the Roosevelt
administration's "appeasement" policy at Yalta and the Truman administration's unwillingness to reverse that policy. McCarthy's charges soon became
the basis for a Republican strategy that capitalized on popular disaffection
with Truman's foreign and internal security policies.

Truman and the Democrats attempted but failed to dismiss McCarthy's
charges as simply partisan politics. To limit McCarthy's appeal, Senate
Democrats, led by Millard Tydings, on February 22, 1950, introduced a
resolution to establish a special subcommittee to investigate the senator's
claim of evidence linking eighty-one State Department employees to Communism. The so-called Tydings Committee did not discredit the Wisconsin
senator. Truman refused to permit the committee to have unlimited access
to the loyalty files of the "eighty-one cases" McCarthy had enumerated on
February 20. Republicans supported McCarthy for reasons of partisan politics. The outbreak of the Korean War in June, 1950 intensified popular
anti-Communism.

Republicans recognized the substantial political benefits of the anti-
Communist issue. Following a Republican Senate Policy Committee meeting
of March 22, 1950, Senator Taft privately advised McCarthy that he should
"keep talking and if one case doesn't work out, proceed with another one."
The Republicans characterized the Korean War as Truman's war—
Congress had not formally declared war in the aftermath of the presidential
action. Truman's limited war strategy, moreover, abjured victory. Why,
many Americans asked, were U.S. military resources not fully used? Why
was General MacArthur shackled, thereby preventing the attainment of
"victory over Communism"? Responding to these doubts, the Republicans
offered a simple explanation: the influence of "Communists in government"!

A combination of popular anger and Republican strategy also resulted
in congressional passage, over Truman's September 22 veto, of the Internal

Joe McCarthy, the junior senator from Wisconsin, in action at Senate hearing (Wide World Photos)

Security Act of September 1950. The so-called McCarran Act authorized the forced detention of deportable aliens who were denied admission to their native lands and barred Communists from employment in defense industries and from securing passports. Communists, Communist-front, and Communist-action groups were required to submit lists of their members and publications and to register as agents of a foreign power with a specially created Subversive Activities Control Board. Whenever the president declared a situation of national emergency, "dangerous radicals" could also be rounded up and held in special detention camps. In companion legislation, Congress enacted Public Law 733 empowering Cabinet officials to dismiss summarily, without hearings or due process, federal employees deemed to be "security risks."

Although the McCarran Act formally established a "preventive detention" program, such a program had already been covertly authorized by Attorney General Tom Clark in August 1948. Ironically, the McCarran Act's procedures reflected a greater sensitivity to constitutional safeguards and due process than those instituted under this independently established program. Unwilling to abide by the McCarran Act's more restrictive standards, in 1950 FBI officials convinced the attorney general to continue "detention" investigations and procedures under the 1948 plan.

An indifference to constitutional rights was not confined to "emergency detention" policy. Since 1940, presidents had authorized "national security" wiretaps in conscious disregard of the absolute ban of the Federal Communications Act of 1934. Presidents rationalized that such information was obtained for intelligence not prosecution and, hence, did not violate the act's ban against "interception *and* divulgence." When the scope and intent of FBI wiretapping was publicly disclosed during the Judith Coplon trial, the administration maintained the practice while unsuccessfully lobbying the Congress for legislation to authorize "national security" wiretaps. At the same time, in February 1952, Attorney General J. Howard McGrath formally advised FBI Director Hoover that the Justice Department could not authorize the illegal installation of microphones (bugs). Yet the FBI continued to install bugs. This was not an atypical practice. In 1952 the CIA (in direct violation of the National Security Act's ban against an "internal security" role) began a mail cover program in New York City, reading the outside of envelopes of mail to and from the Soviet Union.

Covertly instituted, such surveillance programs were never publicly disclosed. In part, national security officials devised sophisticated record-keeping procedures to avert public disclosure. In part, the Congress did not attempt to fulfill its oversight role. Indeed, when the National Lawyers Guild reported on the scope of the FBI's illegal investigations in 1950, the Congress responded by investigating the Guild.

The debate over internal security policy had so narrowed by the 1950s that such traditional defenders of civil liberties, as the conservative Robert Taft and the liberal Hubert Humphrey, denied Communists the protection of established constitutional guarantees. In 1954, for example, Humphrey urged passage of a proposed anti-Communist bill by admonishing his colleagues: "Either senators are for recognizing the Communist party for what it is or they will continue to trip over the niceties of legal technicalities and details." And U.S. Attorney General J. Howard McGrath in speeches before law enforcement and fraternal organizations in 1949 and 1950 emphasized the peril that Communists posed to American liberties and security. "There are today many Communists in America," he warned. "They are everywhere—in factories, offices, butcher stores, on street corners, in private business—and each carries in himself the germs of death for society." To meet this peril, in 1950 the Department of Justice introduced and lobbied for legislation to legalize wiretapping, to repeal the statute of limitations in espionage cases, to grant immunity for testimony involving national security before grand juries and congressional committees, and to expedite prosecution in perjury cases. Without seeking new legislation, President Truman in a July 1950 directive expanded FBI surveillance over left-wing political activists.

Nor did the Supreme Court (reconstituted during the Truman years, with the appointment of four new justices) challenge federal dilution of first amendment guarantees. In two major decisions, *Bailey* v. *Richardson* (1951) and *Dennis* v. *U.S.* (1951), the Court imposed no constitutional restrictions over the procedures which Truman had established to administer a federal employee loyalty program, upheld the constitutionality of the Smith Act, and extended the "clear and present danger" principle of the *Schenck* case (1919) to a new standard of "appreciable probability."

"National security" fears had moved American politics sharply to the right. Exploiting this shift in the 1950 congressional elections, the Republicans gained 5 seats in the Senate and 28 in the House, reducing Democratic majorities to 234-198 in the House and 49-47 in the Senate. In December 1950, moreover, the Senate established its own counterpart to HUAC, the Internal Security Subcommittee of the Committee on the Judiciary. And, to promote Senator McCarthy's campaign, the Republican caucus in 1951 appointed the Wisconsin senator to the powerful Appropriations Committee. Exploiting the unpopularity of summit diplomacy to justify restrictions on executive authority, conservative senators in February 1952 also proposed a constitutional amendment, the so-called Bricker Amendment, requiring congressional ratification of all executive agreements and treaties that affected domestic policy.

By 1952, an open conflict existed between Congress and the president over Truman's executive privilege claims and unilateral conduct of foreign and internal security policy. Indeed, part of Senator McCarthy's and other conservative congressmen's appeal derived from their attack on the secret conduct of foreign policy and the removal of basic decisions from congressional control.

Although such conservative leaders as Robert Taft, John Foster Dulles, and John Bricker may have been disturbed by McCarthy's crude tactics, they supported the Wisconsin senator in order to discredit the New Deal Democrats as well as to reestablish a balance between Congress and the executive. Taft expressed these priorities when he claimed "whether McCarthy has legal evidence, whether he has overstated or understated his case, is of lesser importance. The question is whether the Communist influence in the State Department still exists." For Dulles, the 1952 presidential campaign offered the prospect to initiate a more militant foreign policy. By means of a "psychological and political offensive," Dulles argued, "the United States should make it publicly known that it wants and expects liberation [of Eastern Europe from Soviet control] to occur."

These themes dominated the 1952 presidential campaign. To retain the presidency and control of Congress Democratic leaders attempted to dissociate their party from the incumbent president's policies and failures. In contrast, Republicans directly exploited Truman's unpopularity.

Truman's unpopularity was dramatically revealed by Senator Estes Kefauver's victory over the president in the New Hampshire Democratic presidential primary. Soon after, Truman announced his intention not to seek renomination. No strong candidate, however, emerged before the Democratic Convention. Kefauver was opposed by more conservative elements of the party; Senator Richard Russell was too identified with the South; and Mutual Security Director W. Averell Harriman had too close an association with the Truman administration. A reluctant aspirant, Illinois Governor Adlai Stevenson, eventually won the nomination on the third ballot. A liberal Democrat and an attractive personality, Stevenson was not directly identified with the policies and personnel of the Truman administration. To establish his independence, Stevenson later headquartered his campaign in Springfield, Illinois. This strategy failed. Stevenson not only shared and defended the national security and domestic reform principles of the Truman administration, but President Truman actively campaigned for him and against the Republican nominee Dwight Eisenhower. More important, Republicans succeeded in linking the Democratic nominee to the Truman administration.

In a more surprising development, the front-running candidate for the Republican presidential nomination, Robert Taft, lost the nomination to Dwight Eisenhower. Taft's impeccably conservative record and cold demeanor made him anathema to the Republican party's moderate wing. Convinced that "Taft Can't Win," Republican moderates (led by Senator Henry Cabot Lodge and New York Governor Thomas Dewey) promoted a draft of then-NATO Commander Eisenhower. Although not an announced candidate, Eisenhower defeated Taft by 11,000 votes in the New Hampshire primary, and while not even on the ballot, polled an impressive 107,000 write-in votes in the Minnesota primary. Taft nonetheless remained the more popular candidate among the Republican rank-and-file and went to the party convention commanding 530 uncontested delegate votes of the 604 needed to nominate. A successful convention strategy to deny the seating of Taft delegations from the southern states won Eisenhower the nomination. By capitalizing on the imagery that another Taft, William Howard, had stolen the nomination at the 1912 convention and by effectively employing the medium of television (the 1952 conventions were the first to be covered) to call for an open convention, the Eisenhower forces won a close first-ballot victory.

Eisenhower and the Republicans then won a resounding victory in the final election. Focusing on the issues of Communism and corruption, the Republicans campaigned on the theme of "A Time for a Change." The more extreme campaigned against "Twenty Years of Treason"; the more moderate simply demanded dynamic and effective leadership. Eisenhower shrewdly soft-pedalled his philosophical conservatism, affirming his basic commitment to New Deal policies, yet suggesting limits to the growth of big government and sharp reductions in the federal budget. The campaign

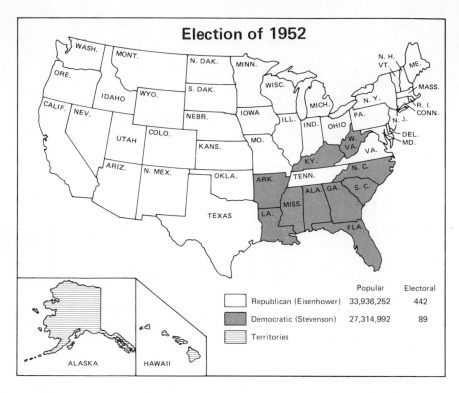

**Election of 1952**

| | | Popular | Electoral |
|---|---|---|---|
| ☐ | Republican (Eisenhower) | 33,936,252 | 442 |
| ▨ | Democratic (Stevenson) | 27,314,992 | 89 |
| ▤ | Territories | | |

turned on foreign policy issues. Eisenhower appealed as an accessible and folksy candidate (campaign buttons proclaimed "I Like Ike"). He also called for liberation from Communism and peace in Korea. The general as politician ably played the contradictory roles of hawk and dove. Eisenhower garnered 442 electoral votes (to Stevenson's 89) and carried the usually Democratic southern states of Texas, Florida, Virginia, and Tennessee. As well, the Republicans captured control of the Congress for the first time since 1946: 48-47 and 1 independent in the Senate and 232-203 in the House—a gain of 2 Senate and 34 House seats.

Ironically, despite his resounding repudiation at the polls, Harry S Truman bequeathed a strengthened presidency to his successor. Throughout his controversial "second" term, foreign and internal security policy decisions were made unilaterally and secretively. Despite McCarthy's assault, President Truman extended classification restrictions in September 1951 and successfully rejected on "executive privilege" grounds congressional demands for loyalty reports. Dwight Eisenhower thus inherited the ambiguous legacy of a more powerful and institutionalized presidency and a congressional challenge to this secretive and unilateral conduct of policy.

# CHAPTER FOUR
# THE GENERAL
# AS PRESIDENT:
## *The Politics and Diplomacy of Stability, 1953–1960*

Although critics dismissed Eisenhower as a leader who "reigned but did not rule," the Republican chief executive resembled Franklin Delano Roosevelt in a striking way. Eisenhower dominated national politics and expanded the authority of the executive branch. Eisenhower's presidency differed from Roosevelt's, however, in three important respects: The changes instituted under Eisenhower centered on the "national security" area, his electoral appeal did not extend to his party, and the Republicans still distrusted a too powerful central government.

The Republicans did not become the majority party during the Eisenhower years. Capitalizing on anti-Democratic sentiments, in 1952 the Republicans had won both the presidency (Eisenhower polled an impressive 55 percent of the popular vote) and control of Congress. Their congressional majority was narrow (48-47, and 1 independent in the Senate and 221-213 in the House) and proved to be short-lived. In the 1954 congressional elections the Democrats regained control of Congress (48-47, and 1 independent in the Senate and 232-203 in the House). The Democrats maintained their majority despite Eisenhower's sweeping reelection victory of 1956 (49-47 in the Senate and 234-201 in the House), and in the 1958 congressional elections increased their Senate majority to 64-34 and House majority to 282-154. Moreover, despite Eisenhower's fiscal conservatism and antipathy to Big Government, New Deal programs persisted and power remained centralized in the presidency.

In 1952, voters responded to the Republican campaign theme of "time for a change"; and the temper of the country was more conservative. Most Americans still endorsed New Deal principles of federal controls over the economy and federal responsibility to promote economic growth. At base, the principal source of this conservative mood was a fear of the Soviet threat to national security.

Fear of Soviet Russia, in turn, contributed to an even more centralized presidency and to a great expansion of the role of the intelligence agencies. During the Eisenhower years, a series of programs were initiated by the CIA and the FBI ostensibly to contain the "Communist" threat. Based principally on vaguely worded executive directives, these programs were secretively initiated and conducted. This secrecy further insulated the intelligence agencies from executive oversight and ultimately created a serious breakdown in constitutional government.

Eisenhower's foreign policy contrasted sharply with its rhetorical call of the 1952 campaign for a bold and dynamic foreign policy to reverse Soviet postwar gains. First, the new administration continued the Truman containment policy but placed greater emphasis on military aid and defensive alliances and less on foreign economic programs. He also relied more heavily on the CIA's "covert operations" capabilities. During the Eisenhower years, U.S.-Soviet tensions moderated slightly despite Secretary of State John Foster Dulles's efforts to erect a worldwide alliance system against Communist expansion. Second, despite the global commitment of the administration's diplomacy, American international influence actually declined during Eisenhower's tenure in office. In part this decline was the result of the rigidity of Dulles's foreign policies and his failure to respond imaginatively to international crises in the Middle East, the Far East, and Latin America. In particular, the Suez War of 1956 intensified Western Europe's desire for greater independence from the United States. In part, the decline in U.S. influence resulted from a natural tendency toward neutralism, especially among newly independent nations. Finally, the Soviet Union's rapidly growing economy, strengthened military arsenal, and technological advances meant that the United States confronted a powerful (if not coequal) rival in science, technology, and global influence. As Soviet military power grew, as Western European nations recovered from the ravages of war, and as former colonies asserted their nationhood, U.S. global influence inevitably diminished.

## THE POLITICS OF IMAGE

Despite his reputation for moderation and nonpartisanship (at the time of his nomination few even knew his party affiliation), Eisenhower was conservative in political philosophy, identified with the corporate business community, and firmly believed in the need to balance the budget. In addition, as an ardent anti-Communist, Eisenhower viewed liberals and radicals with suspicion. In a June 4, 1952, campaign address in Abilene, Kansas, Eisenhower had demanded the elimination from government service of "any kind of Communist, subversive, or pinkish influence."

Not identified with the Republican party's conservative wing, as were Taft and the McCarthyites, Eisenhower could effectively exploit popular dislike of politicians and fears of internal subversion. He could attack subversion without seeming to threaten the accomplishments of the New Deal. Eisenhower also projected himself as an amateur in politics, a disinterested public servant, and an honest man of simple tastes and democratic principles. Yet behind this benign mask lay a shrewd and at times ruthless politician.

Eisenhower was not simply a son of Abilene, Kansas, who read westerns and preferred to play golf. He had grown up in Abilene, but his subsequent career was that of a sophisticated organization and public relations man. Eisenhower did not read westerns, possessed an acute mind, and golfed simply to relax. His meteoric rise in the army during the 1930s and 1940s demonstrated his superior abilities as a publicist and an organizer of men and supplies. A speechwriter for General Douglas MacArthur during the 1930s, Eisenhower was an able press agent and editor. Subsequently, as commander of Allied forces during World War II, he revealed his organizational genius. Involved in fund raising during his thirty-month return to civilian life (in 1948) as president of Columbia University, he established close ties with leaders of the New York business and financial community. Thereafter, his closest friends and associates came from the corporate community. Eisenhower's projected image of simplicity and innocence, the grandfatherly "Ike," thus masked a man of proven organizational abilities who had acquired cosmopolitan values far removed from those of smalltown Kansas.

Cultivating the image of an amateur who was also disinterested in complex issues, Eisenhower delegated authority broadly through a hierarchical staff system. Under the direction of Sherman Adams, the assistant to the president, the White House staff closely monitored congressional and public opinion. White House aides were assigned specific responsibilities—Wilton Persons as congressional liaison, James Hagerty as press secretary, Robert Cutler as national security adviser, and Gabriel Hauge and Arthur Burns as economic advisers. But the White House aides operated within guidelines imposed by a watchful and demanding president. The staff system enabled Eisenhower to acquire expert advice yet make all major decisions.

Eisenhower's use of the National Security Council (NSC) in particular disclosed his penchant for a centralized presidency. Eisenhower met weekly with the council (expanded to include the secretary of the treasury and the director of the bureau of the budget), a step which consciously curtailed the State Department's foreign policy role. Under the direction of Robert Cutler, the president's special assistant for national security affairs, the NSC became the vehicle for implementing presidential policy, insuring that subordinate officials and agencies did not act independently. To monitor CIA covert activities, on March 12, 1955, President Eisenhower issued NSC 5412 requiring that a special NSC Planning and Coordination Group approve "all compatible activities" necessary to destroy "international communism." NSC 5412/2 of December 1955, for example, authorized reducing "international communist" control over "any" area of the world, and assisting nations or groups "anywhere" in the world to react toward U.S. interests. In turn, this required that the CIA develop underground resistance movements and other covert operations.

Because CIA covert operations were either provocative or (as characterized in a 1954 internal report) "fundamentally repugnant" to traditional American ideals, the Eisenhower administration acted secretively. Secrecy became an administration obsession. Eisenhower publicly projected an image of accessibility, but the president carefully monitored the flow of information to the public and the Congress. His regular press conferences suggested his accessibility and yet avoided the pitfalls of embarrassing disclosures. If publicly perceived as an amateur not fully knowledgeable about detail, Eisenhower was in fact fully briefed by twenty to thirty aides before each press conference on potentially troublesome issues. The president's vagueness when pressed on details by the Washington press corps, thus, served to shield his personal responsibility and limit what became public knowledge. Despite his mangled syntax, confused phrasings and rambling responses during presidential press conferences, Eisenhower could be precise and clear. He purposefully projected confusion. Thus, presidential press secretary James Hagerty urged the president to respond "no comment" should any question be raised during a scheduled March 1955 press conference held at the time of the crisis precipitated by the Chinese Communist shelling of the Nationalist-held islands of Quemoy and Matsu. Rejecting this advice, Eisenhower assured his press secretary: "Don't worry, Jim. If that question comes up I'll just confuse them." And confuse them he did!

Queried at a March 23, 1955, press conference about whether the administration would employ nuclear weapons should the United States become involved in a limited war over Quemoy and Matsu, Eisenhower replied:

> The only thing I know about war are (sic) two things: the most changeable factor in war is human nature in its day-by-day manifestation; but the only unchanging factor in war is human nature.
> And the next thing is that every war is going to astonish you in the way it occurred, and the way it is carried out. So that for a man to predict . . . what he

is going to use, how he is going to do it, would I think exhibit his ignorance of war; . . .

Eisenhower's reputation as a man who deferred to expert advisers and delegated authority was also unfounded. In practice Eisenhower followed events closely and ran tight Cabinet and National Security Council meetings. The president dominated these meetings, and as one NSC official who served under Truman and Eisenhower observed, "the mythical Eisenhower, who left decision-making to subordinates, whose mind was 'lazy' and/or not very bright cannot be found in (NSC) records of the most important business he conducted for the nation." The record confirms that Eisenhower made all major policy decisions, whether to oppose the British-French military action in the Suez crisis of 1956 or to achieve Senate rejection of the Bricker Amendment in 1954. Typically, Secretary of State John Foster Dulles, or some other responsible official, announced these decisions and in turn bore the brunt of criticism. Richard Nixon, Eisenhower's vice president, aptly described his chief's technique: "An Eisenhower characteristic was never to take direct action requiring his personal participation where indirect methods would accomplish the same result." Cloaking his taste for political power by frequent golfing, hunting, and fishing excursions, Eisenhower's posturing hid a hardworking and domineering president.

The prevailing Cold War obsession about the threat of Soviet expansion and subversion further reduced Congress's oversight of executive powers. Thus, responding to the Hoover Commission's[1] specific recommendation, in 1955 Democratic Senator Mike Mansfield introduced a resolution to create a joint congressional oversight committee on the CIA. Mansfield presciently noted the need for a greater congressional oversight role, arguing that the CIA's development under tight executive control represented an "arrogation of power on the part of the Executive and a diminution to that extent of the equality between the executive and the legislative." Reported favorably by the Rules Committee on February 23, 1956, Mansfield's resolution was overwhelmingly defeated by the Senate 27-59. The conservative Senate leadership further supported presidential attempts to preclude congressional oversight of intelligence agencies. Senator Richard Russell of Georgia declared that, "If there is one agency of the Government in which we must take some matters in faith without a constant examination of its methods and sources, I believe this agency is the Central Intelligence Agency." Senator Leverett Saltonstall echoed this conception of the adverse costs of congressional oversight: "It is not a question on the part of CIA officials to speak to us . . . [but] our reluctance . . . to seek information and

---

[1] In 1954 and 1955, the commission undertook an intensive investigation of the federal bureaucracy to increase efficiency and reduce waste.

knowledge of subjects which I personally, as a member of Congress and as a citizen, would rather not have."

## CURBING McCARTHY WHILE MAINTAINING EXECUTIVE POWERS AND INTERNAL SECURITY

Since 1950, Republicans had condemned the errors in judgment as well as abuses of power that derived from secret presidential conduct of foreign and internal security policy. To redress this situation, the McCarthyite congressional leadership had championed three measures: restoring the Congress's proper role and reversing Soviet gains through adoption of resolutions repudiating wartime summit conference agreements; amending the Constitution to restrict executive agreements and treaty-making authority; and increasing Congress's role in the internal security area. As a candidate first for the Republican presidential nomination and then for the presidency, Eisenhower had echoed similar concerns. He had specifically promised to repudiate secret unilateral diplomacy, as symbolized by the Yalta Conference of February 4-11, 1945, to consult with Congress prior to formulating foreign policy, and to purge "disloyal" individuals from the federal bureaucracy.

    As president, Eisenhower did seek to harmonize executive-legislative relations. His subsequent presidential actions for the most part repudiated his earlier campaign pledges. In late February 1953, the Eisenhower administration introduced and lobbied for a resolution criticizing the Soviet Union for violating its wartime agreements. Eisenhower acted to avert congressional enactment of a resolution specifically repudiating the Yalta agreements. Republican Senate majority leader Robert Taft quietly killed the administration's weaker Yalta resolution in committee.

    A resolution to repudiate Yalta was a symbolic act, involving as it did an oblique attack on past Democratic diplomacy. Republican Senator John Bricker's proposed constitutional amendment to restrict executive foreign policy authority, formally introduced in 1952 and supported by sixty-five Senators (including forty-four of the forty-seven Republican senators), involved an issue of substance. The amendment required congressional approval of all treaties and executive agreements affecting domestic policy. Powerful conservative groups actively promoted the Bricker Amendment—the American Medical Association feared the introduction of socialized medicine through the World Health Organization of the United Nations and southern segregationists worried that ratification of the UN Covenant on Human Rights might dilute states' rights and the South's system of segregation. Reversing themselves in 1953, Secretary of State John

Foster Dulles and Republican Senator Alexander Wiley of Wisconsin (then chairman on the Senate Foreign Relations Committee) publicly opposed the amendment. Not Eisenhower but Dulles led the opposition to the amendment. The president's apparent neutrality successfully made the issue one involving the effective conduct of foreign policy and not a presidential quest for power. In February 1954, by one vote short of the needed two-thirds, the Senate rejected the Bricker Amendment.

The Bricker Amendment and the Yalta resolution symbolized Congress's challenge to exclusive executive control over foreign policy. As part of their effort to curb executive powers, conservative Republicans had pointedly assailed President Truman's claims to executive privilege in 1948 and thereafter. Senator McCarthy and other conservative Republicans (notably Taft and then-Congressman Richard Nixon) charged that Truman's executive privilege claims frustrated the implementation of an effective internal security program, covered up incompetence and disloyalty, and stymied the creation of a foreign policy that would insure victory in the Cold War. Republican assaults on claimed executive power also sought to discredit the Democrats. "My fellow Americans," Republican House leader Joseph Martin, Jr., thundered, "the record of the last twenty years should convince everyone of us that we must clean house at Washington. The only way that we can get back on the road of real Americanism is to get rid of those responsible for this mess we are in and substitute bold, courageous, intelligent leadership."

Once having obtained the presidency Eisenhower readily abandoned policies aimed at diminishing executive power. On April 27, 1953, Eisenhower amended Truman's loyalty program by executive action and not through consultation with Congress. Eisenhower's "security" program scrapped President Truman's elaborate hearing and review procedures—which had enabled accused employees to defend themselves before being dismissed. Dismissal was no longer based on proof of "reasonable doubt as to loyalty" but on whether the individual's employment was "clearly consistent with the interests of national security." To receive clearance, federal employees had to be "reliable, trustworthy, of good conduct and character, and of complete and unswerving loyalty to the United States." Eisenhower's employee security program was ostensibly based on congressional legislation of September 1950 (Public Law 733) authorizing cabinet officials to dismiss without the right of appeal individuals holding "sensitive" security positions. In effect Eisenhower's order extended this summary dismissal authority to all federal departments. By moving quickly, the president had gained the initiative from Congress. But he had not settled the question of whether Congress or the president should determine national security policy, nor what the role of McCarthyites would be.

Believing firmly in the need to strengthen Congress's internal security role, McCarthyites—particularly Congressman Harold Velde, chairman of

HUAC; Senator William Jenner, chairman of the Internal Security Sub-committee; and Senator Joseph McCarthy, chairman of the Permanent Investigations Subcommittee of the Government Operations Committee—were unwilling to follow blindly even a conservative Republican president. The Republican Senate leadership, moreover, had thought that the obstreperous McCarthy had been effectively constrained with his assign-ment to the relatively insignificant Permanent Investigations subcommittee. McCarthy saw things differently. Hiring a brash young staff director, Roy Cohn, the Wisconsin senator used the subcommittee to investigate State Department security procedures.

Under McCarthy's leadership, the Permanent Investigations Sub-committee held a series of hearings in early 1953 on the Voice of America, at which anti-Communists charged that it was run by "Communists, left-wingers, New Dealers, radicals and pinkos." The senator soon shifted his attention to the State Department's International Information Agency (sub-sequently renamed USIA), to ascertain whether its overseas libraries carried "subversive" literature. Responding to McCarthy's investigation, on March 18, 1953, the State Department banned from United States information centers "the works of all Communist authors," "any publication which con-tinuously publishes Communist propaganda," and the works of art of "any Communists, fellow travelers, etcetera." Overreacting to this order, some frightened agency personnel even burned the books in their libraries of alleged left-wing authors. In a relatively unpublicized commencement ad-dress at Dartmouth College, President Eisenhower obliquely condemned book-burning, advising the graduates: "Don't join the bookburners. . . . Don't be afraid to go in your library and read every book as long as that document does not offend your own ideas of decency." When asked at a subsequent press conference about whether his Dartmouth remarks re-ferred to Senator McCarthy, Eisenhower refused to indulge in "personali-ties" and conceded that he did not object to destroying blatant Communist literature.

The administration at first sought to avert a direct confrontation with McCarthy. As part of this effort, Vice President Nixon, the White House's liaison with McCarthy, urged the Wisconsin senator to explore other issues than the Republican administration's security procedures. Instead, in the fall of 1953, McCarthy's subcommittee initiated an investigation of army security procedures at Fort Monmouth, New Jersey (convicted atomic spy Julius Rosenberg had been employed there in 1944), ostensibly to ascertain why the army had promoted and then honorably discharged Irving Peress, an obscure dentist with radical political views.

Senator McCarthy's harsh questioning of General Ralph Zwicker, the commanding officer at Fort Monmouth, about army security procedures (McCarthy pointedly charged that Zwicker did not have "the brains of a five-year old") during the initial stage of these hearings led Secretary of the Army Robert Stevens to intercede. To protect lower-echelon officers from the senator's harassment, Stevens directed that army officials not testify before McCarthy's subcommittee. Stevens's policy made the hearings into a confrontation between the army and McCarthy.

Hoping to placate the Wisconsin senator, administration personnel quietly arranged a private conference between Stevens and McCarthy. At first eager for a reconciliation, the secretary soon reconsidered and threatened to resign unless the administration supported the army's position. Stevens's threat forced a reluctant administration into a public confrontation with McCarthy over the army's complaint that the senator and his staff had used improper influence to secure preferential treatment for a former consultant to the McCarthy subcommittee, then army private G. David Schine.

During the resultant nationally televised Army-McCarthy hearings (held between April 17 and June 17) McCarthy proved to be his own worst enemy. The senator's tactics and abuse of parliamentary devices raised public doubts about his methods and honesty. Appalled by McCarthy's performance, Republican Senator Ralph Flanders on June 11, 1954, introduced a Senate resolution to censure McCarthy. The Senate that month approved an amended version of this resolution to establish a special committee to investigate Flanders's charges. Chaired by the conservative Utah Republican Arthur Watkins, this committee after a lengthy investigation recommended on September 27, 1954, that the Senate censure McCarthy on two counts of conduct unbecoming a senator. McCarthy in turn accused the committee of aiding international Communism. Even then, the administration did not endorse censure. Vice President Nixon vainly worked behind the scenes to convince McCarthy to apologize publicly and thus avert censure. McCarthy's stubbornness ended all efforts at compromise. Having delayed considering the Watkins Committee's recommendation until after the congressional elections, on December 2, the Senate voted 67 to 22 to condemn McCarthy. Conservative Republicans alone supported the Wisconsin senator.

The Army-McCarthy hearings again raised the issue of executive privilege. On May 17, 1954, Eisenhower directed his staff not to comply with Senator McCarthy's request for information about January 1954 oral and telephone conversations between army counsel John Adams and White House personnel. The administration would not comply: "Because it is essential to efficient and effective administration that employees of the executive branch be in a position to be completely candid in advising with each other in official matters, and because it is not in the public interest that such advice be disclosed." Immediately challenging this claim, McCarthy on May 27 urged all federal employees to recognize that "it is their duty to give us any information which they have about graft, corruption, communism, treason, and that there is no loyalty to a superior officer which can tower above and beyond their loyalty to their country."

Eisenhower's May 17 directive was but one of his administration's forty-five claims to executive privilege. Paradoxically, one legacy of McCarthy's tactics was an increased tolerance for such executive claims and further insulation of executive policy from congressional oversight. In contrast to Truman's, Eisenhower's executive privilege claims encompassed a wide variety of issues, some involving important policy questions and others decisions that if publicly revealed might have been politically embarrassing. Eisenhower's claims also extended beyond individuals who directly communicated with the president to include all executive employees and executive branch reports (both from Cabinet departments and independent federal regulatory agencies). In 1957, for example, the administration rejected a Senate committee request for government plans to maintain civil liberties in the event of a nuclear attack on the United States. In 1958, the administration refused to release a copy of the Gaither Report of November 1957. This report of a special presidential advisory committee assessed the effect of Soviet military capabilities on U.S. national defense spending and civil defense needs.

Tight controls over the dissemination of "national security" information further expanded presidential influence. First, on November 5, 1953, Eisenhower issued Executive Order 10501 which established a new information classification principle "promoting national defense." Eisenhower's order offered no definition of "national defense" or "defense information" and thereby encouraged overclassification. Then, in 1958, the Eisenhower administration established a Censorship Code, headquartered at Western Maryland College, with the authority, subject to issuance of an executive order, to censor radio, television, and newspapers. That same year, a House subcommittee discovered that the army had classified experimental work on "more efficient and effective bows and arrows," as "confidential" and a report on "shark repellants" as "secret."

In 1958 Democratic Senator Joseph Clark demanded an annual presidential report to the Congress on the state of the national security. At present, Clark observed, "The Congress and the public cannot make intelligent decisions without authoritative information yet public information on military matters consists mainly of leaks from the Pentagon and piecemeal bits of information put out in press releases or submitted to congressional committees." Clark's attempt to restore Congress's oversight role was rebuffed as Democratic Senate majority leader Lyndon Johnson warned that "a substantial quantity of classified data" would have had to be released. Johnson further noted that "the basic information necessary for an appraisal of the nation's security is available to the Members of Congress through existing channels in just about the best fashion, even though it has its imperfections."

The administration's unwillingness to challenge McCarthy had also been based on political expediency. Recognizing the senator's value to the Republican party, the president did not wish to antagonize unnecessarily McCarthy's principal supporters in the Republican party's right wing. The Republican right wing still suspected the Eisenhower administration's conservative credentials. The administration's actions in 1953 and 1954—opposing the Bricker Amendment, thwarting congressional attempts to repudiate the Yalta agreements, nominating the former interpreter at the Yalta Conference, Charles Bohlen, as U.S. ambassador to the Soviet Union, and extensive executive privilege claims—further increased these conservatives' doubts about the administration's conservatism. Disgruntled by the president's actions, in early 1954 a number of conservatives formed a new organization, the For America Committee, headed by former Eisenhower aide Clarence Manion. Through this committee, conservatives could advance conservative principles outside the structure of the Republican party. Simultaneously, a number of conservative intellectuals led by William Buckley (a recent graduate of Yale University and coauthor of a sympathetic study of McCarthy) launched a new periodical, *National Review,* as the voice of American political conservatism.

The Administration's fervent anti-Communism also made it hesitant to confront McCarthy. Eisenhower's anti-Communism served several purposes: to discredit the Democrats, to sustain more conservative politics, and, concomitantly, to purge New Deal holdovers from the federal bureaucracy. To accomplish these objectives, the newly inaugurated administration quickly moved in 1953 to rid the federal bureaucracy of New Deal liberals who had gained employment during the twenty-year period of Democratic control of the presidency. Under Truman's loyalty procedures, these civil service appointees could not be dismissed on loyalty grounds unless the government produced substantial evidence. Eisenhower's March 18, 1953, letter to Secretary of Commerce Sinclair Weeks provides insight into his definition of disloyalty. In this letter the president condemned individuals who had advanced to important policy-making posts through "a process of selection based upon their devotion to socialistic doctrine and bureaucratic control practiced over the past two decades."

To eliminate "socialistic" or "bureaucratic" influences, Eisenhower on April 27, 1953, instituted the nebulous "suitability" standard under his "security" program and, on March 31, 1953, reclassified federal positions through executive order 10440, phasing out certain positions and creating new job categories which the new administration could then fill. Deputy Secretary of the Treasury Randolph Burgess summarized the administration's priorities: "Our kind of people are now in power."

The Eisenhower administration's review of atomic scientist J. Robert Oppenheimer's security clearance underscored its more sophisticated McCarthyism. During World War II Oppenheimer had played a major role in recruiting scientists for the atomic bomb project. After the war, and until dissenting in 1950 from the Truman administration's decision to undertake a "crash program" to develop a thermonuclear bomb, Oppenheimer continued to play a major advisory role in nuclear policy. Because of the sensitivity of his position, the atomic scientist underwent several security investigations that focused on his earlier links to radical politics. Until 1953 Oppenheimer had always received a security clearance. A year later his advisory role had virtually ended and the Atomic Energy Commission (AEC) could simply have dropped him as a consultant. Instead, the AEC created a special board to review Oppenheimer's security clearance. (President Eisenhower himself was not convinced that the previous loyalty checks had been conclusive. Their findings did "not mean that he might not be a security risk.") After a lengthy new investigation which uncovered no evidence of disloyalty, the board recommended against continuing Oppenheimer's security clearance because of his politics and judgment on the premise that national security "in times of peril must be absolute."

Oppenheimer's case was not atypical. Security officials depicted Soviet peace feelers in 1953 as a cloak for increased spy activities. Twenty-six states enacted legislation either barring Communists from seeking public office or requiring that teachers, paleontologists, and even wrestlers sign loyalty oaths. The most extreme instances of this obsession involved two security proceedings. In one case, in 1953, William L. Greene, a vice president and general manager of an engineering firm under contract to the Navy Department, was denied a security clearance despite having been cleared four times between 1949 and 1952. Most of the charges against Greene centered on his former wife's political associations (they had been divorced in 1947). In the second case, a soldier underwent a security clearance investigation because of his mother-in-law's political activities. Ludicrously, the soldier's mother-in-law had died when he was ten years old and her death occurred ten years before he met his future wife.

The Eisenhower administration shrewdly exploited the subversive issue for partisan purposes. In his January 1954 State of the Union address, Eisenhower claimed the dismissal of 2,200 "security risks" from the federal government under his administration's "security" program. The Republican National Committee updated these dismissal figures throughout 1954 and until these claims were effectively challenged in 1955. During the 1954 congressional campaign Vice President Nixon crudely red-baited the Democrats. The Eisenhower administration had been "kicking Communists and fellow travelers out of the government by the thousands," Nixon reported; if the Democrats won, he charged, these subversives would regain their former influence. The Communist party, Nixon warned, was working against the

Republican congressional candidates because "the candidates running on the Democratic ticket in the key states are almost without exception members of the Democratic party's left-wing clique which has been so blind to the Communist conspiracy and have tolerated it in the United States." In the closing days of the campaign, Eisenhower echoed Nixon's charges, not too subtly observing that his "administration does not look upon the Communist menace as a red herring."

Partisanship comported with conviction. In April 1954, the administration demanded additional internal security legislation to grant immunity from prosecution to individuals testifying on national security matters before congressional committees and grand juries and authorizing wiretapping in national security cases. Congress approved the proposed immunity bill that year but refused to enact wiretapping legislation. Lacking legislative authorization, the administration continued to authorize wiretaps during so-called national security investigations. On May 20, 1954, moreover, Attorney General Brownell authorized the FBI to install microphones for intelligence gathering involving the "national interest," "internal security and the national safety." President Eisenhower consciously approved FBI investigations of "subversive activities" on December 15, 1953, formalizing this by departmental order 175-59 on March 28, 1959, and since January 1953 encouraged FBI Director Hoover to continue reporting on the dissident activities of American citizens. Encouraged to extend existing surveillance programs, in 1960 FBI Director Hoover personally established a Reserve Index of "prominent" personalities who might adversely influence public opinion. Earlier, in August 1956, the FBI Director on his own planned a so-called counterintelligence program (subsequently expanded) to "harass, discredit, and intimidate" American Communists.

The FBI was not alone engaging in domestic surveillance. In 1953, the CIA (with Eisenhower's subsequent approval) instituted a mail program in New York City to read the envelopes of letters to and from the Soviet Union. Opening these letters in 1956 (in violation of federal law), the CIA after February 1958 began forwarding information obtained through this mail program to the FBI. On May 14, 1954, moreover, President Eisenhower approved an NSC proposal, NSC Action 1114, to censor all foreign Communist propaganda mailed to the United States.

The administration's efforts encouraged Congress to enact further anti-Communist legislation. An administration-sponsored bill purporting to stamp out Communism, the Communist Control Act of 1954, was broadened during congressional debate in August 1954 to impose far-reaching restrictions on individual liberties. "Communist-infiltrated" organizations were denied the privileges of the National Labor Relations Act of 1935, the Communist party was denied the right to appear on the ballot, and the registration requirement (of the 1950 McCarran Act) was extended to "Communist-infiltrated" organizations (a provision specifically directed at left-oriented groups of all sorts). The Communist party and Communist-infiltrated organizations, the proponents of this measure argued, were not entitled to the "rights, privileges, and immunities attendant upon legal bodies."

## THE IMPACT
## OF THE WARREN COURT,
## MODERN REPUBLICANISM,
## AND THE LEGITIMATION OF
## THE WELFARE STATE

As a cautious conservative, Eisenhower kept his distance from two of the most contentious domestic issues of the Cold War years—civil rights and civil liberties. Supreme Court decisions on these issues, however, effectively circumvented the administration's strategy of benign neglect. Under the leadership of Chief Justice Earl Warren (appointed by Eisenhower in September 1953 to succeed Fred Vinson), between 1954 and 1959 the Supreme Court issued a series of rulings that extended individual liberties by restricting congressional, executive, and investigative powers and striking down state-imposed segregation.

In 1957, in *Yates* v. *U.S.* and *Jencks* v. *U.S.*, the Court reimposed constitutional restrictions on governmental prosecution of domestic radicals. In *Yates,* the Court in effect revised the Vinson Court's 1951 ruling in *Dennis* v. *U.S.* In that decision upholding the Smith Act convictions of the eleven leaders of the U.S. Communist party, the Vinson Court had held that the government could punish advocates of revolutionary change. Not directly overturning this ruling, the Warren Court substantially modified the *Dennis* ruling. It reversed the Smith Act convictions of second-echelon Communist party leaders, by holding that *Dennis* prohibited incitement to illegal action and not mere advocacy of revolutionary doctrine. In *Jencks,* moreover, the Court ruled that an accused defendant had the right to examine the pretrial statements made by prosecution witnesses to the FBI.

In *Cole* v. *Young* (1956), *Peters* v. *Hobby* (1954), *Service* v. *Dulles* (1957), and *Greene* v. *McElroy* (1959), the Court limited the arbitrary practice of presidential loyalty programs. It declared that accused employees were entitled to due process during hearings, including the right to challenge directly the veracity of their accusers. In the *Peters* and *Service* cases the Court, in effect, upheld federal loyalty programs but ruled that Truman's Loyalty Review Board had unconstitutionally exceeded its delegated authority. In *Cole,* the most significant of these decisions, the Court held that Eisenhower's security program exceeded the statutory authority on which it had been formally based—Public Law 733. That statute had authorized summary dismissals only for security positions, the Court noted, while the administration had included nonsensitive jobs.

Conservatives bitterly assailed the Supreme Court's civil liberties rulings. This assault paled in contrast to the reaction to the Court's unanimous decision of May 17, 1954, in *Brown* v. *Board of Education of Topeka*. Segregated school systems were unconstitutional, the Court ruled: "In the field of public education the doctrine of 'separate but equal' has no place. Separate educational facilities are inherently unequal." A year later in a related case, the Court required the abolition of segregated systems "with all deliberate speed."

Almost immediately, southern political leaders condemned the *Brown* decision and billboards appeared on southern highways demanding the chief justice's impeachment. Newly formed white citizens councils organized resistance to desegregation: Southern governors and legislatures adopted the policy of "massive resistance" to interpose state power against school integration. The more militant resisters formed the Independent States' Rights party. Democratic Senator J. Strom Thurmond of South Carolina conceived and helped draft the so-called Southern Manifesto. Signed by 101 of the 128 southern U.S. senators and representatives, the manifesto declared "political war against the Court's decision." It pledged "to use all lawful means to bring about a reversal of this decision which is contrary to the Constitution."

This defiance climaxed in September 1957. Responding to a federal court order to integrate the Little Rock (Arkansas) high schools, Arkansas Governor Orval Faubus announced that to "maintain order" the state national guard would prevent nine black students from attending Central High School. When the federal judge ordered integration "forthwith" and black students attempted to attend the high school, guardsmen barred their admission. At first President Eisenhower temporized, claiming that "you cannot change people's hearts merely by laws." Faubus's actions soon forced the president to act. Inviting the Arkansas governor to meet him, Eisenhower affirmed his administration's intention to enforce the laws. Upon returning to Arkansas and pursuant to a court order, on September 20, Faubus ordered the national guard's withdrawal. By then the white population had become so enraged that a mob of 500 that day surrounded the high school. The Little Rock mayor then requested federal assistance. On September 21, Eisenhower federalized 10,000 Arkansas National Guardsmen and dispatched 1,000 paratroopers to Little Rock. Federal troops remained at Little Rock for the rest of the year; the high school, however, was closed in 1958 and 1959, reopening only after another 1959 court order.

Eisenhower's responses to the Little Rock affair reflected his views on desegregation. The President never endorsed the principle of desegregation and did not morally endorse the court's decisions. Instead, in his first press conference following the *Brown* decision, he lamely described the Supreme Court's ruling as the law of the land which must be respected. Not surprisingly, by Eisenhower's second term, only 765 of the South's 7000 school districts were integrated.

The furor over civil rights would not abate. Black Americans had been emboldened by the Supreme Court's decision against Jim Crow.[2] They directly challenged long-established southern segregationist policies with such actions as the Montgomery, Alabama, bus boycott organized by the Reverend Martin Luther King, Jr., which began on December 1, 1955, and the student-led sit-ins to integrate dime-store lunch counters, which began in Greensboro, North Carolina, on February 1, 1960. White and blacks also demanded federal action to remove southern restrictions on black voting. A 1959 study disclosed, for example, that only 8.1 percent of Alabama's black population was registered to vote though blacks comprised 30 percent of the voting age population. Mississippi statistics were starker: Only 3.9 percent of the black population qualified to vote whereas blacks constituted 41 percent of the total state population. Some form of federal action was required, and thus the enactment of the Civil Rights Act of 1957. The act created a civil rights division within the Department of Justice with the authority to intercede on behalf of individuals whose civil rights were violated (whether in housing, education, voting, or law enforcement) and established a civil rights commission to recommend further legislation.

Other developments also exposed domestic divisions during the 1950s. The reactionary John Birch Society, for example, was formed in 1958. Not himself a Bircher, Senator Barry Goldwater articulated some of that society's discomfort with the main drift of American society. The Senator from Arizona criticized the Eisenhower administration's foreign and domestic policies for softness toward Communism and the New Deal heritage. In 1960 Goldwater wrote what soon became the political bible of American conservatism, *The Conscience of a Conservative.*

Reluctantly forced to act decisively in the civil rights area, the Eisenhower administration also sanctioned and even expanded New Deal-style welfare statism. Relying principally on military spending and tax policy, the Republican administration sought to stimulate the economy and promote a more affluent society. Thus, on the one hand, in 1953 and 1954, it liquidated the Reconstruction Finance Corporation, lobbied for legislation granting title to offshore oil to the states (specifically Louisiana and Texas), increased tax depletion allowances for businessmen, and unsuccessfully attempted to reduce the Tennessee Valley Authority's electrical power activities by awarding a generating contract to a private utility group, Dixon-Yates (conflict of interest revelations forced the administration to rescind this contract). On the other hand, the administration established the Department of Health, Education and Welfare, extended Social Security and unemployment compensation benefits to more than seven million additional workers, raised the minimum wage from seventy-five to ninety cents an hour, and continued federal subsidies to agriculture.

[2]See Chapter 7 for a fuller description and analysis of the civil rights movement.

In response to the Soviet Union's successful orbiting on October 4, 1957, of Sputnik, the first unmanned space satellite, the administration won passage of the National Defense Education Act of 1958. It aimed at promoting scientific development and regaining technological primacy over the Soviet Union. The act provided federal aid to secondary and higher education, including a program of graduate fellowships.

Unbalanced budgets remained the norm, except for surpluses of $4.5 billion in 1956 and $2 billion in 1957, owing principally to continued high defense expenditures. During fiscal 1958, for example, defense spending accounted for $45 billion of the federal budget. In fiscal 1959, the federal deficit reached $12.5 billion, the highest peacetime deficit ever, and the total federal administrative budget reached $76.5 billion. Equally important, administration policies indirectly subsidized the construction and automobile industries. The Federal Highway Act of 1956 authorized financing (eventually reaching $30 billion) of a vast interstate freeway system. The new highways facilitated a population exodus to suburban areas, which accelerated the decay of urban America, and stimulated growth in the South and Southwest at the expense of the Northeast and North Central states. Two years of economic recession at the end of the Eisenhower presidency further unbalanced the federal budget. For the Republicans implemented all the New Deal reforms still on the books, which automatically acted as a countercyclical force by providing aid for the unemployed and other federal funds to maintain consumer purchasing power.

## THE EISENHOWER-DULLES LEADERSHIP

Eisenhower's experience in foreign affairs had been one of his strongest assets during the 1952 presidential campaign and, as a result, many had concluded that he would end the Korean War and plot a course of peace and security. As wartime supreme commander in Western Europe, he had adroitly managed a difficult coalition war, a task in many ways more diplomatic than military. He had repeated that feat as the first supreme commander of the newly formed NATO.

During his two-term presidency, Eisenhower became a respected symbol of peace throughout the world. His greatest impact was precisely in foreign affairs, where he helped persuade the American people to accept an unpleasant stalemate in the Cold War. He ended the Korean War without full victory, avoided military involvement in Indochina, and inched East-West relations toward detente.

Some contemporary critics nonetheless concluded that Eisenhower failed the challenges of the 1950s, disdaining bold new approaches to foreign problems. Containment remained heavily military at a time when the post-Stalin era demanded greater flexibility and new policies. To the contrary, Eisenhower did not rely exclusively on military power to advance U.S. policy goals. Instead, under his direction and relying on the CIA, the United States sought to limit radical change overseas by strengthening effective conservative political movements and leaders.

Other contemporary critics complained that Eisenhower was misinformed. Unlike other chief executives, Eisenhower limited his time spent over newspapers and lengthy, detailed reports. Instead, he relied upon his principal staff advisers to keep him informed yet he was erroneously regarded here and abroad, as a chief executive who reigned but did not rule. When illness caused Dulles to resign from the State Department in early 1958 and scandal had forced out Assistant to the President Sherman Adams, a British newspaper cartoon portrayed Ike as a sick and doddering old man leaning for support upon British Prime Minister Harold Macmillan. In fact, Eisenhower was well informed about world events and more in command of the nation's foreign policy than his critics ever knew.

Eisenhower's secretary of state, John Foster Dulles, the grandson of Secretary of State John W. Foster and the nephew by marriage of another, Robert Lansing, had been involved in foreign affairs in various capacities since World War I. He had advised Republican presidential nominees during the 1944, 1948, and 1952 campaigns, and in 1951 had helped draft the Japanese peace treaty. As secretary of state, he worked closely with the president. While other Cabinet officials often found it difficult to obtain direct access, Dulles was in constant and close communication with Eisenhower. It was a unique relationship. As one foreign diplomat expressed it, "We felt that Dulles was the United States and the United States was Dulles. He gave this feeling to the whole world."

From his interpretation of Communist ideology Dulles concluded that there must be no compromise with the godless Soviet leaders or with radical nationalists. He resolved to contain the Soviets by threats of war, to encourage European unity and greater responsibility for its own defense, to employ the CIA to overthrow radical political leaders, and to rely upon superior American moral and material force eventually to liberate countries under Soviet control.

At first, too, the new secretary tolerated the McCarthyites. He appointed Scott McLeod, a close friend of Senator Styles Bridges, as departmental security officer and tolerated McLeod's extensive loyalty investigations. Of the more than 500 employees eventually discharged by the State Department, only eleven were "security risks" (and then because of excess drinking or other personal weaknesses that might invite blackmail) and none were proven disloyal. A number of able foreign service officers, such as John Paton Davis, John Carter Vincent, and John Stewart Service, who had written realistic appraisals about China during World War II, were included among those purged from the diplomatic service.

## THE RHETORIC OF LIBERATION:
## THE PRACTICE OF
## CONTAINMENT

During the 1952 campaign, Eisenhower had demanded a bolder and more dynamic foreign policy and declared that the people were right to distrust a Democratic leadership that had "allowed the godless Red Tide" to engulf millions and that had failed to "see the Red stain sweeping into our Government." Similarly, in a *Life* magazine article and on the stump, Dulles had insisted that by means of a "psychological and political offensive the United States should make it publicly known that it wants and expects liberation [of Eastern European states from Soviet control] to occur." The Western world's firmness, the Soviet system's immorality and internal weaknesses insured a "free world" victory over Communism. Republican campaign promises seemingly insured: a dynamic new policy to liberate Eastern Europe from the Soviet Union; a tougher approach in the Far East which would end the Korean War and "unleash" Chiang Kai-shek's forces from Formosa to invade mainland China; greater European efforts to rearm; a wholesale purge of subversives in the State Department; and adoption of the Bricker Amendment to eliminate executive agreements such as those made at Yalta.

Once in power, the Eisenhower administration failed to carry out its campaign promises. "Liberation" proved illusory; Truman's policy of containment was not reversed. Unwilling to risk a major war to force the Soviet Union out of Central and Eastern Europe, the administration simply watched, when in June 1953 Soviet troops and tanks crushed riots in East Berlin.

The Hungarian Revolution of 1956 graphically demonstrated the administration's dilemma. In mid-October 1956, domestic unrest in Poland had brought a more independent Communist Wladyslaw Gomulka to power. Gomulka eased state repression, restrained the secret police, widened Polish autonomy, and established better relations with the Catholic Church. The first example since Tito of "national communism," the Gomulka government's actions shook the other Soviet satellites, indirectly triggering the revolution in Hungary later that month which brought Imre Nagy to power. A moderate Communist earlier imprisoned by Hungarian hard-liners, Nagy quickly lost control of events. In contrast to Poland, the Hungarian nationalists proclaimed a democracy, their intention to withdraw from the Warsaw Pact, and their neutrality in the Cold War. The Soviet leadership could not tolerate such a direct challenge. After some hesitation, on November 4, 1956, Soviet tanks fought their way into Budapest and brutally smashed the popular uprising. Despite the encouragement given by the CIA-financed Radio Free Europe and its rhetoric of liberation, the Eisenhower administration was unwilling to risk a military confrontation with the Soviet Union. It simply expressed sympathy for the rebels and introduced UN resolutions condemning Soviet military intervention.

As for the other Republican promises of 1952, Chiang was "unleashed" when President Eisenhower announced in February 1953 that the U.S. Navy would "no longer be employed to shield Communist China." This "unleashing" did not bring China's liberation, for without U.S. military assistance Chiang's forces could do no more than launch an occasional raid on the mainland. Within the year the administration released Chiang having concluded a mutual defense treaty with the Nationalists which required among other provisions mutual consultation prior to any ventures in Asia. In return for a U.S. security guarantee of Formosa and the nearby Pescadores Islands, the Chinese Nationalists agreed to stop guerrilla raids on the mainland. When the Chinese Communists threatened to overrun the Tachens Islands, Eisenhower persuaded Chiang Kai-shek to evacuate them. Then, in March 1955 when the Chinese Communists began shelling the Nationalist-held islands of Quemoy and Matsu, Eisenhower refused to commit the United States to any specific military response. Holding firm, yet implying a commitment to defend Formosa, Eisenhower's tactics contained the crisis as the Chinese Communists gradually eased their bombardment of the islands.

Eisenhower's ending of the Korean War did not entail the reversal of Truman's limited war strategy. Upon returning from his Korean visit in December 1952, Eisenhower darkly warned that, unless the truce talks brought results, the United States might retaliate in unspecified ways. Through the Indian ambassador, Dulles hinted to the People's Republic of China that atomic bombs might even be used. New Soviet leaders—Stalin died on March 5, 1953—also helped end the war. Truce talks resumed in April and an armistice was signed on July 27, 1953, but a treaty formally ending the Korean war was never concluded. Given the reality of a potentially unstable armed truce, the United States subsequently concluded a security treaty with South Korea and stationed American troops indefinitely along the armistice line.

## THE "SPIRIT OF GENEVA" AND THE PRACTICE OF COVERT OPERATIONS: DETENTE IN EUROPE, INTERVENTION IN THE THIRD WORLD

The Korean stalemate indirectly confirmed the president's recognition of the realities of Soviet power and thus the inevitability of continued Soviet influence in Eastern Europe and China. Thus, his administration accordingly pursued a policy of accommodation as shown by Eisenhower's "atoms for peace" proposal (outlined in a December 8, 1953, speech at the United

Nations) to create an International Atomic Energy Agency and the Summit Conference meeting of July 1955 in Geneva with the leaders of Great Britain (Anthony Eden), France (Edgar Faure), and the Soviet Union (Nikolai Bulganin and Nikita Khrushchev).

The Geneva summit conference was the direct product of the Eisenhower administration's efforts to reduce U.S.-Soviet tensions. Following Stalin's death, the new Soviet leadership had signalled an interest in resolving U.S.-Soviet differences. Although Secretary of State Dulles remained skeptical about direct negotiations with the Soviets, Soviet agreement to a peace treaty with Austria (signed on May 15, 1955), providing for the withdrawal of Soviet and Western forces and a reunified but neutral Austria, encouraged hopes for progress on a German settlement and for possible arms reductions.

At the Geneva summit conference, Eisenhower advanced another dramatic "open skies" proposal that the United States and the Soviet Union exchange "a complete blueprint of our military establishments" and permit unlimited aerial reconnaissance. No agreement was reached on this measure, as the conferees failed to resolve the complex problems of German reunification and nuclear disarmament. The "Spirit of Geneva," however, marked a thaw in Cold War tensions and reduced the chances of a direct U.S.-Soviet conflict. Consistent with a policy of limited detente, in 1959 Eisenhower invited and Khrushchev agreed to visit the United States. The Khrushchev visit did not usher in an era of continued negotiations; the subsequently scheduled summit conference in Paris of May 1960 was canceled when the Soviet Union shot down a CIA U-2 flight over Soviet territory. In a display of diplomatic ineptitude, the Eisenhower administration first denied that there was a spy flight and then refused to renounce future spying efforts.

As U.S. policy moderated toward the Soviet Union and its European satellites, it hardened in the Third World. This shift necessitated the adoption of a strategy to thwart revolutionary political change. Developments in Indochina illuminated the shift in priorities.

With the end of World War II, Vietnamese nationalists opposed the reassertion of French control over a colony France had ruled since the mid-nineteenth century. Led by Ho Chi Minh, the founder of the Vietnamese Communist party who worked ceaselessly for independence from French rule, Vietnamese nationalists in 1946 proclaimed the independent Democratic Republic of Vietnam. France refused to grant Indochina independence, and a civil war erupted that lasted for eight years. During this lengthy colonial war, French soldiers held the cities and most of the towns, while the rebels controlled the countryside. As part of his containment policy, in May 1950 President Truman authorized limited economic assistance to the French, extended after the outbreak of the Korean War, and recognized the French puppet regime of Emperor Bao Dai. Financing

France's military effort, by 1954 the United States had underwritten about 70 percent of the costs of the war.

Weary of an endless guerilla war in Indochina, the French commander in Indochina, General Henri Navarre, in 1954 fought a decisive battle at the remote fortress of Dien Bien Phu. Navarre's strategy of concentrating French forces at this fortress aimed at stopping Chinese Communist supplies to the Vietminh. The Vietminh responded by besieging the fortress, cutting it off from the outside world, and bringing it under murderous bombardment. France then appealed to the United States for assistance. The Eisenhower administration split on the issue—Dulles and Admiral Charles Radford favored naval air strikes to relieve Dien Bien Phu, Air Force Chief of Staff Nathan Twining even contemplated use of tactical atomic bombs, while Admiral A.C. Davis (who headed the Pentagon's Foreign Military Affairs division) and General Matthew Ridgeway opposed U.S. military involvement. Ridgeway estimated that at a minimum the United States would have to send seven divisions to defeat the Vietminh, and twelve if the Chinese intervened. Although Eisenhower indicated in an April 7, 1954, press conference his support for the "domino theory" principle in Indochina ("You have a row of dominoes set up, and you knock over the first one and what will happen to the last one is the certainty that it will go over quickly."), Eisenhower refused to risk U.S. ground forces in Southeast Asia.

Political considerations proved decisive. Unwilling to commit U.S. troops in ground combat on his exclusive authority, the president conferred with a prestigous group of congressional leaders. The congressional leadership reluctantly agreed to support U.S. involvement but on certain conditions: The administration would have to secure "United Action" in the form of assistance from Great Britain, Thailand, the Phillippines, and the Indochinese peoples. Administration efforts to pressure the British to participate proved unavailing. In the interim, on May 7, 1954, Dien Bien Phu fell.

Defeat at Dien Bien Phu spelled the end of the French military effort to defeat the Vietminh. A new French government was elected, headed by Pierre Mendes-France, which supported an international conference of the interested powers—the People's Republic of China, the Soviet Union, France, and Great Britain—to negotiate an Indochina settlement. The Mendes-France government's determination to conclude a peace succeeded and two pacts were signed in July 1954, the Geneva Armistice Agreement and the Final Declaration of Geneva. A truce between the French and the Vietminh was instituted with a temporary partition and demilitarized zone along the 17th parallel, French troops withdrawing to the south of that line and Ho Chi Minh's to the north. The pacts further permitted the free exchange of peoples desiring to leave either half of Vietnam; created an armistice commission composed of India, Poland, and Canada; and called for supervised free elections to be held by 1956 to reunify the country. Although Vietminh forces controlled an estimated two-thirds of Vietnam,

Ho Chi Minh accepted this compromise, confident of victory in the proposed general election.

The Eisenhower administration did not sign the Geneva agreements—Dulles refused to negotiate directly with representatives of the People's Republic of China. In a separate statement, the administration supported the idea of free elections and warned against "any aggression in violation" of the Geneva accords. From the outset, the president's policy was to establish an independent, anti-Communist government in South Vietnam. To achieve this result, the administration helped bring Ngo Dinh Diem to power, an ardent anti-Communist nationalist not compromised by identification with the French, and provided him with conventional military and economic assistance. In addition, through the CIA the administration secretly assisted South Vietnamese police officials to establish internal security in the South. Diem's repressive and unpopular policies, coupled with his refusal to hold the promised unification elections, led to the outbreak of civil war in 1959.

The CIA's covert operations role was not confined to shoring up an anti-Communist government in South Vietnam. Following a March 1953 NSC meeting, President Eisenhower and Secretary of State Dulles approved a plan to employ the CIA to overthrow the nationalist Iranian premier Mohammed Mossadegh and restore the shah to power. Again with White House approval, in June 1954 the CIA engineered a coup to overthrow the Arbenz government in Guatemala and to install a right-wing government headed by Colonel Carlos Castillo-Armas. Again at Eisenhower's direction, the CIA: in 1953 promoted Ramon Magsaysay's candidacy for presidency of the Philippines, in 1957 supported dissident military officials seeking to oust Indonesian president Achmed Sukarno, funded anti-Communist politicians during the 1957 Singaporean elections, and in 1960 supported elements seeking to overthrow Dominican Republican strongman Rafael Trujillo. Strongly opposed to the radical nationalism of Congolese Premier Patrice Lumumba, the CIA sought his overthrow, and even planned to assassinate him. Concerned over the policies and radicalism of Cuban President Fidel Castro (who successfully overthrew Fulgencio Batista in January 1959), President Eisenhower on March 17, 1960, authorized the CIA to train and arm Cuban exiles for a prospective invasion of Cuba to overthrow the Castro government.

## THE U.S. AND THE MIDDLE EAST:
## ISRAEL, THE ARABS,
## AND OIL DIPLOMACY

At the minimum embracing the Arab-speaking lands of Asia and Egypt, and at the maximum also including Iran, Turkey, and North Africa, the Middle East is unified only by the Moslem religion. Oil links many of the region's states and further defines their relationship with the Western powers, who were more dependent upon Middle Eastern oil after 1945—between 1938 and 1955 oil exports to Western Europe through the Suez Canal increased from five million to sixty-eight million tons.

This dependence coincided with the weakening of Western European influence in the Middle East. France had been pushed out of Syria and Lebanon after World War II, leaving Britain alone to uphold Western interests in the Middle East. Having liquidated much of her empire elsewhere during the early postwar years, Britain might also have done so in the Middle East except for her economic dependence on oil. Consequently, Britain struggled to retain influence in this vital area.

Israel's creation in 1948 added the final explosive element to an already treacherous situation. Israel constituted one of the few examples of a state deliberately created in pursuit of an idea, Zionism—a national Jewish home to replace the one destroyed by Roman dispersions of the population in the first century, A.D. Founded in 1897 by Dr. Theodore Herzl at a congress in Basle, Zionism was a reaction to European persecutions of Jews in the nineteenth century. It also absorbed the Western doctrines of liberal nationalism and self-determination. During World War I, another prominent Zionist, Dr. Chaim Weizmann, obtained the Balfour Declaration from the British government. The British promised Jews a "national home" in Palestine on the condition that the non-Jewish peoples already living there would not be harmed. The establishment of the British mandate after World War I opened the area to Jewish immigration and between 1922 and 1944 the ratio of Jews to Arabs increased from one to eight to one to two—from 83,790 Jews and 600,000 Arabs to 528,000 Jews and 1 million Arabs.

Arabs resisted Jewish immigration. Britain was thus torn between her promises to the Zionists and need for Arab oil. Responding to Arab pressures, in 1939 the British government limited immigration to 75,000 during the next five years, and terminated it completely thereafter. As a result Zionists fought the British.

Despite the explosive potential of these developments, the Truman administration's initial postwar policy toward the Middle East drifted with events, the State Department at first following the British lead in Palestine. Well-organized Jewish organizations challenged this policy, commanding as well considerable influence within the liberal wing of the Democratic party and a sympathetic American public opinion heightened by recent publicity of Hitler's genocide policy toward European Jews. Then in 1947, a weary Britain decided to yield the Palestine question to the United Nations for solution and to surrender its mandate over the area. Under U.S. pressure, the United Nations divided Palestine into a Jewish and an Arab state.

War resulted when British forces formally withdrew from Palestine in May 1948. Arab armies from surrounding countries promptly invaded Palestine intending to crush the newly proclaimed Jewish state of Israel. Instead, the numerically inferior Jewish forces quickly smashed the invaders. Compelled by defeat to sign a truce with Israel, the Arabs would not conclude a treaty recognizing the new state's existence. Some 700,000 Arabs fled or were encouraged to flee Israel and settled in refugee camps along Israel's borders in the Gaza Strip and in Jordan. Encouraged by Egypt and other Arab states, many of these refugees remained committed to a war of revenge to exterminate the Jewish state.

Responding to the waning of British influence, the United States had assumed the primary burden of keeping the Middle East and its vital oil in the Western camp. In 1951, the Truman administration promoted the Middle East Defense Organization to limit Communist penetration. But Egypt and the other Arab countries declined to join this alliance, having concluded that it would perpetuate Western predominance. More important, the corrupt Egyptian regime of King Farouk was overthrown in 1952, bringing to power the radical nationalist Colonel Gamal Abdel Nasser.

The first of a new generation of Arab nationalists, Nasser saw his mission as to unify the Arab world. In 1954 he persuaded Britain to withdraw all its forces from Egypt. Promising to maintain former British bases on a standby basis, Nasser reaffirmed the 1888 Convention of Constantinople that had called for unimpeded passage through the Suez Canal. With Britain's consent, the Eisenhower administration promised Egypt economic aid and eventually, in December 1955, offered $270 million to help finance Egyptian construction of the Aswan High Dam on the Nile. Heretofore pro-Israeli, administration policy shifted slightly as the president sought to demonstrate Western friendship to the Arabs and alert Israel to U.S. intentions to pursue a more even-handed Middle Eastern policy.

Eisenhower-Dulles policy in the Middle East was based largely on power politics and containment of Soviet power. Accordingly, in 1955 under U.S. leadership, Great Britain, Iran, Iraq, and Pakistan signed the Baghdad Pact—an alliance intended to strengthen the area against Soviet expansion and to buttress Britain's position in Iraq. The pact disturbed the Arab world, especially Nasser who regarded it as an undesirable extension of NATO to the Middle East and a British device to promote Iraq as a rival to his leadership in the Arab world. Egypt managed to keep the rest of the area out of the new alliance. Alarmed by the pact, the Soviet Union also intervened actively in Middle Eastern politics.

A new blow to Western hopes resulted from Egyptian-Israeli hostilities. In February 1955, Israeli forces launched a large-scale raid in the Gaza Strip, in retaliation for numerous border clashes. Catching the Egyptian army totally unprepared, Israeli forces inflicted a humiliating defeat. Enraged and abased by this defeat, Nasser intensified the border war and requested Western arms aid. In accordance with the Tripartite Declaration of 1950, Britain and the United States refused. The Egyptian president then turned to the Soviet bloc and in September 1955 concluded a deal with Czecho-slovakia for $200 million in arms.

Nasser's flirtation with the Soviet Union caused Britain and the United

States to reexamine their policies. Unmoved by Nasser's hints that the Soviet Union had offered more generous aid for construction of the Aswan Dam, the Eisenhower administration was further disturbed when in May 1956 the Egyptian president recognized the People's Republic of China. On July 19, 1956, Dulles brusquely and undiplomatically withdrew the Aswan Dam aid on the grounds that the project was unsound. Nasser responded on July 27 by nationalizing the Anglo-French–owned Suez Canal.

Nasser had only broken a contract with the privately chartered Suez Canal company. Yet British Prime Minister Eden concluded that Nasser must be dealt with firmly. Maintaining that Egypt had violated international law, including the 1888 Convention for unimpeded use of the canal by all nations, the British attempted to disrupt canal transit by ordering all Western pilots off the job. The Egyptians, nonetheless, managed to operate the canal.

In the midst of the 1956 presidential election campaign, Eisenhower particularly feared the outbreak of war, having also decided that force was unjustified and that Britain's case was weak. Instead of using force, Eisenhower and Dulles proposed a managerial board for the canal and a canal users association to negotiate terms with Nasser. Unmoved by the Eisenhower-Dulles approach, British Prime Minister Eden decided to act without consulting or informing Washington.

On October 29, Israeli forces invaded the Sinai. Britain and France concurrently sent Israel and Egypt an "impartial ultimatum" to withdraw from the area around the Suez Canal. Israel promptly agreed, but Egypt refused. Israel's invasion had been carefully prearranged to justify Anglo-French intervention. On October 31, 1956, the British sent bombers into the area and then on November 5 British and French forces seized the Suez Canal and bombed targets along it.

To forestall Soviet action, and to teach Britain and France that they could not act independently of Washington, the Eisenhower administration worked through the United Nations to resolve the Suez crisis. Joining with the Soviet Union, Secretary of State Dulles secured passage of a UN resolution condemning the Anglo-French resort to force and calling for a cease-fire. Under American pressure, feeling the effect of an Arab oil embargo, and fearing Soviet military intervention, on November 6 Britain and France accepted a cease-fire and began to withdraw their forces. Israel also withdrew and a truce was instituted under UN supervision.

Only Israel emerged from the Suez crisis with clear gains, having opened the port of Eilat on the Gulf of Aqaba and also having captured an ample supply of Czech-Egyptian war materials. Moving quickly to exploit this unanticipated opportunity, the Soviet Union extended financial and technical assistance to Egypt for the Aswan Dam. The administration's diplomacy failed to enhance its standing in the Arab world and instead contributed to a deterioration in U.S.-British-French relations.

To forestall the further extension of Soviet influence in the Middle East, having confused aggressive Egyptian Pan Arabism with pro-Communism, in early 1957 the Congress passed a joint resolution, the so-called Eisenhower Doctrine, authorizing the president to extend military and economic aid to any requesting Middle Eastern nation to resist Communist aggression. Hailed as a bulwark against Communist expansion, the Eisenhower Doctrine further extended U.S. security commitments to protect the existing nonsocialist states. The doctrine was first invoked in the spring of 1957 to bolster Jordan against Egyptian threats. Then, in July 1958 responding to a request from Lebanese President Camille Chamoun, the president dispatched 1700 marines to Lebanon to suppress another crisis instigated by Nasser. Strengthened by this show of force (an additional 14,000 troops were sent including troops armed with tactical nuclear weapons), Chamoun reestablished order and U.S. troops withdrew three months later in October.

The Lebanese intervention was exceptional. Eisenhower preferred to exercise American influence in the Middle East through arms sales and economic leverage rather than direct military intervention. Saudi Arabia and Lebanon, in effect, became dependent on U.S. arms and support for protection against more radical Arab nationalists. The State Department, moreover, supported the interests of private American oil companies in Arabia and other mineral-rich Persian Gulf states.

Under Eisenhower the United States had supplanted Britain as the protector of Western oil interests and the antagonist of radical Arab nationalism. Eisenhower attempted to hold the oil-rich Arab states in the Western camp at the same time that he guaranteed Israel's independence and territorial integrity. This delicate diplomatic balancing act persistently involved the United States in Middle East turmoil as Arab-Israeli conflict refused to abate.

The entire diplomatic pattern of the Eisenhower years, moreover, revealed the president's virtuosity in balancing contradictory tendencies. On the one hand, Dulles promised to roll back the iron curtain and, on the other hand, Eisenhower recognized the legitimacy of Soviet interests in Eastern and Central Europe. Dulles encircled the Soviet Union with hostile alliances and military bases, threatening the Communists in Indochina with massive retaliation; Eisenhower restrained the military and tolerated the use of force only where real military conflict was unlikely, as in Lebanon in 1958. Dulles proclaimed a holy war against godless Communism; Eisenhower sought to reduce tensions with the Soviets and acclaimed the "Spirit of Geneva."

The president presided less cautiously over the steady diminution of U.S. global influence. Rejecting radical nationalism, Eisenhower relied on the CIA to destabilize leftist third world governments and to defend more conservative, anti-Communist regimes. For a time these efforts succeeded. But in the long run, CIA intervention complicated politics in such third world countries as Vietnam and Iran and bequeathed to subsequent administrations insoluble diplomatic dilemmas. In addition, the Eisenhower administration neglected to address the future problems which Japanese and Western European economic recovery posed for U.S. economic and strategic interests. As Japan and Western Europe prospered economically, as the Soviet Union, the People's Republic of China, and other socialist states grew more stable, and as anti-Western, anticolonial national liberation movements intensified, the United States suffered a relative loss in power and influence—despite being wealthier and militarily more powerful in 1960 than it had been in 1952. The Eisenhower administration thus bequeathed to its successors a restructured world environment, one in which the United States remained the strongest economic and military power but one less able to use its power effectively than at any time since 1945. For the next two decades, the limits of American power would be severely tested and sometimes circumscribed.

# CHAPTER FIVE
# ECONOMIC GROWTH AND A CONSUMER SOCIETY, 1950–1970

For a full generation after World War II, the United States enjoyed an economic boom and a widely based prosperity unparalleled in its modern history. Uncommonly harmonious relations among private corporations, trade unions, and the federal government created a situation of steady economic growth and general affluence. The titles of two books written by the economist-ambassador John Kenneth Galbraith captured the essence of the stable, prosperous social-economic universe Americans thought had been built in the 1950s and 1960s: *The Affluent Society* (1958) and *The New Industrial State* (1967).

Throughout the 1950s the United States economy dominated much of the globe. Though less dependent on foreign trade for economic growth than most other industrial nations, the relatively small percentages of United States domestic production and capital that entered international trade had an enormous impact on the economies of smaller, less productive nations. Despite the fact that America's gross national product expanded relatively more slowly than other rapidly industrializing societies, the United States' productive base was so immense that between 1949 and 1960 absolute real GNP increased from $206 billion to over $500 billion, a rise of nearly 150 percent. Such economic power, especially in relation to weaker, less industrialized societies, allowed the United States to set the terms of trade. Thus

American corporations during the 1950s purchased raw materials cheaply and sold manufactured goods dearly. As America grew wealthier, raw material-producing nations in Latin America, Africa, and Asia became relatively poorer.

But, in the mid-1960s, the United States found itself threatened economically by intensified competition in the global marketplace. More efficient and aggressive West German and Japanese industrialists seized overseas markets once the preserve of American businessmen. These nations, more dependent than the United States on external sources of raw materials, bid up the price of such goods as oil, copper, and rubber. Under the pressure of foreign competition and rising raw materials prices, the dollar gap of the 1950s (when foreign nations purchased more from the United States than they could afford) became the dollar shortage of the 1960s (when our expenditures overseas exceeded earnings). America's trade surplus shrank, in the 1970s falling into a deficit. The mark and the yen challenged the dollar. The world's most affluent society found itself by the end of the 1960s in an unexpected economic predicament.

How did the domestic economy change as the United States evolved from a position of global economic supremacy to one in which it faced stringent international competition? Which industries prospered, and which declined? Who prospered at home, and who suffered? Which individuals, groups, and institutions wielded economic power, and which did not?

## THE NEW GROWTH INDUSTRIES

During the 1950s some of the old standbys of industrial America—railroads, coal mining, textiles, and shoe manufacturing—continued a decline that had begun in the 1920s. Railroad freight traffic fell steadily before the inroads of highway trucking, and passengers discarded long-distance trains in favor of more rapid air or cheaper bus transportation. By the end of the 1960s nearly the entire rail network in the Northeast, including the giant Penn-Central, had gone bankrupt. Coal found itself unable to compete with oil, natural gas, nuclear power, and water power; the nearly 600,000 miners employed at the end of World War II had fallen to about 100,000 by 1970. Cotton and woolen manufacture succumbed to synthetic fibers and domestic production to cheaper foreign manufactures. The shoe industry wrote an equally sorry chapter. Endicott-Johnson, the world's largest shoe manufacturer, had employed about 28,000 production workers in its New York "Southern Tier" factories in the late 1940s; by 1970 the production force had dipped below 4,000, the company began to dismantle its mills, and it even purchased shoes from Rumania for sale in its American retail outlets. Such instances of economic decline caused permanent depression in many New England towns and Appalachian coal patches. Again in the 1950s, as in the 1920s, economic sores festered on a generally healthy economic body.

If parts of New England and Appalachia declined economically, other regions of the nation prospered as never before. Wherever chemicals, business machines, electronics, and computers were manufactured the economy boomed, for these were the postwar growth industries par excellence. They were the new industries fit for survival in a "new society." Their economic growth based on technological and scientific advances, electronic-chemical firms stressed research and development programs (almost half of which were financed by the federal government), hired thousands of new graduates from the nation's universities, and served as the employers for a technocratic-scientific elite.

E. I. DuPont de Nemours & Co., Dow, and Monsanto prospered by manufacturing the synthetic goods that increasingly transformed the United States into a plastic society. Women wore their nylon stockings, people cooked on their Teflon pots and pans, men donned Dacron suits and Orlon shirts, and cars rolled on synthetic tires. Electronics, the child of wartime technological innovations, transistorized the postwar world. As tiny transistors replaced bulky tubes, teen-agers walked everywhere holding the ubiquitous portable radio, and homebodies carried small TVs from room to room and house to patio. It was a society in which stereophonic sound replaced high fidelity phonographs only to be displaced in turn by quadraphonic sound. The electronics industry promised to turn every home into a private concert hall; indeed some new houses were built with sound systems wired into every room. And electric eyes now opened and shut garage doors.

Meantime, automation and its associated business machines produced still greater profits and affected the economy more substantially than plastics and electronics. What Ford and General Electric symbolized in the 1920s, IBM and Xerox personified in post–World War II America. Ever since the industrial revolution, machinery had been replacing human labor in manufacturing. But where humans once operated the new machines, in the postwar era of automation such companies as IBM produced machines that controlled themselves as well as other machines. Automation, based on the same simple feedback principle that operated home thermostats, controlled steel strip mills, auto assembly lines, and entire petro-chemical complexes. Computers, the next stage in the process of automation and first introduced commercially in 1950, had the ability to remember, sort materials, and make decisions; computers could also write poetry, compose music, play chess, and simulate strategy in a football game. So varied were the computer's uses that they were utilized by hotel chains, insurance companies, banks, airlines, and even universities (by the 1960s college students were identified by their IBM numbers) to simplify increasingly complex paper transactions. Where automation once threatened only blue-collar industrial workers, it now endangered the job security of millions of white-collar clerks. Even politicians, eager to predict beforehand the results of elections, worshipped at the shrine of IBM.

While electronic data processing assisted businesses in coping with a mounting flood of paper, xerography multiplied endlessly the copies of vital, and not so vital, documents. Carbon copies became a relic, as copying machines reproduced documents in any form, fashion, or substance; copying machines could even produce documents indistinguishable from the original. Photocopying machines eased the labors of research scholars, simplified the reproduction of business records, and ironically, in some cases undermined secrecy in business and government. Without it there might have been no *Pentagon Papers,* Jack Anderson and other muckrakers would have had far less grist for their journalistic mills, and Watergate's ramifications would have remained murkier still.

One reason for the success of the new growth industries was their close link to the Department of Defense, postwar America's largest single business contractor. The Pentagon supplied a lavish market for electronic and chemical manufacturers, as its deadly nuclear missiles with their elaborate guidance systems relied on synthetics, transistorized modules, and advanced computers. Even the more mundane hardware used by infantry, artillery, and nonnuclear aircraft depended heavily on electronic components and computerized guidance. NASA, too, provided an economic bonanza for the world of electronics. Without transistors, computers, and chemical fuels, there would have been no flight in space, nor man on the moon. Between government contracts and consumer demand for household appliances (household use of electricity tripled in the 1950s), the growth industries prospered enormously.

American agriculture changed as well in the postwar era. Farming became a big business. Agricultural productivity rose more rapidly than demand for foodstuffs for most of the first two postwar decades, forcing millions of smaller farmers off the land; and large farmers prospered as a result of government subsidy programs and their own efficiency. Because production rose so rapidly, prices for agricultural goods declined, and profits could be made only by lowering unit costs of production through intensive application of fertilizers, use of costly new farm machinery, and introduction of sophisticated managerial techniques. Smaller farms simply lacked the resources and the capital to purchase fertilizer, acquire new machinery, and hire costly managerial experts. They also lacked enough land to make the use of expensive new machinery profitable or to join the soil bank. The latter was a program intended to promote soil conservation by paying farmers cash subsidies to let some of their land lie fallow. In other words, because most federal farm programs and subsidies were directly proportional to farm size and productivity, large farmers received proportionately more benefits than small farmers. The beneficiaries of federal largesse, the big farmers also possessed the land, capital, and knowledge necessary to grow food and fibers most efficiently. Consequently the percentage of owner-operated farms rose, and the size of the typical farm increased substantially. Cotton production shifted away from the old South, where it remained profitable only on the extremely large plantation, to the immense corporate, irrigated, farms of Texas, Arizona, and southern California. Farming in such prosperous agricultural states as California, Arizona, and Florida was justly labeled "agribusiness." In some cases industrial corporations, Tenneco among others, purchased large farms. These corporate farmers were in an extremely advantageous position when the international terms of trade shifted after 1970 in favor of agriculture.

## THE NEW MERGER MOVEMENT

As old industries declined and new ones thrived, the concentration of economic power in fewer corporate hands accelerated again after World War II. (The trend toward concentration had first become apparent in the 1880s, reached epic proportions from 1897 to 1904, and seemed to culminate in the 1920s.) During the 1950s, despite a previous half-century of federal antitrust legislation aimed at preserving industrial competition, the fifty largest firms swallowed 471 competitors without government demurrer. And during the prosperous 1960s the corporate merger movement picked up added speed as it assumed new dimensions. By the end of the 1960s the movement toward economic concentration consolidated power in banks and financial institutions more rapidly even than in manufacturing corporations. In an economic landscape marked by millions of competing firms, a single giant—American Telephone and Telegraph—controlled assets that equalled the combined holdings of one million smaller business enterprises.

Not only did large businesses continue to merge and consolidate economic power; their share of business sales, income, and profits also rose. The top one hundred industrial corporations, which possessed 25 percent of all corporate wealth in 1929, owned 31 percent by 1960. In the auto industry, the remaining smaller, independent domestic auto manufacturers fell by the wayside in the 1950s. Only the big three—General Motors, Ford, and Chrysler—survived successfully (American Motors retained a minuscule share of the domestic market), and each of them was among the ten largest enterprises in the nation. General Motors, the world's largest, industrial enterprise, had assets, expenditures, and revenues greater than any American state and many foreign nations. It made almost as much profit per car as it paid out in wages, and it raised car prices by $3.75 for every dollar added to its wage bill. Its very size and economic power enabled GM's managers to target (i.e., plan) a 20-percent profit on capital after taxes and to reach that goal by operating company plants at full capacity for only thirty-six out of fifty-two weeks. Such power and planning enabled it to achieve, by 1965, over $2 billion in annual profits.

In effect, then, by the 1960s the United States had a two-level economy. At one level, millions of small firms with minimal assets struggled to survive competitively. "Mom and Pop" stores, service stations, TV-appliance repair businesses, and small contractors worked long hours to turn a profit. More failed annually than succeeded. On the second level, .1 percent of the larger industrial corporations—500 firms—accounted for one-third of all corporate activity. And within this group of 500, the top 50 industrials achieved aggregate sales equal to the total of the bottom 450, while the profits of the top 10 firms equalled nearly half the profits of the remaining 490. As the economist Robert Heilbroner has suggested, if some catastrophe obliterated the nation's 150 largest enterprises, society would come to a standstill and the American economy would be effectively destroyed. "A tiny group of immense corporations," writes Heilbroner, "constitutes a bastion of formidable economic strength within the sprawling expanse of the American economy—indeed . . . it forms a virtual economic system within an economic system."

Corporate concentration had not brought pure economic monopoly. In fact, the share of the market controlled by the largest firms in their primary fields seemed to stabilize and in some cases shrink during the 1950s and 1960s. Expansion, nonetheless, carried many firms outside their customary markets into totally unfamiliar areas of enterprise. International Telephone and Telegraph, the most notable exemplar of such new trends, acquired hotel chains, auto rental agencies, bakeries, insurance companies, and even book publishers. During the 1960s, conglomerate corporations proliferated. The once independent publishing firms of Alfred A. Knopf and Holt, Rinehart and Winston became respectively parts of the RCA and CBS empires. Oil companies purchased coal mines, and natural gas firms bought farms. Retail supermarket chains even offered vacation travel packages to their customers, and CBS, for a time, owned the New York Yankees.

Several factors induced the trend toward conglomerate enterprises. As had happened in previous decades, firms with surplus resources—whether capital, labor, or managerial—sought new and more profitable outlets in existing fields of economic activity. For some firms the opportunity to acquire business enterprises in unrelated sectors of production or sales was a form of economic insurance. Losses in one area of the economy might be compensated by gains in another. Some acquisitions were rendered attractive by federal tax laws that practically underwrote the complete cost of corporate expansion. In other cases, mergers profited promoters and those who could benefit from the resulting rise or decline in stock prices. Finally, expansion being the central force behind corporate capitalism, many firms in saturated or fully developed sectors of the economy believed that they had to acquire assets in rising sectors or face company decline.

More disturbing to many observers of the economy than the trend to conglomerate corporations was the growth during the 1960s of the multinational enterprise. Not that corporations had previously lacked transnational ambitions; as early as the 1920s, the large oil companies had established a global economic empire in which oil executives wielded considerable diplomatic power. Beginning in the 1950s and quickening rapidly in the following decade, numerous large American corporations built production facilities overseas. Instead of manufacturing their goods at home and exporting them abroad, multinational companies manufactured products overseas and sometimes imported them into the United States. This trend could work both ways, as evidenced by the decision of the French tire maker, Michelin, to open a factory in South Carolina. Before long, Volkswagen purchased a Chrysler plant in Pennsylvania, Sony assembled television sets in California, Kawasaki built motorcycles in Nebraska, Datsun a truck plant in Tennessee, and a British firm absorbed that venerable American institution, Howard Johnson's.

The emergence of multinationals posed a set of hard problems for American policy makers. Union officials had to consider how to bargain with corporations that threatened to shift work from more highly paid, unionized American workers to cheaper, nonunion foreign laborers. Government officials faced the problems of how to determine the multinational corporation's impact on international trade and tariff policies, how its foreign operations affected domestic tax liabilities, and how antitrust legislation applied to transnational enterprises. Trade union leaders and government officials, however, gave no sign of being able to shut the lid on the Pandora's box opened by the multinational corporation.

## WHO HOLDS POWER?
## MYTHS AND REALITIES

Several beliefs about the nature of the American economic system gained credence in the postwar era. First was the concept that the United States during the Eisenhower years had built a "people's capitalism." "People's capitalism" stood on two economic legs: (1) The reality of ever-rising real incomes and the effective abolition of poverty by the affluent society, and (2) the rapid spread of stock ownership among the mass of Americans, whether by direct purchase or through mutual funds. A grain of truth buttressed both beliefs, but economic realities hinted at a more complex and less sanguine situation.

Rising incomes during the 1940s and 1950s did lift many Americans above the poverty level and gave them material comforts unimaginable during the Great Depression. The depression and the war in fact stimulated a marginal redistribution of income away from the top 20 percent of the population to the remainder. But such improvements cloaked substantial inequalities in income and wealth that grew again after the Korean War. By

1953 the share of income received by the top 20 percent of the population rose, as did the share of the top 5 percent of citizens. In 1957 the top 20 percent earned 45.3 percent of all income, and the top 5 percent received more than the bottom 40 percent combined. By the end of the 1960s the top 2 percent of income receivers enjoyed annual incomes ten times greater than the nation's average.

This functional economic system, which preserved privilege at the top, did not challenge poverty at the bottom. In 1959, at the end of the affluent Eisenhower years, a Census Bureau statistician estimated that, depending on precisely where one drew the poverty line, between 20 percent and 40 percent of American families lived in poverty. Michael Harrington's *The Other America* (1962), the book that triggered the Kennedy-Johnson war on poverty, was remarkably reminiscent of Robert Hunter's *Poverty* (1904), yet the intervening sixty years had seen Progressivism, a New Era, the New Deal, the Fair Deal, and the New Frontier. After all this, the world's wealthiest nation remained haunted by the biblical prophesy that "the poor ye shall always have with you."

Just as poverty persisted, even in a "people's capitalism," actual ownership of capital and wealth remained concentrated among a small elite despite wider stock ownership. A study by a University of Wisconsin economist estimated that in 1954, 1.6 percent of the adult population held 90 percent of corporate bonds and nearly all state and municipal bonds. Students of the modern corporation have shown that as few as 200 to 300 families effectively possess stock control of the 150 supercorporations. Moreover, the top 2 percent in income level of all American families own between two-thirds and three-quarters of all corporate stock, a concentration of ownership which has persisted since 1922. By 1970 many more Americans may have owned a few shares of stock but a small elite of wealthy individuals and families, labeled the "super rich" by Ferdinand Lundberg, exercised effective economic power.

**Distribution of Family Income, 1947–1970**

|                 | SHARES |      |      |      |      |      |
|-----------------|--------|------|------|------|------|------|
|                 | 1947   | 1950 | 1955 | 1960 | 1965 | 1970 |
| Lowest Quintile | 5.0    | 4.5  | 4.8  | 4.8  | 5.2  | 5.4  |
| 2nd Quintile    | 11.9   | 12.0 | 12.3 | 12.2 | 12.2 | 12.2 |
| 3rd Quintile    | 17.0   | 17.4 | 17.8 | 17.8 | 17.8 | 17.6 |
| 4th Quintile    | 23.1   | 23.4 | 23.7 | 24.0 | 23.9 | 23.8 |
| Highest Quintile| 43.0   | 42.7 | 41.3 | 41.3 | 40.9 | 40.9 |
| Top 5%          | 17.5   | 17.3 | 16.4 | 15.9 | 15.5 | 15.5 |

Defenders of the American economic system now publicized another concept: the notion of altruistic management. Adolph A. Berle, Jr., who together with Gardiner Means, had warned Americans early in the 1930s about the dangers inherent in an economic system that separated business management from ownership and hence promoted corporate lassitude and irresponsibility, in the 1950s asserted that corporate executives had developed a conscience. In his *20th Century Capitalist Revolution* (1955), Berle proclaimed that corporate management, staffed largely by university graduates who operated the firm but did not own it, preferred public service to classical profit making. The modern corporation with a conscience served the local community through United Fund contributions, supported local cultural and recreational programs, and sometimes pampered its employees. The popular observer of American mores, John Brooks, noted: "The big, coldly menacing grizzlies of 1939 [are] the superbig, smiling, approval-seeking pandas of 1964." "The capitalist robber baron," added another commentator, "has turned out to be a love-starved aunt cramming cake into eager little mouths."

The concept of public-service, non-profit-oriented managements with a conscience conflicted with several economic realities. First, many top executives not only managed their companies but also owned large shares of the stock, at least 10 percent in the one hundred largest industrials. Second, the actual income and economic security of executives depended on the profit-making potentialities of their firms, and most high executives were not bashful about raising their own salaries. In 1964 the incomes of the key men in the ten largest corporations ranged from $300,000 to over $600,000, with most of that income dependent on bonuses and incentive payments related to corporate profits. These men also cherished the power that flowed from corporate growth, which in turn derived from earnings and profits. Perhaps the Marxist economist Paul Baran essentially captured the difference between the late nineteenth-century robber baron and the modern manager. "The one stole from the company," he wrote, "the other steals for it."

Like most modern industrial economies, the United States in the 1960s operated an economic system based on planning by business and government elites. In the words of John Kenneth Galbraith, "the mature corporation is an arm of the state." It was a system in which private executives and public officials allied themselves to manage aggregate demand, induce price stability, insure corporate profits, and stimulate economic growth. Government used its monetary and fiscal authority to sustain aggregate consumer demand and its coercive power to stabilize wages and prices. In return, corporate officials served the avowed public goal of an ever-rising GNP. While government and corporations bolstered each other, individual executives like Charles E. Wilson of General Motors (first secretary of defense in the Eisenhower administration), Neil McElroy of Proctor and Gamble (Wilson's successor as defense secretary), and Douglas Dillon and John J. McCloy of Wall Street (key members of the State Department–national security complex) regularly passed through a revolving door that carried them in and out of public service. Cabinet officials were drawn from the leading law firms and corporations; in turn the corporations recruited new executives from the government, especially from among military men. Generals Omar N. Bradley, Douglas MacArthur, and Lucius Clay, became corporate directors, and scores of army colonels and navy captains became business directors and purchasing agents.

By the 1950s the federal government was far and away the largest single consumer in the economic marketplace. Federal expenditures for all goods and services, which had been only $3.5 billion in 1929, had reached $57 billion in 1965 and had increased from 1.7 percent of GNP in 1929 to 8.4 percent in 1965. Federal budget decisions determined the difference between economic recession and boom, between corporate retrenchment and expansion. The Kennedy administration publicly asserted the federal government's economic role by its adoption of Keynesian economics. The Keynesian theory calls for the government to regulate aggregate demand by stimulating consumption and inducing prosperity through tax cuts and federal deficits and retarding inflation and checking demand by tax increases and budget surpluses.

In practice, however, the new economics worked effectively in only one direction. The Kennedy administration could reduce taxes in order to stimulate demand and promote employment. But the Johnson, Nixon, and Ford administrations could not raise taxes in order to dampen demand and check inflation. Keynesian economics also produced warped results. Lower taxes and higher deficits benefited the privileged proportionately much more than the underprivileged. And when the government sought to dampen runaway prosperity, the poor, as usual, paid the price in terms of rising unemployment. The bulk of direct government expenditures, moreover, went to the creation of weapons of destruction, for military-related expenditures provided the fulcrum for the Keynesian system.

The Cold War admirably suited the needs of the domestic economy. Government expenditures for housing, health, education, or income maintenance precipitated class and group conflict and subverted the politics of consensus. But few dared to question the cost of defense, for, as the cliché puts it, the price of freedom is never too dear. A *New York Times* letter to the editor warned about a 1968 proposal to end hunger in the United States: "Does Senator McGovern seriously mean that he is willing to risk annihilation of the entire United States just to subsidize the cost of solving the hunger problem?" Such beliefs bolstered an economic system in which, during the 1960s, half the government's funds went for military purposes, and the

Defense Department had accumulated assets greater than the nation's seventy-five largest industries and spent more than the whole federal government had before the Great Depression. Military expenditures regularly surpassed the cash total of federal personal income taxes, accounted for one-quarter of federal public works and employed some 3.2 million workers in defense industries and another 1.1 million as civilian employees of the Defense Department and armed services. Defense spending in the mid-1960s financed 30 percent of all manufacturing jobs in Kansas, 28 percent in Washington state, and over 20 percent in five other states. And the military subsidized one-third of all American research. Defense Department-sponsored programs saved the Litton Industries nuclear shipbuilding venture from bankruptcy, kept Grumman Aircraft alive on Long Island, and financed the research and production programs of such other aeronautical firms as North American Aviation, McDonnell Douglas, and General Dynamics as well as their direct and indirect subcontractors.

American industrialists, workers, and consumers seemed caught in an economic web. "The imperatives of organization, technology, and planning operate," wrote John Kenneth Galbraith, to make "much of what happens . . . inevitable and the same."

## A TAMED LABOR MOVEMENT

In the late 1940s the American labor movement, grown fat on its wartime membership gains and strengthened by the outcome of the 1945-1946 strike wave, seemed a new power in the land. A spokesman for the movement declared: "American labor unions have become a social power in the nation and are conscious of their new import." And an academic authority on labor-management relations observed in 1948 of the labor movement: "It means that the United States is gradually shifting from a capitalistic community to a laboristic one—that is, to a community in which employees rather than businessmen are the strongest single influence." He also prophesied that the newly powerful union movement had placed the nation "on the threshold of major changes in its economic and political institutions."

Such promises and prophesies were never realized. Why?

Trade unionism did not shrink back to pre–World War II levels, nor was it paralyzed as it had been from 1923 to 1933. With the exception of a few years in the late 1950s marked by relatively high unemployment, the labor movement grew absolutely. In 1970 American unions claimed almost 21 million members, about 40 percent more than they had in 1945-1946, and 15 percent more than at their relative peak in 1954.

Yet the absolute growth in the number of union members cloaked a real, substantial loss in momentum and influence. The enormous expansion of the labor movement—which began during the New Deal, accelerated during World War II, and climaxed during the Korean War had recruited primarily among workers in the nation's basic industries: autos, steel, coal mining, agricultural machinery, electrical machinery, and appliances, that is, the manufacturing sector. Beginning in the mid-1950s, this sector of the economy stopped growing in terms of employment. As the demand for the products of these industries grew less rapidly or even fell, and as automation replaced human labor, the number of coal miners, steelworkers, and autoworkers, among others, declined. This was immediately reflected in the membership of such giant unions as the United Auto Workers (UAW) and the United Steelworkers (USA), both of which lost their capacity for growth. The United Mine Workers of America declined from the largest and most militant union during the years 1933-1946 to a small, accommodationist organization.

Meantime, employment grew rapidly in those sectors of the economy and among those workers traditionally most resistant to unions. White-collar workers, whether in service or trade occupations, multiplied in number. More so than their blue-collar counterparts, white-collar employees identified with their corporations or employers. An increasing proportion of the new labor force was also female, and many women workers had customarily experienced a mutually antagonistic relationship with a labor movement controlled by aging, blue-collar origin, paternalistic men. Employment opportunities also expanded in the South and those parts of the West hostile to unionism. Finally, much of the growth occurred in areas of public employment where unions and collective bargaining were banned or among small employers in extremely competitive sectors of the economy impermeable to trade unions.

Thus, although growing absolutely, the labor movement declined as a proportion of the even more rapidly growing total labor force. And that relative decline portended an even bleaker future for American trade unionism.

The political balance in postwar America also shifted against the labor movement. Committed to the Democratic party since 1936, in the 1940s and 1950s labor leaders found themselves integral parts of a political organization grown cooler to their movement's still ardent courtship. The southern wing of the Democratic party, moreover, frequently allied in Congress with conservative Republicans to pass antilabor legislation. One such bill, the Taft-Hartley Act of 1947, substantially restricted the rights unions had won under the Wagner Act. Taft-Hartley made it much more difficult for unions to grow in the South and Southwest or among traditionally antiunion firms.

It was just such economic and political setbacks which caused the American labor movement, split into two competing centers (AF of L and CIO) since 1936-1938, to reunite in 1955. The newly merged AFL-CIO's president, George Meany, promised a reinvigorated labor movement and an aggressive organizing campaign.

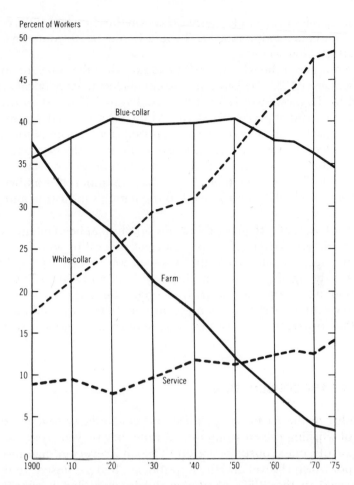

Percent of Workers

Blue-collar

White-collar

Farm

Service

1900  '10  '20  '30  '40  '50  '60  '70 '75

Occupation Distribution of the Labor Force *(Bicentennial Statistics Pocketbook,* 1976)

Meany's promises proved to be empty words. Instead the AFL-CIO behaved, in the words of the labor economist Richard Lester, as "a sleepy monopoly." Its affiliates and leaders preferred ease and security in administering what they had to the costs and risks associated with bold innovations. A reunited labor movement led no organizing crusade. Nor did it blaze a new political path for organized labor.

Beginning in the 1960s, however, white-collar and service workers, especially public employees, joined unions as never before. Among the fastest growing trade unions in the country were the American Federation of State, County, and Municipal Employees (AFSCME), the American Federation of Teachers (AFT), the Retail Clerks, and the Amalgamated Butcher Workmen. Even so, the growth of white-collar and service trade unionism failed to keep pace with employment growth in those sectors of the economy. Nor did these gains compensate for the loss of membership among unions in the manufacturing sector.

The merger of the AFL-CIO did not alter the labor movement's political practices after 1955. Despite a persistent decline in its political influence, indicated by the passage in 1959 of the Landrum-Griffin Act which further curtailed trade union prerogatives, the AFL-CIO remained a captive of the Democratic party. All efforts to push organized labor in a more independent direction failed. As one of the most astute students of the twentieth-century American labor movement, David Brody, has observed, the movement operates on the "assumption that labor's place was inherently limited, that its sphere was necessarily circumscribed in the nation's industrial and political life."

By the late 1960s, then, workers and unions had been integrated into a corporate warfare-welfare state. A variety of federal programs established minimum wages, stabilized income, insured job security, provided social security for the aged, infirmed, and dependent, and redistributed a small part of national income to the truly needy. The major unions and their leaders, meantime, negotiated long-term contracts with binding no-strike clauses that provided stability for large enterprises and job security for workers.

## AFFLUENCE AND CONSUMPTION

The stability of the American political and economic system as well as the absence of working-class discontent and militancy flowed from the successful creation of a mass consumer society. The car in every garage and chicken in every pot which Hoover and the Republicans had promised Americans in 1928, arrived in the 1950s. And now it also included beefsteaks, color television, stereophonic sound, and suburban split-levels.

Mass consumption depended on constantly rising real wage levels, a condition the United States economy sustained between 1945 and 1960. By 1956 the real income of the average American was more than 50 percent greater than it had been in 1929, and by 1960 it was 35 percent higher than it had been in the last year of World War II.

How the typical American spent his increased earnings was determined as much by external factors as by intrinsic, real personal needs. Indeed, the larger the income an individual earned the more choice he had in its disposal. As growing numbers of citizens satisfied their need for food and shelter, the manufacturers of attractive but nonessential goods competed lustily for the consumer's dollar.

To sell the autos, refrigerators, dishwashers, stereo sets, and other appliances that rolled off production lines, manufacturers resorted to Madison Avenue and intensive advertising.[1] Between 1946 and 1957 expenditures on advertising increased by almost 300 percent, rising to over \$10 billion annually. Not only did the money devoted to advertising rise significantly, but the lords of Madison Avenue also developed more sophisticated selling tactics. Successful advertising was complicated when consumers had to select from among breakfast cereals and cars that differed neither in price nor utility and also had to be convinced to buy products never before manufactured. Employing all the tools of normal (and abnormal) psychology, advertisers alerted consumers to the psychic benefits of larger cars, sweeter-smelling underarms, striped toothpaste, and Marlboro—the man's cigarette. Brighter teeth, Madison Avenue implied, guaranteed every wallflower a desirable husband, and the cigarillo won every man a buxom and accommodating female. Able to allocate money and talent to the one-minute television spot, advertisers bombarded viewers with irresistible commercials. Madison Avenue sales campaigns got such good results in the marketplace that in time many candidates for public office substituted the one-minute television spot for the half-hour platform speech. By the 1960s,

Index of Median Family Income and Per Capita Income in Constant Dollars: 1947 to 1977 (Bureau of the Census, *Current Population Reports, Consumer Income,* Series P-60, #118, 1977, p. 5.)

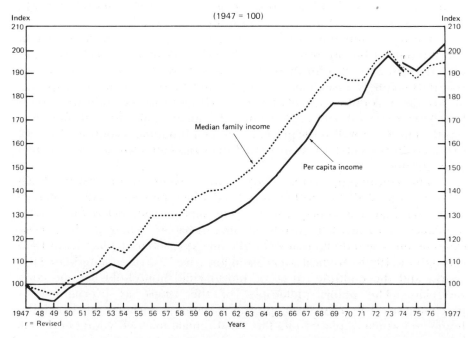

[1]The term *Madison Avenue* became a synonym for high-powered advertising created by advertising agencies, many of which had their offices on New York City's Madison Avenue.

Madison Avenue sold presidents as well as Pontiacs, congressmen as well as Cadillacs.

More than advertising was required to create the postwar consumer society. Regardless of the reality of rising wages, millions of citizens still lacked income sufficient to satisfy their demand for goods. A 1950 Census Bureau survey of over seven thousand families, for example, showed that 60 percent having earnings of $4,000 or less spent more than they earned. Even those workers whose incomes exceeded their current expenses seldom had a margin of savings adequate to sustain the cash purchase of such costly durables as autos and large home appliances. Only by borrowing money on the assumption that higher future earnings would render repayment painless could most citizens satisfy their desire for cars and dishwashers.

As advertising stimulated the demand for consumer goods, the nation's financial institutions financed their purchase. Between 1946 and 1957, private indebtedness increased by 360 percent—in contrast, total public debt rose by only 11 percent and the federal debt actually declined. More remarkable still was the rise in consumer installment indebtedness; the estimated annual installment credit outstanding soared from just over $4 billion in 1946 to over $34 billion in 1957. Automobile installment credit alone rose from under $1 billion to in excess of $15 billion. The propensity to buy now and pay later made the cash registers ring. Detroit produced over five million new cars in 1949 and in the peak year of 1955 sold nearly eight million autos, a record unsurpassed until the late 1960s.

For those individuals whose earnings rose annually, consumer credit and installment buying provided a relatively easy means to achieve rapid material affluence. But for those Americans whose income failed to rise, or rose only haltingly, installment buying became more an economic trap than an avenue to comfort. Unable to save sufficient cash to underwrite their purchases, these unfortunate consumers frequently failed to earn enough to pay the interest as well as the principal on their installment contract. In some cases, credit costs effectively increased the original purchase price by one-third or more.

The consumption craze took many shapes in the 1950s. Such economists as Walt W. Rostow suggested that when men and women in America's "high mass consumption society" satisfied their desire for cars and appliances, they invested surplus income in babies. Whatever the precise cause no one could doubt that a population explosion took place from 1945 through the 1950s. Medical science and improved nutrition lengthened life spans, and the multiple (three or more) child household became commonplace. The public philosophy of the 1950s, as proclaimed by psychologists, TV comedians, preachers, and politicians, sanctified the home and woman's place in it. The ideal female married young and well, bore a large brood, and remained home to create the perfect environment for keeping the American family together. The sanctification of the family and the idealization of the woman as mother and homemaker further promoted the growth of a consumer society. Larger families required bigger houses with more appliances to simplify "mom's" work and increased purchases to provide for the children. Before long many one-car families would become two-, three-, and in rare instances even four-car households.

If affluence enabled many Americans to enjoy unsurpassed material comforts, millions of citizens still struggled to make ends meet. If new recruits joined the "jet set" and flew to vacations in Rio, Biarritz, and Monaco, many workers, like the Bronx couple that *New York Times* reporter A. H. Raskin investigated, who lived half an hour by subway from Times Square saw "less of Great White Way than the average farmer from Pumpkin Corners." John K. Galbraith lamented in *The Affluent Society* the ubiquity of public squalor amidst America's opulence and hinted at the persistence of poverty. Nonetheless, regardless of how unequally and inequitably the fruits of affluence were distributed, many of those Americans who did not share fully still felt themselves more comfortable in the 1950s than they had been in the 1930s and more fortunate than non-Americans. As Raskin's Bronx worker remarked: "We're a lot better off than we would be anywhere else in the world. We may not get everything we want, but at least we can choose what to do with our money. In other countries they don't even have a choice. No matter how bad things are, we're better off than they are."

## THE TRIUMPH OF THE SUBURBS

The emergence of an affluent mass consumer society saw the reassertion of a pattern of residential mobility and settlement that had been retarded by depression and war. In the 1950s, as also had happened in the 1920s, millions of citizens deserted the cities for the suburbs. Except in the South and Southwest where urban population continued to grow as a result of the annexation of adjacent land, the bulk of metropolitan population growth occurred in the suburbs. By 1960 in most northern metropolises, suburban residents outnumbered central city occupants, and as people fled the urban core, so, too, did businesses, trades, and professions. The "Miracle Mile" in Manhasset on Long Island's North Shore brought Fifth Avenue to the suburbs, just as similar suburban shopping centers elsewhere attracted downtown's most prestigious retailers to new locations with ample parking space and affluent consumers.

Suburban development stimulated a housing boom of unprecedented dimensions. As of 1960, one-fourth of all the housing in the nation had been constructed in the previous decade, during which annual new housing starts regularly exceeded the growth of new households. In the 1950s, for the first time in history, more Americans owned their homes, albeit usually with heavy mortgages, than rented dwelling space.

The reasons for this exodus to suburbia might have remained constant from the 1920s to the 1950s; after 1945, however, the opportunity to flee the city had expanded significantly. The desire for a private home with a lawn and garden in a suburban arcadia had long been an integral aspect of popular culture. The economic costs and occupational impracticality of suburban life, however, had put it beyond the reach of most Americans. All this changed in the postwar world, as federal credit and highway policies, technological innovations, and a mass consumer society reshaped metropolitan America.

In the postwar world, as automobile ownership became general, Americans had been liberated from dependence on mass public transit. The possession of a private car snapped the link that hitherto had connected the individual's home to his place of work via public transit. Through federal and state highway programs funded by fuel taxes, limited access highways were constructed that linked new suburbs and older central cities. The prospect of smooth, unimpeded traffic flow on safe, modern highways and in private cars led passengers to abandon subways, trolleys, and buses and to move from the city to the suburbs. Americans were now free to reside wherever their incomes allowed, and suburbia was also opening up to a wider range of incomes.

Federal policies enlarged the suburban housing market by providing generous mortgage loans to World War II veterans and by insuring the mortgages marketed by private lending agencies. The self-amortizing mortgage, whereby the homeowner paid back his original loan at a fixed monthly rate (comparable to rent) over a twenty- to thirty-year term, became the common means to home ownership. Federal tax policy also stimulated suburban expansion, for citizens received a generous income tax deduction for the interest charges and real estate taxes paid on their homes. The availability of long-term credit and the inducement of tax advantages drew comfortable middle-class Americans to suburbia. Working-class citizens needed a further inducement, the chance to purchase a home within their means. Here the firm of Arthur Levitt and Sons provided one solution, doing for the housing market what Ford had done for autos. Just as Ford offered a basic car in a single color at a low price, Levitt sold a standardized dwelling unit in one color—white—at a price within the reach of thousands of working-class Americans. His original "little boxes" constructed in the first Levittown in central Long Island soon had counterparts in New Jersey and Pennsylvania.

Suburbia, in general, and Levittown, in particular, occasioned a new image of American society, one consonant with the concept of a mass consumer public. Suburbia, in the words of social critic and planner, Lewis Mumford, offered the prospect of

> a multitude of uniform, identifiable houses, lined up inflexibly, at uniform distances, on uniform roads, in a treeless communal waste, inhabited by people

of the same class, the same income, the same age group, witnessing the same television performances, eating the same tasteless pre-fabricated foods, from the same freezers, conforming in every outward and inward respect to a common mold.[2]

In the "little boxes made of ticky tacky," about which Pete Seeger sang, lived William F. Whyte's "organization men" who in their haste to adjust smoothly to their fellow junior executives became as undifferentiated as the houses in which they dwelled.

Critics of suburbia mounted a contradictory attack against the emerging character of national life. On the one hand, they charged suburban residents with uniformity, dullness, and unthinking accommodation to neighborhood mores. On the other hand, they indicted suburbanites, as did John Keats in *The Crack in the Picture Window*, for alcoholism, adultery (wife-swapping was said to be the favorite indoor suburban sport), and

A new lifestyle (Shel Hershorn/Black Star)

[2]Lewis Mumford, *The City in History,* Copyright 1961 by Lewis Mumford. Reprinted by permission of Harcourt, Brace Jovanovich, Inc.

juvenile delinquency. Whatever the substance of the criticism, it seemed to miss the mark, for suburban growth proceeded unabated.

In fact most social criticism portrayed a fictional suburbia, not its reality. By the late 1950s American suburbs contained as many differences as similarities; there was no single ideal-type suburban community. Communities of upwardly mobile young executives who preferred accommodation to conflict, uniformity to individualism, such as William F. Whyte located in Chicago's environs, did exist. So, too, did communities of wealthy senior executives and rentiers, whose incomes and security enabled them to experiment with architecture and engage in eccentric behavior. At the other end of the suburban spectrum, one could find working-class developments whose residents had moved from the city but had scarcely altered their life style; they still voted Democratic, preferred baseball to ballet, and the company of relatives to that of neighbors. Even the allegedly undifferentiated, standardized world of Levittown contained, as the sociologist Herbert Gans discovered, a universe of strikingly individualized homes. Levittowners wasted no time in applying personal touches and preferences to the standardized homes and to creating a society in which, according to Gans, they felt very much at home and comfortable.

More disturbing for the future of American society than suburbia's alleged propensity to uniformity, alcoholism, and adultery was the impact of suburbia on racial divisions. Primarily a white phenomenon, the flight to suburbia transformed the typical American metropolis into a white cupcake with a black filling. Between 1950 and 1960, nonwhite population increases accounted for more than 30 percent of the urban growth in the nation's fifty leading metropolises; by 1960 blacks formed nearly a fifth of the residents in 212 standard metropolitan statistical areas. By 1970 every city in the state of New York except Rochester, had experienced decline in its total white population. In that same year, the population of Washington, D.C., was 71.1 percent black, and Newark, N.J., Gary, Ind., and Atlanta, Ga., had populations more than 50 percent black. Seven other major cities had black populations in excess of 40 percent. The suburbs, in contrast, experienced an increase in nonwhite population of from only 4.2 percent to 4.5 percent. In suburban Washington, for example, only 7.9 percent of the total population was nonwhite. This residential transformation laid the foundation for the creation of the two nations—one white and one black—that the Kerner Commission warned against in its report on the ghetto riots of the 1960s.

## DEMOGRAPHIC CHANGE

Just as population redistributed itself between city and suburbs, it shifted between rural and urban districts, east and west. Even during the peak agricultural prosperity of World War II, millions of Americans had left the countryside for jobs in defense-related urban industries. In 1943 alone, three million people deserted farms; and in eight of the thirteen years between 1942 and 1954, more than a million Americans a year gave up farm life. After 1957 the drift from the countryside accelerated, depositing millions of former agrarians, white as well as black, on the American cities' doorsteps.

In another population shift, many midwesterners and easterners moved west. California accounted for one-fifth of the nation's population increase in the 1950s, and by 1963 surpassed New York as the most populous state. Oregon and Washington also received their share of migrants, as did Alaska and Hawaii, both of which achieved statehood in 1959. Nothing so graphically revealed the westward drift than an event in 1958 that rendered the impossible possible: The Brooklyn Dodgers deserted their hallowed Ebbetts Field for sunny Los Angeles, where a new mass market promised greater riches for the team's management. That same year the New York baseball Giants left Manhattan for San Francisco, and soon major league baseball teams, once limited to an area north of the Ohio River and east of the Mississippi River (St. Louis excepted), had franchises in Kansas City, Atlanta, Houston, Dallas (its suburbs in fact), Oakland, San Diego, and Seattle. Other professional sports also drifted south and west to follow population, the lucrative television market, and the consumer dollar.

Population redistribution took several unexpected forms. The South, which for a century had exported its surplus population, began in the mid-1950s to attract newcomers. Population growth was most striking in the boom space-defense industries region along the Gulf Coast from Houston, Texas, to Mobile, Alabama, and the retirement-vacation haven, Florida. By the 1960s, even the interior South, from Virginia to Alabama, benefited from the migration of industries and people, with industry expanding more rapidly in the rural South than elsewhere in the nation. By the 1970s major European manufacturers were considering the construction of plants in South Carolina and Virginia.

Population figuratively exploded in the postwar world. There were one-third again more Americans in 1960 than in 1940. The birthrate, which had begun to increase markedly during the war, took off afterwards, rising steadily each year until by 1956 it approached the levels common before the 1920s and the introduction of modern contraceptive techniques. In the 1950s, none of the factors operated that had previously countervailed high birth rates and thus retarded population growth. Modern medicine continued to reduce the incidence of infant mortality; war-stimulated advances in antibiotics, and surgical methods rendered infections less fatal; and medical breakthroughs such as an antipolio vaccine ended one of the last of the childhood epidemic diseases. For everyone—infant and adult, men and women, whites and nonwhites—life expectancies rose, until by 1960 the average life expectancy neared the allotted biblical three score and ten.

Millions of Americans in the postwar years also began to fill a changed working world. Blue-collar work remained the dominant form of employment for men, the largest number of whom earned their wages in manufacturing, mining, and construction. Almost 50 percent of the male labor force toiled at traditional blue-collar vocations, a percentage that scarcely shrank in the postwar decades, though the proportion of unskilled manual laborers fell precipitously. Although blue-collar workers remained the core of the work world, the outlines of what some observers considered a "new working class" became manifest in the 1950s. As the proportion of Americans engaged in agriculture and in self-employment trades and professions declined further, the number of citizens filling salaried professional and technical positions rose from only 4.3 percent of the work force in 1900 to 14.4 percent in 1970; at the same time the proportion of workers employed in white-collar clerical and sales jobs soared by 1970 to 23.4 percent of the labor force. By 1960 service, clerical, and technical workers in the so-called white-collar trades outnumbered blue-collar laborers. As more and more women entered the labor force, they filtered into clerical, sales, and service occupations (in 1970 almost 80 percent of female workers fell in those three categories), a form of work that commentators suggested created a different ambience and consciousness from blue-collar labor.

The emergence of a "new working class" in the 1950s and its rapid growth thereafter raised significant questions about the future of American society. By and large the new occupations required a longer formal education than traditional blue-collar jobs. Indeed, a college degree rather than a union-card often became the means to opportunity. The increasing importance of white-collar workers, especially in the professional and technical areas, led some sociologists to conclude that the era of militant labor unionism and employee-employer confrontations was ending. Professional workers and their white-collar associates, it was said, identified with management, not with each other, and assumed that their future security was implicitly linked to the growth of the firm. Other commentators suggested that the educated salariat in command of society's most vital resource—knowledge—would ultimately use their brainpower to seize economic and social control from the money managers and profit makers. In time the new "meritocracy" would play the role once prophesied for it by Thorstein Veblen: The professional technocrats would manage an economy based on production for use, not profit, for creation, not destruction. Still other critics thought such images of the "professional meritocracy" to be fairy tales. These critics elaborated a different scenario for the future in which the technocrats, aware that they had knowledge but not power, intelligence but not autonomy, joined forces with the blue-collar unionists to struggle against corporate management for workers' control. Which vision of the role of the "new working class" would materialize only the future would tell.

If the social impact of the transformed occupational universe seemed unclear as the 1950s drew to a close, the importance of formal schooling for individual social and economic advancement had become self-evident. By the 1950s only a rare worker in the under-30 age group had less than a high school education, and increasing numbers had had some higher education. By 1970, over 30 percent of American males and 20 percent of females had gone to college, with almost 20 percent of blue-collar workers and over 80 percent of the "new working class" also having attended college (over 65 percent of the technocrats completed at least four years of college). More young Californians attended college in the 1960s than the entire French university population, and in some years new college registrations in the United States exceeded Britain's total student body in higher education.

During the 1950s the rising college enrollment induced social optimism; it seemed to presage a social order in which once-excluded individuals and classes would rise to positions of government, corporate, and professional power. By the mid-1960s, however, when universities had become as much a part of the mass society as other American institutions, pessimism began to replace optimism, anxiety conquered certainty. Indeed, by 1970, as riots, bombings, and deaths paralyzed the nation's campuses, some citizens perceived higher education more as a threat to the social order than as a panacea.

However productive and finely integrated the American system appeared, it was not flawless, flaws that grew as the 1960s passed into the 1970s. Technology could send a rocket to the moon but it could not eradicate slum housing. It could put men in space yet not render work more humane and satisfying. The economy could produce unprecedented national wealth but not end poverty. Industry could manufacture sophisticated weapons of destruction but could not produce consumer goods that would work well or last long. Keynesian economics, as practiced by federal officials, could stimulate demand but not erase unemployment or halt inflation. As the 1960s ended, the economy seemed mired at a high permanent level of unemployment (still the primary cause of poverty aside from old age and illness) yet faced with an escalating rate of inflation that seemed impermeable to cure. Thus, as the 1970s began, the economic system came under attack from dissatisfied consumers, discontented workers, inflation-ridden pensioners, and low-income citizens.

# CHAPTER SIX
# MASS CULTURE
# AND ITS CRITICS

The affluence of the 1950s and 1960s laid the basis for what came to be known as "mass culture." Never before had so much music, drama, and literature been accessible to so many people as a result of fundamental changes in the presentation of entertainment and enlightenment. Television, the long-playing record, improved sound-reproduction equipment, and paperback books brought a plethora of cultural forms within reach of the great mass of Americans.

Once again, as had happened during the 1920s, Americans celebrated their exceptional prosperity. A new hedonism symbolized by oversized, overpowered cars crammed with options and adorned outside with two-tone color patterns, vinyl tops, and fins captivated consumers. Americans relished a culture of consume, dispose, and enjoy. We were, in the words of the historian David Potter, "people of plenty."

Not everyone, to be sure, joined in the American celebration. Some critics raised questions about the quality of life. Whereas once left-wing intellectuals had lamented the ubiquity of poverty and exploitation, they now bewailed a consumer society in which shoppers had become as indistinguishable from each other as the merchandise they purchased.

A few critical voices cried out in the wilderness. The industrial sociologist William F. Whyte portrayed in scholarly detail the culture of the prototypical success story of the 1950s, the rising young corporate executive, the hero of best-selling novelist Sloan Wilson's *The Man in the Gray Flannel Suit*. Whyte showed these young executives as insecure, status-driven people who lived transitorily in suburban developments housing only their own kind, and as "organization men" who molded their personalities to suit the corporate image. The radical and idiosyncratic scholar, C. Wright Mills, discerned a bleak future in his 1951 book, *White Collar*. He described a society of men and women who worked without autonomy or direction, who strived only for status, and who lived as dependent beings, not free citizens. In *White Collar*, one glimpsed an American mass potentially susceptible to producing fascism, as their Italian and German likes had in the 1920s and 1930s.

David Riesman, the premier critic of mass society, early on diagnosed the new American disease in *The Lonely Crowd* (1950). Americans once, he wrote, had been an inner-directed people, men and women who could distinguish right from wrong, who could chart their own directions and goals in life. Now, Americans had become an other-directed people, who lacked their own internal moral compasses. The great mass of postwar Americans lost themselves in a "lonely crowd" to which they looked for values and personal decisions. The independent democratic citizen had become a cypher in the clutches of an anonymous mass society.

Such tendencies toward mass society caused a minority of Americans to worry that the nation had lost its sense of purpose amidst a flood of consumer goods. They wondered if mass society could rise above the level of a car dealer's showroom.

But the great mass of Americans shared no such worries. Those who could, consumed as never before, and those who could not, aspired to do the same.

## THE AGE OF TELEVISION

No aspect of postwar America so transformed popular styles and tastes as television. Across the nation, regardless of region, class, or race, television brought its viewers simultaneously the same images, jokes, songs, and standardized mid-American speech patterns. Television was the perfect cultural homogenizer.

In 1946 only 17,000 homes had television sets and these were limited to the few major metropolitan centers that had transmitting stations. By 1949 almost three million sets were sold annually; and by 1954 two-thirds of American families possessed a TV set. A new symbol—the television antenna—dominated the American skyline, whether on a New York tenement roof, a Mississippi sharecropper's shack, or a California ranch-style house. The multiset family had become more common than the multicar family by the 1960s, and by the 1970s color television surpassed black and white as the preferred type.

For adult entertainment, Saturday night around the tube replaced Saturday night at the movies, and for children Saturday morning TV viewing replaced Saturday afternoon at the movies. Private and public television personalities emerged and vanished with startling rapidity. Sergeant Bilko (Phil Silvers), who dominated situation comedy in the 1950s, as the con-man leader of a group of comic sad sacks in the pre-Vietnam peacetime army, was probably unknown two decades later to most admirers of "Archie Bunker"; Lucille Ball ("I Love Lucy"), the quintessential dumb, helpless, yet singularly superior "little woman" gave way to Mary Tyler Moore, the cool, talented, and capable modern career woman; and Molly Goldberg, the first-generation Jewish immigrant tenement "yenta"[1] was replaced by "Maude," her affluent, suburban reincarnation. Charles Van Doren, a culture hero of the vastly popular quiz show, "The $64,000 Question," became the first of a long line of idealized Americans who were shown to lack integrity when it was revealed that the knowledge that won him a fortune derived from rehearsed answers to expected questions. Television also transported its viewers as easily from the staged drama of a national political convention to the unstaged assassination of a president on the streets of Dallas; from a view of the "flower children" of Haight-Ashbury to the politicized children of 1968 being clubbed by Chicago police; from the naturally scarred terrain of the moon to the man-raped landscape of Vietnam. Nothing, high or low, comic or tragic, real or imagined, escaped the camera eye.

Television seemed an integral part of the disposable consumer culture. As stations competed for the largest potential audiences and the greatest amount of advertisers' dollars, they replaced stars and favorite series with startling speed. One season's hit became the next year's turkey. Standardization became the hallmark of television, as each year police dramas or westerns or quiz shows or situation comedies dominated prime-time television. The shows changed—the sponsors remained the same. Television had displaced Hollywood (though Hollywood soon produced the bulk of TV fare) as the great American dream and money-making machine.

Throughout all the changes of the 1950s and 1960s only Marshall Dillon (James Arness of "Gunsmoke") and Ed Sullivan endured. And even they faded from the screen as the 1960s passed into the 1970s.

As television viewing occupied more and more Americans for more and more hours, questions arose about its impact on the audience. Did steady viewing hinder schoolchildren's ability to read and write? Were adults becoming less able to distinguish image from reality and also less sociable as the TV habit increasingly bound them to the house? Had rigged quiz shows made people less sensitive to moral corruption? Did the constant stream of

[1] A Yiddish slang expression describing a female busybody or gossiper.

violence and sexual innuendo emanating from the home screen render people more prone to violent behavior and sexual exploration? Had the endless hours of mass entertainment totally debased culture in the United States?

Much ink, tons of print, reams of paper, and hours of congressional hearings were consumed in seeking to answer such questions. Yet experts disagreed and findings contradicted each other. Moreover, the more the prim and the righteous cried out against sex and violence, the more the mass of viewers sought them out, and the more readily the networks provided such programs. During the 1950s women on television had to dress modestly, married couples used twin beds, and when Elvis Presley appeared on the Ed Sullivan show the cameras avoided his hips and pelvic area (male bumps and grinds were ruled unacceptable for a prime-time audience). By the end of the 1960s all this had changed. Couples, married or not, shared beds, singers shook, rattled, and rolled their bodies in full view, and the ABC network rose to the top of the Nielsen ratings by featuring scantily clad, nubile young women in what were known euphemistically in the trade as jiggle, or t and a (tits and asses), shows.

Still, whether television altered sexual and other social practices or merely reflected such changes in the larger society remains in doubt. Unquestionably television affected Americans enormously. What that affect was between 1950 and 1970 remains debatable.

## THE OTHER CULTURE

Just as one could point to television as the source and reason for the debasement of culture in the United States, one could just as easily find signs of a cultural renaissance. If people spent most of their leisure time watching mindless TV programs, more people than ever before listened to classical music, patronized art museums, attended live theater, and purchased books.

Affluence and technology held promise as well as peril for culture. The increasing scale and dispersion of wealth in the United States made it possible for cities such as Houston and Minneapolis to become lively centers for the performing arts. Symphonic music and live, original theater flourished in both cities. Even the unlikeliest places enjoyed live performances by leading artists and groups, as the growth of colleges and universities dotted the landscape with new symphony halls, grand stages, and eager audiences. The New York City Ballet and the Metropolitan Opera annually visited Bloomington, Indiana, the home of Indiana University. And Isaac Stern performed in Fort Hays, Kansas, a far smaller college town.

For those who could not attend live performances, high-fidelity records and improved sound equipment brought the finest music directly into the living room and den. Indeed, consumers spent more on records and stereo sets than on professional sports entertainment. In some cases, television itself took classical dance and fine drama into the home.

The wealth which built performing arts centers in such places as Houston, Minneapolis, and Milwaukee also provided the funds to erect art museums and fill them with paintings, sculptures, and other artifacts of the high culture. If provincial art museums could not acquire masterpieces comparable to those on display in the great metropolises, wealthy provincials could travel easily to the great museums. Jet-air transport came of age in the late 1950s and early 1960s and enabled the affluent from America's hinterland to enjoy museum-theater weekends in New York or Boston, Chicago or Minneapolis, San Francisco or Los Angeles.

Literature shared in the cultural boom. During the 1950s book sales doubled. New methods of production and promotion stimulated the publishing business. Low-priced, mass-produced paperbacks widened the potential market; their sale in supermarkets, drugstores, and airport terminals altered merchandizing for the mass market. Equally important was the growth in the college student population. On campuses everywhere teachers assigned their students a variety of inexpensive paperbacks in place of the traditional textbook.

To be sure, the new book publishing methods and merchandizing techniques flooded the market with much dross and just plain trash, enough to cause the sometime radical and film critic Dwight MacDonald to lament a cultural Gresham's law under which "bad stuff drives out good, since it is more easily understood and enjoyed." Such jeremiads were only partly true.

First of all, the paperback revolution made available to college students and other readers complete, unexpurgated versions of literary classics hitherto costly and of limited circulation. But it was not only Shakespeare and Thomas Hardy, Tolstoy and Dostoyevsky, Moliere and Proust, Dreiser and Hemingway, who found a wider audience. William Faulkner, the greatest of American southern novelists, won new paperback readers. And the emerging generation of American novelists, one of the more impressive in United States history, attracted a larger reading public than their literary forbears. J.D. Salinger's adolescent hero-manque, Holden Caulfield of *The Catcher in the Rye*, became the personification of teen-age trauma for millions of high school and college students. Philip Roth's hero in *Goodbye Columbus* symbolized the coming-of-age for upwardly mobile ethnics, the first-generation graduates of municipal and state universities, who greedily sought their share of America's wealth. John Updike's novels, especially *Rabbit Run*, painted the plight of lower middle-class WASPs unable to come to terms successfully with an affluent society. John Cheever's short stories also focused on WASP culture. Cheever's characters did achieve the American dream—successful executive status, personal wealth, and fine homes in the best suburbs. Yet they found success empty. Moreover, such southern regional writers as Flannery O'Connor and Eudora Welty were now read by a national audience.

The 1950s and 1960s saw the flourishing of ethnic as well as regional forms of literature. It was the period in which Philip Roth, Bernard Malamud, Saul Bellow, and Herbert Gold wrote their best books and enjoyed their widest popularity. And a Jewish-American novelist, Joseph Heller, early in the 1960s wrote the novel which best caught the absurdities of World War II and postwar America and whose title—*Catch 22*—became the phrase used to describe all absurd bureaucratic rules.

The prominence and success of these writers led some dyspeptic non-Jewish critics to complain that you can't read the "great American novel" without a Yiddish-English language dictionary.

At this same time Mario Puzo began to publish his stories of Italian-American life, which culminated in the late 1960s with his smash bestseller, *The Godfather,* made even more famous and profitable in the 1970s by the two Hollywood films of the same title.

Yet the literary group which attracted the most attention and publicity during the 1950s were those known as the "beat generation." Why that was so is hard to say. For the best known of the "beats," Jack Kerouac, the novelist, and Allan Ginsberg and Lawrence Ferlinghetti, the poets, scarcely rank as the literary equals of Updike, Bellow, and Malamud, or of the poets Robert Lowell and Stanley Kunitz. Nor did their novels and books of poetry outsell those of their literary superiors, let alone those who purveyed more popular trash.

Society's concern with the beats probably flowed from two interrelated causes. However much their life-styles conflicted with the central mores of Eisenhower's America, the "beats" posed no direct threat to conservative political and social dominance. They may have despised the work ethic, ridiculed the conventional middle-class family, celebrated homosexuality, and turned on to drugs. But rather than challenge directly and collectively the prevailing system, the beats preferred to drop out of society and to pursue their own individual pleasures or forms of Oriental mysticism. Only a small, select group during the 1950s, the values and life-style of the Kerouacs and Ginsbergs were at the heart of the 1960s counterculture, many of whose adherents proudly bore the title *beatniks.*

## YOUTH CULTURE

By the 1950s the offspring of the wartime and postwar baby boom were beginning to enter adolescence and create a bulge in the teen-age population that peaked in the late 1960s. Once again, as had happened two generations earlier during the 1920s, adults began to decry teen-agers who no longer respected their parents and their values and who smoked too much, drank too much, and experimented too much sexually. Worse, youths seemed to be creating their own social world in which teen-age peers, not parents, teachers, or priests, set the norms and goals of behavior.

Teen-age culture seemingly epitomized the Eisenhower-era cultural void. Pampered, petted, and pandered to in a society in which to be young was to be beautiful, teen-agers spent billions of consumer dollars, $22 billion in 1963 alone. A singular teen-age society had evolved with its own highly ritualized dress and grooming, behavioral, and sexual patterns. The cut of a boy's hair, the style of a girl's dress, the nature of a young couple's relationship placed them within a stylized social context. Teen-agers rocked around the clock with "Bill Haley and his Comets," and gyrated to the beat of Elvis Presley's diluted black rock music. If popular music still seemed conventional, tame, and sedate compared to what followed in the 1960s, this was the music the young John Lennon and Paul McCartney listened to in Liverpool, England. The Beatles also drew their own name and inspiration from the emerging American rock star of the late 1950s, Buddy Holly and the Crickets. The crew cut distinguished the "jock" from the long, slick-downed hair of the "greaser," while the neat trim bedecked the "square." Teen-agers might have watched the same TV programs, purchased similar records, and adored cars, but their sartorial styles suggested quite different social ambitions and futures.

A film of 1973—"American Graffiti"—distils graphically the teen-age culture of the late 1950s. The movie's smalltown California teen-agers (ca. 1962) endlessly cruised the town's main street in a wierd, almost surrealistic, parade of cars; they drift in and out of the drive-in hamburger stand; and tune their car radios to an all-night disc jockey who serves as the resident divine. Such forms of teen-age behavior caused that astute student of adolescent psychology, Kenneth Keniston, to observe in 1962, "I see little likelihood of American students ever playing a radical role, much less a revolutionary one, in our society." Despite the film's portrayal of an apparently monochromatic adolescent culture, it also captured the subtle individual differences latent among 1950s teen-agers, which prefigured the youth and student rebellion of the late 1960s and early 1970s.

## A SECOND GOLDEN AGE
## OF SPORTS

The 1950s, like the prosperous 1920s, produced an unprecedented boom in spectator sports, especially at the professional level. Prior to this period baseball was the only regularly scheduled professional sport which drew substantial attendance. College football and basketball games attracted millions of fans annually, outdrawing the professionals. By the end of the 1950s, however, professional football, basketball, and ice hockey had all become widely attended, national-level events. And this proved only a foretaste of the future.

The blossoming of professional sports was largely the result of the simultaneous conjunction of basic economic, technological, and sociological changes. Steadily rising real wages joined to a shorter working week widened immeasurably the potential market for paid sports events. Improved forms of artificial lighting enabled baseball clubs to schedule most of their games at night, further widening their potential market. Only William F. Wrigley's (the chewing-gum magnate) Chicago Cubs refused to install lights in their ballpark. Jet-air travel made it possible for professional sports teams to follow the population flow west and south and thus truly to nationalize all major-league sports. Finally, television, which many commentators thought would wreck paid spectator sports, as individuals chose to watch games at home, had precisely the opposite effect. Television promoted professional sports, especially NFL football, widened their audiences, and enriched their treasuries.

Perhaps as important as the economic and technological changes were the sociological ones. Prior to the 1940s all professional sports, except boxing, followed the color line in race relations. In baseball Afro-Americans had to play in their own league where only the ball was white. In football, nonwhites had even fewer options and in basketball a select few could earn good money playing for the Harlem Globetrotters, whose talents as clowns dominated their athletic skills.

Between 1946 and 1955 the race line in professional sports collapsed. In 1946 Branch Rickey, president of the Brooklyn Dodgers, signed Jackie Roosevelt Robinson, a former UCLA multisport great, to a major-league baseball contract, the first American black ever. A year later, Robinson played for the Dodgers as a regular, and before the decade's end he won the National League's Most Valuable Player award. Enduring an unending stream of petty and also substantial racial incidents and slurs, Robinson persevered. His triumph blazed the path for the Afro-Americans who soon followed him to the major leagues: Roy Campanella, Larry Doby, Willie Mays, and Henry Aaron, who, before he retired, broke the most venerable record in baseball, Babe Ruth's career mark for home runs.

What these men pioneered in baseball, others did in football and basketball, and even in tennis, where the dress, balls, and competitors had always been only white. By the mid-1950s, professional football teams eagerly competed for black stars, and, by the end of the decade, the most famous and successful NFL star was a black man, Jimmy Brown, still the greatest running back in the history of the game. Basketball was somewhat slower than baseball and football in breaking the color line. When it did so, it transformed the racial complexion of its teams even more rapidly and fully. Basketball became the black man's game par excellence, as the careers of Oscar "Big O" Robertson, Elgin Baylor, Wilt Chamberlain, and especially Bill Russell (who became a successful championship coach as well as player) attested. In tennis a black woman, Althea Gibson, won the national women's championship at Forest Hills in 1957 and 1958, and a decade later Arthur Ashe emerged as one of the world's top-ranked men.

Breaking the color line produced two benefits for professional sports.

First, it created an additional audience among nonwhites, now a more urban people and concentrated in precisely those cities with major-league franchises. Second, it improved noticeably the quality of competition, further attracting spectators.

Whatever the precise conjunction of circumstances which produced it, none could deny that by the end of the 1950s spectator sports, live and on television, were big business. The National Basketball Association, which had a shaky first decade after its formation in 1946, was by the late 1950s stable, prosperous, the beneficiary of a national TV contract, and poised for franchise expansion. Sunday NFL football became the most widely watched television program, a football star became in 1959 the subject of a prime-time documentary, "The Violent World of Sam Huff," and by the mid-1960s Coach Vince Lombardi and his Green Bay Packers were national culture heroes. Football seemed so profitable that a rival league, the American Football League (AFL), was formed in 1960 to chase fan and television dollars. When in 1967 the champions of the two rival leagues met in the first "Super Bowl," it quickly became the most widely publicized and money-making single event in team sports history.

Minor sports were not bypassed. Golf gained its share of TV time, and Arnold Palmer became a household name and, in the bargain, a multimillionaire. Tennis shed its amateur pretenses, opened all major competitions to professionals (indeed most players turned professional immediately), and created its own stable of athlete millionaires.

With spectator sports such a profitable enterprise, athletics permeated all aspects of society. Colleges chased the sports "buck" as avidly as professional franchises, making bigtime college athletics a semiprofessional enterprise. A host of sports entrepreneurs offered, for a fee, specialized athletic camps whose "products" might win college scholarships or lucrative professional contracts. And parents avidly organized little league teams in baseball, football, and basketball (and, in the 1970s, soccer), for youngsters to develop and refine their playing skills. In the United States where the virtues of competition were extolled and to be Number 1 was everyone's goal, athletic champions were a breed of self-made royalty.

## THE CULTURE OF CONSENSUS

The hard edges of the Cold War and the tensions of McCarthyism had been softened in the United States of the late 1950s by the smiles, platitudes, and tranquility of the Eisenhower era. It was a time to consume, to achieve, and to celebrate.

Intellectuals and writers who for much of the twentieth century had been at war with a materialistic, bourgeois America now also joined the celebration. *Partisan Review,* a literary-intellectual journal which had served at the end of the 1930s as a voice for non-Stalinist Marxists, in the 1950s sponsored a symposium entitled, "Our Country and Our Culture." In it one contributor declared, "For the first time in the history of the modern intellectual, America is not to be conceived of as a priori the vulgarest and stupidest nation of the world."

Indeed, the America of the 1950s was a country in which private foundations generously subsidized free-lance intellectuals and many of those same intellectuals gladly served such government agencies as the Central Intelligence Agency through the Congress for Cultural Freedom. Cultural anti-Communism united intellectuals, trade unionists, and such socialists as Norman Thomas in a common front with corporate executives and federal officials.

What had happened to American intellectuals and social critics was aptly caught in the substance and title of *Commentary* editor Norman Podhoretz's 1968 autobiography. The son of Jewish-immigrant parents, himself born and bred in the Brownsville, Brooklyn, ghetto, Podhoretz had made his way to Columbia University and from there to the apex of the New York literary-intellectual universe. His journey through life was surely, as he titled it, a case of *Making It* in America.

Formal academic works reflected a similar influence. Where once history books stressed have-nots versus haves, farmers versus bankers, section versus section, and city versus country, in the 1950s they spoke of consensus and shared values. David Potter perceived abundance as the single most influential factor in the American experience, and he entitled his interpretive history of America *People of Plenty*. In 1956 Richard Hofstadter won the Pulitzer Prize for a study, *The Age of Reform,* which emphasized the relative absence of class conflict, the priority of status over class, and the basic American commitment to private property, the profit motive, and capitalist institutions.

Economists, too, saw social harmony and material abundance as the new reality. In their view, the Keynesian economic revolution had given them the tools to fine-tune the economy in order to maintain full employment and price stability. Students no longer had to look to classical economics or its Marxist repudiation for solutions to contemporary problems.

None celebrated America's success more lustily than political scientists and sociologists. Both academic groups saw democracy, especially in America, as a completed, successful experiment. Full democratic rights were in place, all adults had basic citizenship, and all were formally legal before the law. No single, unified group ruled or dominated society to the detriment of others. Instead, a variety of equally balanced interest groups competed with each other for public favors and influence with the state which acted as an honest broker among them. This system came to be known as pluralism to distinguish it from authoritarianism and totalitarianism.

According to the political sociologists, pluralism was not a belief system comparable to socialism, communism, or fascism. It was rather a simple practice of balancing harmoniously competing claims and rights in an affluent, democratic society, which had, as the sociologist Seymour Martin Lipset claimed in his book *Political Man,* abolished all class politics based on irreconcilable isms. Indeed, as Daniel Bell proclaimed in a collection of essays published in 1960, the United States had seen *The End of Ideology.* One essay in the collection analyzed trade unionism as "The Capitalism of the Proletariat," and another, "Crime as an American Way of Life," dissected criminal activities as an ethnic version of "making it." The passions which had generated mass socialist parties, the Bolshevik Revolution, Fascism in Italy, and Nazi in Germany, Bell proclaimed as dead. The new generation, he wrote, "finds itself . . . within a framework of political society that has rejected . . . the old apocalyptic and chiliastic visions."

John F. Kennedy's election as president symbolized the marriage of "new generation" intellectuals to the power of the American state. The new president invited Robert Frost to read a poem at the inauguration. The historian Arthur Schlesinger, Jr., served as White House scholar-in-residence; the economic historian Walt W. Rostow acted as a foreign-policy planner; the economist John Kenneth Galbraith went to India as ambassador; and the historians Samuel Eliot Morison and Henry Steele Commager sang the praises of "Camelot" on the Potomac.

Not that voices of dissent and criticism were silent in the 1950s. Not at all. The *New Republic* and *Nation* magazines maintained their long traditions of left-liberal social and political commentary. In the 1950s a group of anti-Stalinist Social Democrats founded *Dissent,* a journal which tried to keep alive in America the perspectives associated with Western European labor and social democratic parties. For the more orthodox on the left, there was always *Monthly Review,* in which Paul Baran and Paul Sweezy subjected contemporary American and world developments to the scrutiny of Marxist economics and theory. But in the 1950s and early 1960s their audiences were relatively small and their sometimes strident criticism of affluent America no more than tiny voices in the wilderness.

It was this reality that led C. Wright Mills to cry out as early as 1951 that "political expression is banalized, political theory is barren administrative detail, history is made behind men's backs."

In reality, the affluent mass culture of the 1950s that bred a quiet generation of organization men lost in the void of a "lonely crowd" was more ephemeral than it first appeared. Indeed it was shot through with unseen cracks and flaws. John Kenneth Galbraith may have bemoaned the widespread public squalor amidst the private affluence; for more than thirty million Americans even affluence was beyond reach. Rural life decayed apace, urban ghettoes spread and festered, nonwhite Americans remained at best second-class citizens and at worst the hapless victims of social and economic discrimination, and most wage-workers, regardless of skin color, endured as objects of external authority. Wealth and poverty, the ideal of equality versus the reality of inequality, authority against freedom remained inextricably at war in affluent America. During the 1960s, the social tinder represented by poverty and racialism, ignited in the form of urban race riots and the impassioned militancy of the New Left and the radical feminist movements.

# CHAPTER SEVEN
# THE NEW EQUALITY,
# THE REVOLT OF NONWHITES,
# YOUTH, AND WOMEN

In 1945 and 1946, black veterans left a segregated army to resume civilian life in a segregated society—one in which they were denied equal public accommodations, where restrictive real-estate covenants closed much of the housing market to them, and in which a dual labor market confined them to the least secure and lowest-paid jobs. Almost a decade later, in 1953 and 1954, black veterans returned home from a newly integrated army and a war in Korea to a society that still treated nonwhites as second-class citizens. The black man in white America could still expect in 1954 what James Baldwin hyberbolically described as his fate:

> The rope, fire, torture, castration, infanticide, rape; death and humiliation; fear by day and night, fear as deep as the marrow of the bone; doubt that he was worthy of life since everyone around him denied it; sorrow for his women, for his kinsfolk, for his children, who needed his protection, and whom he could not protect; rage, hatred, and murder, hatred for white men so deep that it often turned against him and his own, and made all love, all trust, all joy impossible.[1]

[1] James Baldwin, *The Fire Next Time*, Copyright © 1970 by The Dial Press. Reprinted by permission.

Other domestic minorities suffered their own singular indignities. In the Southwest, stretching from Texas to southern California, Americans of Latin, mostly Mexican, origin—the Chicanos—occupied the lowest, most despised rungs of the social ladder. Marked as inferior by virtue of color, language, and culture, Chicanos existed to serve as field hands and domestics. The Indian tribes that had survived the late nineteenth-century frontier wars were for the most part on reservations, invisible subjects of a dominant society that denied them adequate shelter, food, education, and opportunity.

Nonracial groups also experienced discrimination. Women, society ordained, belonged in the home to raise children and consume industry's products. Men and women with socially "unacceptable" patterns of sexual behavior had to disguise themselves and live furtively in society's dark corners. And students, from the kindergartens to the graduate schools, marched to the beat of their teacher's drum.

Until 1954 an order in which nonwhites, women, and students occupied inferior positions seemed to hold. Nonwhites deferred to whites, women to men, and students to teachers. Then, with amazing rapidity, the old order cracked. Black Americans arose to demand the equality that had eluded them since the end of the First Reconstruction. Brown Americans, too, organized and struggled to gain equal civil, social, and economic rights. Betty Friedan resurrected the old feminist battle cries of the 1920s, calling on women to come out of the kitchen and do as men did. And students, who initially allied with rebellious blacks, carried the tactics of the civil rights revolution into the nation's classrooms and campuses.

What caused the old order to crack? Why did individuals and groups that traditionally accepted the roles society defined for them now rebel? What did the protesters seek and how did they plan to accomplish their aims?

## THE CIVIL RIGHTS REVOLUTION

No simple answer suffices to explain the eruption in the 1950s of protest against racism and its spread to epidemic proportions in the 1960s. Demographic changes, political realignments, and exigent foreign policy needs coalesced to break the shackles of segregation and to spark militant protest. As blacks left the South for the North in an ever-swelling stream beginning with World War II, they became more influential politically. Because many settled in compact urban communities where no poll taxes, unfair registrars, or veiled threats denied them the right to vote, Afro-Americans developed the political muscle to influence state, local, and national elections. In 1948 Harry Truman risked a southern white defection from the Democratic party and endorsed civil rights. Black voters played a decisive role in Truman's upset victory, and he repaid them by desegregating the armed services and recommending civil rights legislation.

But Truman's policies conflicted with the realities of congressional politics in which southern Democrats and northern Republicans joined forces to defeat administration civil rights bills. In 1954, the Supreme Court broke this political deadlock when declaring, in *Brown* v. *Board of Education of Topeka,* the principle of "separate but equal" facilities (in this case public schools) unconstitutional. For Afro-Americans the promise exceeded the reward. The Eisenhower administration failed to endorse the Court's decision, and southern whites organized a bitter resistance that used courts, politics, and violence to thwart school desegregation. But this time Afro-Americans demanded the reward as well as the promise, the substance as well as the shadow of change; they now had the leadership and the will to fight for the rights so often denied them in the past; and they were no longer willing to let things take care of themselves, nor for the law to wend its slow course.

A year after the Supreme Court condemned segregation, black Americans in Montgomery, Alabama, acted decisively to achieve their civil rights. When a Montgomery seamstress named Rosa Parks refused to surrender her seat in the front of a bus to a white man in December 1955, she ignited the modern civil rights revolution. Her subsequent arrest by local police brought to prominence the man who for the next decade symbolized the movement: Martin Luther King, Jr. The son of an Atlanta clergyman, King had been trained for the pastorate at Boston University before coming to his first ministerial post in Montgomery, the right man at the right time in history. Under his leadership, Montgomery Negroes participated in a months-long boycott of the city's bus lines, which terminated in the first in a series of victories against Jim Crow.

Although the NAACP continued to adjudicate in its traditional manner and win numerous legal decisions outlawing segregation in the South, its tactics lacked the militancy, color, and impact of mass direction action. Newspapers, magazines, and TV cameras preferred the drama of action in the streets to more solitary courtroom struggles. King's tactics and ideas became contagious, spreading first throughout the South and later into northern ghettoes, though seldom achieving the success in the North that was obtained in the South.

The movement Rosa Parks sparked and Martin Luther King kindled into flame blazed more brightly in February 1960 when four black students from North Carolina Agricultural and Technical College sat down at a Woolworth's lunch counter in Greensboro, North Carolina, to demand equal service. Thereafter, despite being spat on, beaten, burned, and insulted, young black students continued to sit in and demand equal service, a goal that they won at the lunch counters of more than 126 southern cities by the end of 1960. In April 1960 at a conference called by King, the black college students formed the Student Non-Violent Coordinating Committee (SNCC), which became the spearhead for the civil rights revolt.

At first, committed to the principles and tactics of King, SNCC united young whites and blacks in a militant but nonviolent direct action movement aimed at eradicating the last vestiges of segregation. After desegregating lunch counters, whites and blacks rode together on interstate buses, waded in at southern pools and beaches, and checked in at motels and hotels. Always a step ahead of the existing law, these young people typically met violent resistance until their courage caused legislators to enact new laws or courts to declare existing laws unconstitutional. In the face of ever-present violence, the protestors compiled an enviable record of nonviolent behavior reminiscent of an earlier generation of American radicals whom historian Howard Zinn called to mind when he titled his history of SNCC: *The New Abolitionists*.

The New Abolitionists, like their antebellum predecessors, waged a reform crusade steeped in Christian theology. It was no accident that a minister, King, personified the movement and that its impact was greatest in the South where blacks remained most closely linked to the church. From the Christian precept of redemption through suffering and the Gandhian concept of passive resistance, King forged a nonviolent strategy directed toward convincing white Americans that the victims of segregation were more Christian and moral than their oppressors. Encouraging his followers to apply the principle of Christian love, King advised them never to stoop so low as to hate the enemy. "We must use the weapon of love," he implored. "We must have compassion and understanding for those who hate us."

Heeding King's singular synthesis of Christian and Gandhian ideals, his followers—black and white, young and old—marched from victory to victory. King's army could not be halted, in spite of jail sentences for their leader in Birmingham and Atlanta, resistance to classroom integration by the governor of Alabama (George Wallace, who barred the way at the University of Alabama), Sheriff "Bull" Connor's police dogs in Birmingham, or the violence of Alabama state troopers at Selma. The more violent the opposition the more nonviolently the civil rights protestors behaved and the more aid and encouragement they received from much of northern white America. In the summer of 1963 over 200,000 blacks and whites gathered on the mall in Washington, D.C., to sing of how they would overcome their oppression, and to listen to King's "I have a dream" of a day "when the sons of former slaves and the sons of former slave-owners will be able to sit together at the table of brotherhood."

In 1963 the day of King's dream did not seem far distant. It was a time when President Kennedy issued executive orders desegregating interstate transport and federally financed housing, a time when he sent to Congress the most advanced civil rights legislation in a century. Kennedy's assassination in November did not retard the civil rights movement. The new president, Lyndon B. Johnson, pushed through Congress the civil rights bill stalled in committee during Kennedy's last months. And when Johnson in a 1965 speech on civil rights pledged that "We Shall Overcome," his words carried concrete meaning. By 1965 the legal Jim Crow system was a shambles. Thousands of public schools had been desegregated or were under court orders to do so; public facilities, theaters, restaurants, hotels, and transit lines, had been desegregated; and a series of congressional acts stretching from 1957 to 1965 had restored voting rights to southern blacks. In 1965 as in 1867, national law guaranteed black men and women their full civil rights—from the polling place to the toilet. On paper, a revolution, a Second Reconstruction, had been consummated.

## FROM CIVIL RIGHTS
## TO BLACK POWER

In a real sense, the United States stood in 1965 where it had in 1867. Having once again decided to guarantee blacks their full civil rights, the nation had to decide whether to offer Afro-Americans the economic and social opportunities that would render legal rights meaningful.

The answer in 1965 appeared to be the same as it had been a century earlier: *No!* In 1966, the veteran black radical and civil rights crusader Bayard Rustin summed up the place of black Americans twelve years after the *Brown* v. *Topeka* decision. "Negroes today," Rustin wrote, "are in worse economic shape, live in worse slums, and attend more highly segregated schools than in 1954." Statistics buttressed his indictment: black unemployment was double that of whites (almost 32 percent among black youths), and the gap between white and black wages had widened; in northern open-occupancy cities and states blacks lived in deteriorated ghetto housing; and the Health, Education and Welfare Department reported that 65 percent of first grade black pupils attended schools from 90 to 100 percent black. "The day-to-day lot of the ghetto Negro," concluded Rustin, "has not been improved by the various judicial and legislative measures of the past decade."

This economic record caused frustration among northern blacks who realized that the great expectations aroused by the civil rights movement had brought few material rewards. As America grew more affluent and the consumer society enveloped all, the gap widened between what blacks desired and obtained, what they expected and received. For the mass of ghetto blacks reality remained dirty homes on filthy dope-ridden streets in noisome neighborhoods that offered only inferior schools and dead-end jobs for its volunteers. These realities gave new meaning to the warning novelist James Baldwin had hurled at white America in 1963: "God gave Noah the rainbow sign. No more water, the fire next time!"[2]

[2]*The Fire Next Time.*

Black and white together, acme of the Civil Rights Movement at Washington Monument Reflection Pool, August, 1963 (Wide World Photos)

The year 1965, the apogee of the civil rights movement, saw the fire ignite. Los Angeles's black ghetto (Watts) exploded in a frenzy of rioting. Rioters looted and burned white-owned businesses, leaving much of Watts a smoldering ruin. From Los Angeles the fire spread the following summer to Chicago and to New York's Harlem, where rioters also looted and burned, again focusing on white-owned enterprises. But this was only a prelude to the summer of 1967 when Newark, New Jersey, and Detroit blew up. Rioters, police, and troops killed over twenty-six and wounded more than twelve hundred (mostly black) in Newark, while in Detroit forty-three died and two thousand were wounded. Vast sections of both cities' black ghettoes burned to the ground; both were occupied by troops armed with machine guns and tanks. Encircled by local police, well-armed soldiers, and overhead helicopters, black rioters (and nonrioters) were tightly confined to their ghettoes as the fires of rage smoldered out. Surveying Detroit from the air,

Michigan Governor George Romney observed: It looks like "a city that has been bombed."

The ghetto riots raised more questions than they answered. Why, for example, should violence erupt after a decade of progress for black Americans? Why begin in the tree-lined, single-family-home ghetto of Watts and then spread to Newark, which had received proportionately more antipoverty money than any other city, and Detroit, where blacks commanded better jobs and higher wages than elsewhere? Why had black and white unity collapsed in the spectacle of blacks burning white property and attacking white persons? What explained black rage against white America?

The nation's leaders pursued a traditional course to answer those questions: the appointment of special commissions to investigate the violence. In California, the McCone Commission analyzed Watts, and three years later President Johnson created the Kerner Commission to investigate racial violence nationally. Both commissions discovered the same facts and

The fire next time, Brownsville (Leo de Wys, Inc.)

reached similar conclusions. They saw a society in which racial divisions were widening and the threat of domestic turmoil rising. They agreed that the civil rights movement had stirred expectations among blacks that American society refused to satisfy, and the Kerner Commission appended a scathing indictment of what it labeled as "white racism." It was easier to locate the roots of violence, to condemn white racism, and to prophesy the emergence of a dual society than to propose specific policies that would assuage black rage and satisfy frustrated expectations. Not unexpectedly, a year after the Kerner Commission reported, a black veteran returning to the United States from a tour of duty in Vietnam observed that: "The rights we fought [for] for somebody else just don't exist for us."

Even before blacks ignited their ghettoes in fire, veterans of the civil rights movement had begun to rethink tactics and strategy. What, they asked, were the actual results of passive resistance and civil rights legislation? What had King's reliance on nonviolence, the white man's conscience, and Christian charity brought?—the bombing of a black church in Birmingham and the death of four young black girls; the brutal murders in Mississippi in the summer of 1964 of James Chaney, a southern black, and Michael Schwerner and Andrew Goodman, white northern college student civil rights activists; the Orangeburg, South Carolina, massacre in which state police shot down unarmed black college students; and finally the April 4, 1968, assassination of Martin Luther King. The words of black writer Julius Lester, not King, now resonated among young blacks. "Love?" asked Lester. "That's always better done in bed than on picket lines and marches." Civil rights marchers used to sing "I Love Everybody," Lester recalled. "Now they sing,"

> Too much love,
> Too much love,
> Nothing kills a nigger like
> Too much love.[3]

Having shifted perceptions on the realities of American society, blacks moved from passivity to resistance, protest to politics, integration to cultural nationalism. Power, not prayer, brought change. And most blacks needed social and economic power as much as civil rights laws. But how could society's mudsill gain economic improvements? Only political power promised betterment—the use of the vote to influence government to redistribute wealth to the advantage of poor blacks, especially through preferential employment practices.

Lacking a voting majority of their own, black leaders at first turned to the Democratic party as the vehicle for coalition politics. In the summer of 1964 SNCC workers labored in the rural regions of Mississippi and other

[3]Alfred F. Young, ed., *Dissent*, Copyright 1968 by Northern Illinois University Press. Reprinted by permission.

Deep South states to register black voters. Rejected by the regular Democratic party in Mississippi, blacks organized the Freedom Democratic party and petitioned the 1964 Democratic convention and congressional Democrats to purge the remnants of "lily-white" organizations from the party replacing them with the FDP. Blacks won only a minimal compromise at the Atlantic City Convention that offered them recognition but not power. To many, the rewards of coalition politics appeared illusory.

In this milieu "black power" emerged as a new slogan and program among militant blacks. In Alabama SNCC rejected coalition politics and formed the Black Panther party, a political organization totally independent of the regular Democratic party, to organize black voters first in Alabama, then the South, and ultimately the nation. Simultaneously black SNCC leaders purged their white student allies who, it was alleged (rightly so in many cases), patronized rural blacks and undermined their independence and initiative. In the summer of 1966 a new young black leader captured the headlines as he shouted, "black power." That man, Stokely Carmichael, a West Indian immigrant, exceptional student at Howard University, and an impassioned orator, personified the rising assertiveness of black Americans and their desire to control their own destiny. To rejected white liberals who charged Carmichael with "reverse discrimination" he responded: "Once again, responsibility is shifted from the oppressor to the oppressed."

Carmichael's assertion of black independence had many echoes in the Afro-American community. CORE, originally founded by idealistic white and black liberals and dedicated to racial harmony and integration, purged white members at the same time that SNCC did. And even Bayard Rustin, long-time exponent of integration and coalition politics, counseled white critics of "black racism": "It is both absurd and immoral to equate the despairing response of the victim with the contemptuous assertion of the oppressor."

What, in fact, did "black power" mean and what were its aims? Obviously it did not mean legal change and the achievement of equality before the law. Nor could white liberals easily identify with it. It was instead a self-interest movement to serve black-defined concepts of their own welfare based on the belief that what is good for blacks is good for democracy. At the simplest level, black power meant black votes for black candidates serving black needs. In that sense it scarcely differed from the customary American practice of ethnic politics. At a deeper level, however, it contained an antiintegrationist, separatist core. "The white man," wrote Carmichael, "is irrelevant to blacks, except as an oppressive force." Integration was a delusion; whites were not urged to integrate black schools and neighborhoods but blacks were to integrate white institutions, implying black inferiority and white superiority. Integration, asserted militants, has meaning only when it works both ways. Experience had taught black militants that there was no existing political group with which "to form a coalition in which blacks will not be absorbed and betrayed." "Only black people," asserted Carmichael, "can convey the revolutionary idea that black people are able to help themselves." Black power advocates further insisted that they sought not simply an equal place for the Afro-Americans in white society but also a totally noncapitalist national society. It would be a society, they said, "in which the spirit of community and humanistic love prevail."

By the late 1960s, "black power" assumed more impact as a cultural than a political movement. Young northern blacks, in particular, rejected the tradition of skin bleaches and hair straighteners, the custom of black men and women seeking to act white. They now wore their hair natural (the so-called Afro style), donned dashikis, praised soul food and soul talk, and proclaimed that to be black is to be beautiful. Among the poorest, most despised residents of northern ghettoes a new religious movement spread, Black Muslim faith. Founded by Elijah Muhammed, it preached that whites were devils and blacks were Allah's anointed. Whatever its theological deficiencies, the Black Muslim faith saved many Negroes from drugs, made them proud and self-sufficient, and gave them self-respect. It also gave northern black America its most representative spokesman, Malcolm Little, better known as Malcolm X. Before his assassination in 1965, Malcolm X, who by then had broken with Elijah Muhammed, promised to link the black Muslims of the United States to traditional Islam and to make it more than a blacks-only movement.

Cultural nationalism manifested itself in a variety of ways. The successful black dramatist and poet, LeRoi Jones, discarded integrationist themes (as well as a white wife) for antiwhite ones and changed his name to Imamu Amiri Baraka. The basketball star, Lew Alcindor, converted from Christianity to Islam, changing his name to Kareem Abdul-Jabbar. Most spectacularly the brilliant and iconoclastic young heavyweight boxing champion Cassius Clay joined the Black Muslim faith, rejected the draft (for that exercise of his conscience he was stripped of his title for three and a half years), and changed his name to Muhammad Ali.

Ironically, those black militants who sought to build a society based on community and love increasingly turned to the rhetoric of despair and violence. H. Rap Brown, who replaced Carmichael as chairman of SNCC in 1967, advised blacks to get guns and remember that "violence is as American as cherry pie." When black militants on the West Coast organized the Black Panther movement in Oakland, they carried rifles as a symbol of their manhood. Police became known as "pigs," and Panther newspapers suggested that the only good "pig" was a dead one. When Detroit and Newark burned in the wake of Carmichael's impassioned cry for black power and policemen were shot down in the aftermath of Rap Brown's fiery speeches and the creation of the Black Panthers, Carmichael's earlier observation that "to most whites, black power seems to mean that the Mau Mau are coming to the suburbs at night," assumed new meaning.

As the ghetto fires burned out and the police and the courts undermined the Panthers, many black leaders questioned the rhetoric of violence. Rustin asserted that the speeches of Carmichael, Brown, and Bobby Seale "isolate the Negro community, and encourage the growth of anti-Negro forces." As a small minority of the larger society and a smaller minority of the voting population, how could Afro-Americans progress without white allies? Where blacks were a majority they could practice black power and elect sheriffs, school superintendents, and mayors. Even then, what good was a black mayor of a black community on the verge of bankruptcy, as seemed to be the case in Newark? The black community of Gary, Indiana, depended on U.S. Steel, and blacks in Detroit relied on white-owned auto companies and banks.

Afro-Americans at the end of the 1960s found themselves in an unenviable predicament. A decade and a half of civil rights protest had raised consciousness and stirred expectations. Leaders like Malcolm X had taught them that "black is beautiful," and they came to show open pride in their skin color, culture, and life-style. Opportunities for individual blacks were never better. They dominated professional basketball, and coached as well as played; ever since Jackie Robinson had broken the color line in baseball in 1947 and Emlen Tunnell a few years later in football, black men had starred in professional sports in numbers out of all proportion to their percentage of the population. The movies and TV began to cater to black audiences to whom they offered cool, black versions of Superman, Batman, and James Bond. Ivy League colleges recruited black undergraduates; universities sought black professors; and corporations hired black executives. In short, in the 1960s more blacks than ever before broke into the American middle class. Yet, despite real economic progress during the 1960s, by the start of the 1970s the median black family income was just 59 percent of that earned by whites, 33 percent of the total black population still lived in poverty, and black unemployment remained twice as great as for whites. In 1970 as in 1950, Afro-Americans depended on white society for advancement, for whites controlled the economy and the power that flowed from wealth. If whites refused to yield power or position, how could a group doomed to minority status by its dark skin itself alter the social and economic order?

## POWER! POWER! POWER!

The demand for power and the resurgence of cultural nationalism, which blacks had initiated, soon reverberated among other minority groups in American society. Brown and red Americans began to question pluralism and to suggest, as blacks had previously, that the concept of pluralism cloaked a society based on white, bourgeois dominance. Americans of Indian and Hispanic origins could succeed socially only by discarding the language and culture of their ancestors. Even then only a minuscule minority rose above society's doorsill. Most red men and brown men remained mired as deeply as blacks in poverty and despair.

Concentrated in the cities and farmlands of the Southwest, where they supplied most of the region's low-paid labor, Americans of Hispanic origin began to assert themselves in the 1960s. Segregated in slums, stripped of their language in school, dominated by Anglo public officials, and doomed to a life of ill-paid stoop labor in California's "factories in the fields," the Chicanos fought back. Led by Cesar Chavez, a disciple of professional radical Saul Alinsky, field workers in California formed a labor union in 1963. Chavez, however, transformed the farm workers' struggle into a cultural as well as a labor battle. With support from Catholic priests, student radicals, and mainstream organized labor, Chevez led *La Causa* against California's powerful agricultural interests in a fight for union recognition and improved working conditions. Denied the right to picket en masse and unable to pursue traditional strike tactics, the agricultural workers took their crusade to the nation's supermarkets asking consumers not to purchase California grapes and lettuce. The boycott, endorsed by Walter Reuther, George Meany, and Robert F. Kennedy among others, worked. By 1966 Chavez's union had negotiated labor contracts with the largest grape growers in California, Chicano field workers for the first time had an effective organizational voice, and the union prepared to challenge lettuce growers as well as Arizona and Texas ranchers.

Whereas Chavez allied with white liberals, endorsed coalition politics, and practiced traditional trade unionism, other Chicano leaders argued for their version of black power: *La Raza*. Rejecting the Puritan ethic and other white American values, advocates of *La Raza* demanded Chicano-only political organizations, the teaching of Spanish and its southwestern American dialects in the public schools, Chicano studies in the universities, and a Latin cultural alternative to the dominant national culture. Pluralism had meaning, militant Chicanos asserted, only if brown Americans could freely and with pride practice their own traditional culture.

Indians, too, began to remember and respect their past. They wrote books like Vine Deloria, Jr.'s *Custer Died for Your Sins* and were the subjects of bestsellers such as Dee Brown's *Bury My Heart at Wounded Knee*. Young Indians no longer reflexively accepted assimilation into American society as the only path to follow. Militants revived tribal customs and asserted that Indians had a right to traditional culture. By the late 1960s Indians took to a figurative warpath; they occupied Alcatraz Island in San Francisco Bay, which they offered to buy from the federal government for $24 (in beads and cloth); they invaded the Indian Bureau offices in Washington, and challenged federal power in the village of Wounded Knee, South Dakota. They, too, demanded "native American" studies in the universities, preferential hiring, and government reimbursement for what white men had stolen from Indians in the course of three centuries.

The advocates of the various forms of minority power confronted a dilemma that had puzzled generations of American radicals: whether to seek immediate reforms by accommodating the prevailing power structure or to refuse concessions and seek a total revolution; whether to work through such existing institutions as trade unions and major political parties or to form pure, independent revolutionary organizations. Effectiveness depended on delivering the goods, extracting substantial concessions for minorities from dominant groups. Such material gains flowed most readily from alliances with the labor movement and the Democratic party. But those radicals who practiced "coalition politics," such blacks as Bayard Rustin and Julian Bond and such white ex-Socialists as Tom Kahn and Albert Shanker, president of the American Federation of Teachers, found their influence diffused whether in the Democratic party or the AFL-CIO. Coalition led to collaboration, which in turn weakened radicalism. Yet those radicals who remained true to a revolutionary commitment and refused to accommodate to the established order scarcely fared better. Some black revolutionaries, notably Stokely Carmichael and Eldridge Cleaver, fled into exile overseas; others, including Angela Davis, H. Rap Brown, and Huey Newton, experienced the full force of the law. After a long and harrowing legal trial, Davis won an acquittal, Brown was convicted and sentenced to prison for armed robbery, and Newton for a time remained a fugitive from justice on a murder warrant. Most American radicals in the 1960s, regardless of their skin color, age, or sex, failed to devise a strategy that enabled them to participate effectively in society without sacrificing their commitment to a new society.

For "brown," "red," and "black" power advocates the dilemma of the typical American radical was compounded. Indians and Chicanos, like Afro-Americans, were a minority in an overwhelmingly white society, and they also lacked substantial wealth and capital. Political and economic realities caused some influential Indian and Latin spokesmen, especially those who had made substantial progress in their own careers, to criticize cultural nationalism as "reverse racism" and to insist that assimilation and integration were the only answers to the dilemma of American racial minorities. As the 1960s ended, the meaning of pluralism remained problematic, and the future of nonwhite minorities in a white society seemed uncertain.


## REBELLION ON THE CAMPUSES

As the old order cracked and its leaders could not decide how to respond to the demands of protesting minorities, further fissures rendered the American consensus. College students who had at first joined with southern blacks to challenge white supremacy returned to their campuses unwilling to tolerate what they now considered an equally outmoded and authoritarian academic order. Student publications began to refer to the student as "nigger," the impotent subject of academic masters.

The "silent generation" of Eisenhower-era college students gave way in the 1960s to a more militant, radical, and concerned breed of young scholar. Partly subsidized by the League for Industrial Democracy (the descendent of the pre–World War I Intercollegiate Socialist Society), a group of University of Michigan undergraduates met in the summer of 1962 at Port Huron to found a new student political society: Students for a Democratic Society (SDS). Like their pre–World War I predecessors at Harvard and other elite schools, these were the children of privilege at war with a society which consigned millions to poverty and even more to a bare living. "We are the people of this generation," proclaimed the Port Huron statement, "bred in at least modest comfort, housed now at universities, looking uncomfortably to the world we inherit." To change a world which they saw as scarred by selfish consumerism, gross manipulation of people, and extreme privatism, the founders of SDS called for social action, participatory democracy, and the rebirth of community.

For the next decade SDS remained at the center of campus discontent, the new political radicalism, and student activism. It produced a generation of student leaders—Tom Hayden, Todd Gitlin, Mark Rudd, Bernadine Dohrn, among others—who left their imprint on the decade. It also was largely responsible for fostering a cohort of "new left" academics and for making Marxist studies once again respectable.

At the University of California, Berkeley in 1964, militant students under the leadership of Mario Savio confronted the nation's greatest multiversity, protesting that it treated its students as identical cyphers on a mass-production educational assembly line. The Berkeley Free Speech Movement demanded a university in which students had autonomy, in which faculty served students, not corporations and governments, and in which education questioned rather than buttressed the social order. At Berkeley and elsewhere where militant students failed to win all their demands, "free universities" and "alternative classrooms" were created off campus to enable committed students to toy with ideas alien to the traditional university.

The real external world also impinged on the students in hitherto cloistered universities as it had long since done on faculty who moved regularly between classrooms and corporate boardrooms and government agencies as highly paid consultants. Students questioned educational institutions whose representatives served military agencies and business corporations as much as the quest for knowledge. The civil rights movement, which once had taken idealistic students away from campus, now hit home, as administrators recruited blacks for the formerly exclusively white university world. And most important, as the war in Vietnam intensified, making conscription an ever-present reality to the male student, campus life grew more embittered. Antiwar protest, primarily a white phenomenon though endorsed by such blacks as Martin Luther King and Julian Bond, distracted attention from the problems of black "liberation" and weakened the black-white alliance forged in the civil rights movement.

To radical students in the late 1960s American universities were an integral part of an oppressive, imperialistic society. College ROTC programs trained the officers who staffed a global armed forces; social scientists advised the government on counterinsurgency techniques and wrote scenarios for counterrevolution; and scientists developed the sophisticated, deadly weapons of modern warfare. Frustrated and embittered, student radicals burned ROTC facilities, and in some cases even armed themselves. In the spring of 1968 militant Columbia students shut the university down. By occupying buildings and ransacking the president's office, thus coming under police attack, they brought the academic year to a premature end. The following academic year armed black students split the Cornell University campus and pressured a shaky administration into concessions. Then, in the spring of 1970, the intensification of the Vietnam war as a result of the Cambodian invasion that May precipitated a nationwide explosion. Students protested, marched, struck, and closed scores of campuses weeks before the term ended; and tragically, at Kent State in Ohio, National Guard troops killed four students and wounded more than a score during a protest against the invasion. "The Fire Next Time" seared the nation's campuses in 1970 as frustrated radicals resorted to the torch and the bomb in such places as Santa Barbara, California, and Madison, Wisconsin.

By the end of the 1960s many young student radicals had become as frustrated as their nonwhite counterparts by an inability to transform society. Unable to bear political impotency, minuscule followings, and government surveillance, some young activists turned to violence and a furtive underground life. In 1969 SDS split into factions, the most militant of which, calling themselves first Weathermen and then Weatherpeople (after the theme of a Bob Dylan song), took to violent street actions (the 1969 "days of rage" in Chicago) and random bombings (three Weatherpeople blew themselves up in a March 1970 Greenwich Village townhouse bomb factory). Mark Rudd and Bernadine Dohrn, two of the faction's leaders, were indicted by federal and state governments. In response, they assumed aliases, went underground, and moved from one crash pad to another, before reemerging at the end of the 1970s. Meanwhile, Tom Hayden, an organizer of the demonstrations at the 1968 Democratic convention and one of the "Chicago Seven," moved to California, married the actress Jane Fonda, and became an adept practitioner of Democratic coalition politics.

The fires of radicalism also burned out on the campuses, leaving behind a mixed prospect. In some ways the university in 1970 was not what it had been in 1960; in other ways it remained much the same. Most college administrators no longer sat in loco parentis; students had won the right to live where they desired, to be free of curfews, to have coed dormitories, in

The war on the campuses, Columbia University, May 22, 1968, 2:30 a.m. (Wide World Photos)

short to be treated as adults. Students also obtained experimental new courses, a voice in rating their teachers and, in some cases, seats on university policy making committees. Nonwhites and females, both as students and instructors, became more visible on college campuses. While political radicalism abated, the counterculture associated with hard-rock music, hallucinogenic drugs, and proletarian-style dress continued to attract students and separate them and other youths from their more conventional elders. Still, on most campuses effective power rested with faculty and administrators, who were overwhelmingly white and male. Moreover, the majority of students entered traditional academic programs in order to pursue customary careers.

## THE WOMEN'S MOVEMENT

Of all the movements that rent American society women's liberation was potentially the most threatening to the social fabric. Females not only protested their exploitation at work, within the household, and in bed; they also found themselves pushed into subordinate positions in the civil rights and student radical movements. (Stokely Carmichael once remarked: "The position of women in our movement should be prone.") Having learned that gender distinctions remained as demeaning as ever, young women schooled in the militancy of the 1960s now criticized male domination in marriage, the home, and the nuclear family.[4] And these militant young women from the "new left" found eager allies among many affluent suburban and professional career women.

What factors revitalized feminism in the 1960s? First, and quite obviously, the general protest against inequality echoed among women long forced to tolerate subordinate social positions. The whole structure of women's place in the economy and society, moreover, was shifting. Beginning in the 1950s women began to take jobs once closed to them and this process accelerated in the 1960s. For the first time women in substantial numbers entered the skilled trades. The number and proportion of women in the professions also rose rapidly, doubling in the law and tripling in engineering. More women than ever worked in diverse occupations and new sorts of females toiled for wages and salaries. Married women, with and without young children, and older women (45-54) joined the labor force in unprecedented numbers.

Despite all this apparent progress, women still faced severe discrimination in the job market. Professional females had fewer opportunities than men, earned lower salaries, and rose less often in the corporate hierarchy. Working-class women earned only about 59 percent as much as men and were still clustered largely in gender-specific, low-wage jobs. At the end of the 1970s the typical working woman remained a clerk-typist, retail clerk, household domestic, nurse, or teacher. Moreover, most working-class

**THE DIVISION OF LABOR**

Employment by sex (16 years and older, seasonally adjusted)

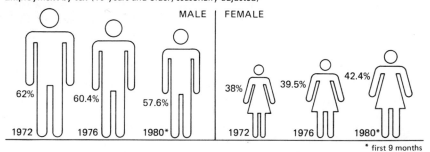

The Division of Labor (The New York Times, November 2, 1980. © 1980 The New York Times Company. Reprinted by permission.)

[4]The nuclear family consists of the parents and their children occupying a household in which no other related or unrelated individual dwells and in which there are no boarders or other nonfamily residents.

women took such "undesirable" jobs not to earn "pin money" or to establish careers but to enable their families either to survive or to achieve an "American standard of living."

With women of all ages and classes occupying a more central place in the job market and many younger women dissatisfied with their subordination in radical movements, the time was ripe for a new wave of feminism. When Betty Friedan published *The Feminine Mystique* in 1963, many women, not just suburban housewives, agreed with her assertion that women no longer had to feel "like freaks for not having that orgiastic bliss while waxing the floor." Three years later, in the fall of 1966, Friedan organized the National Organization of Women (NOW), the first truly feminist organization founded in half a century. A year later, NOW drew up a Bill of Rights for Women, which quickly became the heart of the new women's movement. Two of NOW's rights—the Equal Rights Amendment and "the right of women to control their reproductive lives"—stimulated a decade of controversy and conflict that remained heated into the 1980s.

Even before the formation of NOW, women had begun to achieve modest feminist goals. In June 1963, Congress, at the recommendation of President Kennedy's Commission on Women, passed the Equal Pay Act. The next year the Civil Rights Act of 1964 forbade discrimination on the basis of sex as well as race. And in 1970 the House of Representatives finally approved the Equal Rights Amendment and submitted it for state ratification. Meantime, in several states, women won the right to abortion and to control over their own bodies. The Supreme Court in the 1970s invalidated many state laws which restricted the right to abortion.

Yet women's liberation, like black protest, red power, and student radicalism, brought change without revolution. For every female who preferred lesbian relationships, scores still chose heterosexuality. For every woman who scorned marriage, many more aimed ultimately for matrimony, however many unsanctified relationships preceded. And for every women who preferred communal life and extended families, scores freely chose the private residence and the nuclear family. But as more and more women entered the labor force, traditional sexual roles necessarily became less distinguishable. Men could no longer claim to be sole breadwinners, or to wear the pants, and especially among the middle class, they had to share household duties from marketing to diapering.

Perhaps the most visual changes in American society during the 1960s were the sexual ones. If the counterculture won any lasting triumphs, it was in the realm of sexual liberation. The contraceptive pill removed the remaining anxiety from premarital sex, and widely distributed manuals, books, and films tutored inexperienced lovers in the varieties of sex. Male and female homosexuals came out of hiding to proclaim their gayness and demand their rights, an event unthinkable a decade earlier. Everywhere surface sexual differences vanished, as men, including professional athletes, let their hair grow, donned gaily colored clothes, and wore rings and beads. Women, meantime, put on pants.

The changes in sexual mores and reproductive rights produced a predictable reaction. Just as happened a century earlier during the struggle over women's suffrage, some women organized to fight their more militant sisters. Phyllis Schlafly, a self-proclaimed suburban Illinois housewife, emerged as the Betty Friedan of the female right. Committed to the defense of women's traditional role in the home and primary function as wife-mother, Schlafly and other like-minded women formed a host of political action committees which stymied ratification of the ERA at the state level and also sought to ban abortion.

Although American society during the 1960s in the title of a popular history of the decade seemed to be *Coming Apart,* the various minority rebellions produced an equally powerful reaction by a diverse, conservative majority. Those whom Richard M. Nixon referred to as his "silent majority"—affluent middle-class homeowners, well-paid and unionized workers, insecure whites fearful of losing their privileges to nonwhites, and traditional women—coalesced to guard the American center. The white

Out of the kitchen, 1970 (Richard Lawrence Stack/Black Star)

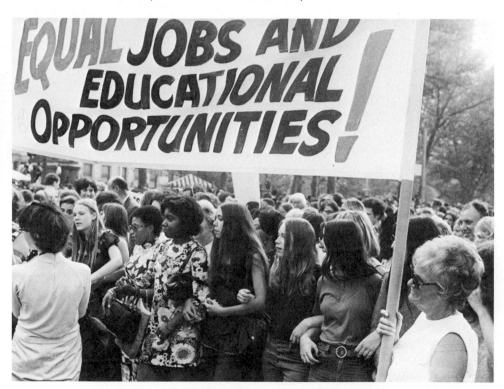

majority shared presidential adviser Daniel Patrick Moynihan's belief that it was time nonwhites received a little "benign neglect." Moynihan meant that blacks should no longer appear openly as the primary concern and beneficiaries of federal programs, and that minority groups would progress best in the future by disappearing from the headlines, controversy, and public view. The silent majority also seemed indifferent to the killing of four students at Kent State University, and it joined a rising chorus of criticism aimed at students and universities. And the silent majority had its sexual fears assuaged by the Supreme Court's 1973 decision which granted local majorities the right to define acceptable sexual mores on the stage, in films, and in books.

The upheaval of the 1960s had erupted in a time of relative economic prosperity and full employment. As turbulence abated during the 1970s, economic expansion gave way to contraction, a sense of affluence to a feeling of discomfort. As economic crisis took precedence over cultural issues, though the latter remained extremely divisive, questions arose about how long the center would hold.

# CHAPTER EIGHT
# A NEW AGE DAWNS:
# *John F. Kennedy*
# *and the Promise*
# *of Camelot, 1960–1963*

A charismatic leader, John Fitzgerald Kennedy is remembered nostalgically for enlivening national politics during the 1960s. Yet, Kennedy was as much a prince of ambiguity as a prince of Camelot; his presidency both intensified and mitigated Cold War tensions and reluctantly advanced reformist programs. As candidate and president, Kennedy did not forthrightly challenge the socioeconomic inequities of the sixties—notably, poverty and racial injustice. His New Frontier programs were cautious and never ardently pressed. His internal security policies widened FBI investigative authority while encouraging FBI Director Hoover to act insubordinately. His foreign policy was more adventurist than Eisenhower's as the CIA's covert operations role expanded and focused on the third world.

Kennedy's actual record of ambivalent, cautious leadership was not surprising. The image of Kennedy as a bold reformer emerged only after his assassination on November 22, 1963; his prepresidential career was decidedly conventional. As a U.S. senator from 1952 to 1960, Kennedy had sponsored no major legislation and his voting record had been mixed. A supporter of social welfare legislation and known as a friend of labor unions, he had often voted with conservatives on financial and internal security matters.

Kennedy's rise as a national political leader during the 1950s was more the consequence of his wit and engaging personality, the publicity he gained from writing a best-selling book, *Profiles in Courage* (published in 1956), and his prominent role in Senate investigations of labor racketeering. Undertaking an extensive speechmaking effort between 1957 and 1959, crisscrossing the country to address a variety of organizations, the Massachusetts senator in the process developed invaluable political contacts in all parts of the nation, and capitalized on his Catholicism (in 1952 and 1956 many Catholics had broken their traditional Democratic ties over the Communist issue). At the same time, Kennedy adopted more liberal positions on foreign and domestic policy.

As the recognized front-runner for the Democratic nomination (he held a commanding lead in the Gallup poll), Kennedy encountered two principal obstacles. First, he had to dispel the conventional wisdom that a Catholic could not be elected president. For him, the primaries were crucial to prove his political appeal. Second, he had to overcome the candidacies of other more prominent Democrats—Lyndon Johnson (Senate majority leader), Stuart Symington (an influential senator and former air force secretary), Hubert Humphrey (leader of the Senate liberal bloc), and former Illinois Governor Adlai Stevenson (the Democratic presidential candidate of 1952 and 1956). All these men had had longer, more distinguished careers in congressional and party politics.

These contenders did not directly challenge Kennedy. Johnson and Symington avoided the primaries, as both senators lacked popular support. Already a twice-defeated candidate, Stevenson was scarcely a likely nominee. He too did not enter the primaries, though he tacitly authorized a last-minute draft effort. Hubert Humphrey was the only major candidate whom Kennedy faced in the primaries.

In 1960, Humphrey commanded the allegiance of many liberal Democrats whose support Kennedy needed to win the nomination. Seeking to force the issue early, Humphrey invited Kennedy to enter the Wisconsin primary, an invitation posing grave risks given Humphrey's strength in the upper Midwest. In a well-funded and efficiently organized campaign, Kennedy decisively defeated Humphrey. But the Wisconsin results did not settle as an issue the question of Kennedy's Catholicism. (Humphrey ran best in predominantly Protestant rural areas and Kennedy best in heavily Catholic urban areas.) The next primary, in heavily Protestant West Virginia, assumed new importance. There, the same tactics and organizational efforts resulted in an even more decisive Kennedy victory.

The West Virginia and Wisconsin primaries eliminated Humphrey as a contender, partially stilled the Catholic issue, and enabled Kennedy to consolidate his political base. His demonstrated popularity and organizational efficiency eventually insured him a first-ballot victory. To strengthen the Democratic ticket, Kennedy asked Lyndon Johnson, his chief convention opponent for the nomination, to accept the vice-presidential post. Johnson was a perfect running mate. The Senate majority leader from Texas was an experienced politician with solid support in the South and from important Democratic leaders in Congress and state politics. He also was a rural Protestant with strength in a region, the Southwest, essential to Democratic success.

Kennedy's Republican opponent was the incumbent vice president, Richard Nixon. Nixon exploited the vice presidency to consolidate his political base and become the acknowledged front-runner for his party's nomination. For one, Eisenhower's nonpartisan stance as president and foreign policy decisions minimized the president's direct contacts with the Republican party's conservative leadership. Since 1953, Vice President Nixon had served as the administration's liaison with the party leadership and Republican conservatives. In addition, New York Governor Nelson Rockefeller's withdrawal in 1959 eliminated any serious challenge to Nixon from the Republican party's liberal wing. Nixon's nationally televised debate with Soviet Premier Nikita Khrushchev at the American trade fair in Moscow contributed to his image of strong anti-Communist leadership, further enhancing his appeal to the party's right wing. To balance the ticket and as a concession to liberal Republicans, candidate Nixon chose as his vice-presidential running mate the U.S. ambassador to the United Nations, Henry Cabot Lodge, Jr. (an important leader in 1952 of the draft-Eisenhower movement).

The 1960 presidential campaign was marked by one novel development, the scheduling between September 26 and October 21 of a series of four nationally televised debates between the two candidates. Although the format for each session was precisely drawn, the debates did not sharply distinguish the candidates' specific positions on the issues. The major Nixon-Kennedy differences, which emerged during the debates, and more generally the campaign, were those of style, emphasis, and personality. Kennedy stressed the need for dynamic leadership to get "the country moving again," reestablish the nation's international influence, and improve the quality of life in America. In contrast, Nixon exploited Eisenhower's popularity, commending the Republican president's successes in bringing peace and prosperity out of the "mess" he had inherited from Truman and pledging to continue these policies. Nixon emphasized his experience and ability to stand up to the Russians, stressed his Democratic opponent's youth and wealth, and blamed the Democrats for inflation. If Nixon affirmed "We never had it so good," Kennedy maintained "We can do better."

Emphasizing his own anti-Communism, Kennedy asserted, "I run for the presidency because I do not want it said that in the years when our generation held political power America began to slip. I don't want historians writing in 1970 to say that the balance of power in the 1950s and 1960s began to turn against the United States and against the cause of freedom." In the first televised debate, Kennedy deemed nonessential the defense of

Quemoy and Matsu (islands that served as defense outposts for the Nationalist Chinese government on Formosa). To avoid an unnecessary war, the Nationalists should abandon these "indefensible" islands. Responding aggressively, Nixon charged that the issue was not territory: "I oppose handing over to the Communists one inch of free territory." In a later debate, in contrast, Kennedy condemned the Eisenhower administration's Cuban policy as "too little and too late" and specifically called for a four-point program including an "attempt to strengthen the non-Batista, democratic, anti-Castro forces in exile, and in Cuba itself, who offer eventual hope of overthrowing Castro." Condemning this stance as adventurist, Nixon now accused Kennedy of wanting to intervene illegally in Cuba, denounced Kennedy's "policies and recommendations" as "probably the most dangerously irresponsible recommendations that he's made during the course of this campaign," and instead advocated nonintervention and respect for self-government.

The television debates were not without significance. Television offered possibilities for a new campaign strategy. Brilliantly exploiting television's potential, Kennedy projected an image of efficiency, detailed knowledge, and vibrancy. He recognized the distinction between scoring points and winning audiences (which Nixon did not, believing himself the superior debater). A Roper poll later revealed that, of four million Americans who admitted having been influenced by the debates, three million voted for Kennedy. Television had made its mark—in the process transforming political campaigns as issues and political philosophy became less important than personality, appearance, and image.

Kennedy's Catholicism was indirectly accentuated by the absence of sharp policy differences between the candidates. Public knowledge of Kennedy's religion increased from 48 percent in May 1959 to 87 percent in August 1960, rising slightly higher thereafter. Early in the campaign, prominent Protestant ministers directly questioned whether Kennedy would subordinate his national responsibilities to church discipline. To dispel these and more scurrilous charges, Kennedy outlined his views on church-state relations in a September 12 speech to the Greater Houston Ministerial Association. Declaring his belief in "an America where the separation of church and state is absolute" and in "a Chief Executive whose public acts are responsible to all and obligated to none," Kennedy added that he thought it no more proper for a Catholic prelate to tell a Catholic president how to act than for a Protestant minister to tell his parishioners how to vote. Fundamentalist Protestant ministers continued to emphasize Kennedy's Catholicism, while the frequency of Richard Nixon's denials that Kennedy's Catholicism was an issue, indirectly called attention to Kennedy's religion.

In some areas, particularly rural Indiana and Oklahoma, Kennedy lost votes because of his religion. But Kennedy's Catholicism was an asset in urban and ethnic areas. Kennedy's appeal was principally to Americans

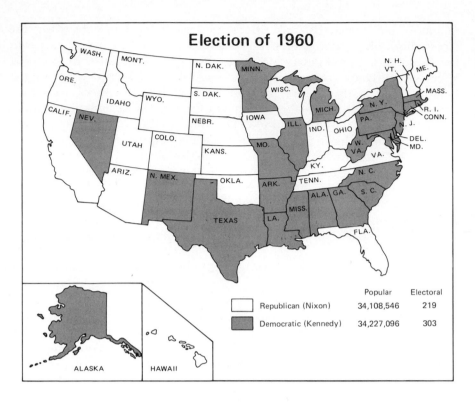

## Election of 1960

| | Popular | Electoral |
|---|---|---|
| Republican (Nixon) | 34,108,546 | 219 |
| Democratic (Kennedy) | 34,227,096 | 303 |

ALASKA   HAWAII

dissatisfied with the status quo. The final outcome was a razor-thin Kennedy victory. Of a total 68,412,709 votes, Kennedy polled 118,550 more votes than Nixon (34,227,096–34,108,546). Because he won the major industrial states (Nixon won more total states, 26–24), Kennedy's electoral college margin was wider, 303–219. The closeness of the presidential race did affect congressional contests, as the Republicans recovered slightly from the devastating setback of the 1958 elections: gaining two seats in the Senate (64–36) and twenty-two seats in the House (263–174).

Kennedy had campaigned on the need for bold and resourceful leadership to get "the country moving again." Through a dynamic anti-Communist foreign policy, he promised a peace based on strength. The Eisenhower administration's fiscal conservatism and reduced defense expenditures, the Democratic candidate charged, had contributed to a "missile gap" that seriously affected the U.S. military position vis-à-vis the Soviet Union. As an alternative, Kennedy outlined his administration's foreign policy priorities, to increase defense expenditures (conventional and nuclear) and extend economic and military assistance to anti-Communist governments in Latin America, Africa, and Asia.

In his inaugural address, Kennedy enunciated his administration's priorities, based on the principle of "ask not what your country can do for you; ask what you can do for your country." In his acceptance speech at the Los Angeles convention where he coined the "New Frontier" phrase, the Democratic nominee articulated his conception of responsibility: "All mankind awaits our decision. A whole world waits to see what we will do. We cannot fail their trust. We cannot fail to try." This role could be realized, Kennedy believed, not through a revised set of national priorities or the redistribution of wealth and power but rather by new and expert leadership: "Most of the problems that we now face are technical problems, are administrative problems. They are very sophisticated judgments which do not lend themselves to the great sort of 'passionate movements' which have stirred this country so often in the past." "A new generation of leadership was needed," Kennedy averred, "new men to cope with new problems and new opportunities."

## A STRENGTHENED PRESIDENCY

Kennedy's speeches were not simply rhetorical flourishes; they reflected his conception of the president's leadership role. To Kennedy, the president was not simply coequal to the Congress or the repository of the public will. The president's function was to "lead, inform, correct, and sometimes even ignore constituent opinion." In a 1960 speech to the National Press Club, Kennedy affirmed that the next president "must be prepared to exercise the fullest powers of that office—all that are specified and some that are not." A Department of Justice memorandum of January 17, 1962, drafted to justify the constitutionality of the president's authorization of the CIA's covert involvement in the Bay of Pigs affair, captures more starkly this expansive conception of presidential powers: "Just as 'the power to wage war is the power to wage war successfully,' so the power of the President to conduct foreign relations should be deemed to be the power to conduct foreign relations successfully, by any means necessary to combat the measures taken by the Communist bloc, including both open and covert measures." In Kennedy's view, the United States' economic, social, and diplomatic problems resulted from the Eisenhower administration's failure to provide leadership. To rectify this, Kennedy moved to centralize power in the presidency.

On the one hand, to rationalize decision making at the Pentagon, on October 1, 1961, President Kennedy created the Defense Intelligence Agency (DIA). This new agency would coordinate the intelligence reports of the various military intelligence agencies and draw up a consolidated military intelligence budget. On the other hand, reacting to the failure of the Bay of Pigs operation, on April 27, 1961, President Kennedy appointed General Maxwell Taylor to head a special study of existing programs "in the areas of military and paramilitary, guerilla and anti-guerrilla activity which fall outside of war." Implementing this group's recommendations, President Kennedy created a review agency to direct CIA covert operations. His immediate policy objectives were to overthrow the Castro government in Cuba and undermine Vietcong resistance to the Diem government in South Vietnam.

Kennedy held frequent press conferences and enjoyed the give and take with the Washington press corps. Yet his attitude toward the media was sometimes defensive and belligerent. He viewed the media as instruments to be manipulated to shape public opinion, heighten the president's moral leadership, and control events. Equating the national interest with his administration's policies, Kennedy addressed the public through televised press conferences, periodic nationwide television and radio addresses, and personal television appearances such as Jacqueline Kennedy's tour of the White House and the president's informal discussions with selected television commentators.

The press could not be fully controlled. It could and did uncover administration mistakes and the actual bases for policy decisions. Insofar as its independence threatened the administration's preference for secrecy in the planning and execution of "national security" policy, a confrontation ensued. Following the Bay of Pigs debacle of April 17–19, the president lamented that press reports often presented "the nation's foes" with information otherwise obtainable only through espionage. In an April 27, 1961, speech to the American Newspaper Publishers Association, he urged editors before printing stories to ask not only "is it news?" but also "is it in the interest of national security?" Speaking on December 6, 1962, to a national journalist fraternity in the aftermath of the Cuban missile crisis, Assistant Secretary of Defense for Public Affairs Arthur Sylvester spoke of news as "part of the weaponry" available to the government in the Cold War and affirmed the government's "right, if necessary, to lie to save itself, when it's going up into a nuclear war. That seems to me basic—basic."

Kennedy also attempted to control the dissemination of news concerning administration policy. During the Cuban missile crisis, Pentagon and State Department officials' press contacts were tightly restricted. At the same time, White House aides were further required to clear all their communications with newsmen with White House press secretary Pierre Salinger and then to report back in writing the subject of those communications. Soon forced to abandon these procedures, the president nonetheless on two occasions in 1961 and 1962 directed the FBI to investigate the sources of leaked "national security" information to the press.

Kennedy's reliance on secrecy to sustain executive initiative also diluted the Cabinet's independent authority. As president, Kennedy did not turn to his Cabinet for advice on major policy issues, having concluded that there was no sound reason why the postmaster general should sit through a briefing on Laos. Kennedy's Cabinet appointees, moreover, reflected a diminution of the Cabinet's function: individuals of recognized administrative ability who lacked an independent political base. Robert McNamara of the Ford Motor Company was appointed secretary of defense, not Senator Henry Jackson or Senator Stuart Symington; Dean Rusk of the Rockefeller Foundation was appointed secretary of state, not Adlai Stevenson or Chester Bowles. Rusk and McNamara, if able administrators, lacked the nationwide constituency or political base of a Symington or a Stevenson. Kennedy's other Cabinet appointments followed the same lines. The most controversial of these was his nomination of his brother, Robert Kennedy, as attorney general. Robert Kennedy's nomination raised questions of nepotism and competence—the attorney general-designate had had no prior legal experience, having served as counsel to various congressional committees after graduation from law school. No less important, Robert Kennedy had played a major role in his brother's campaigns for the Senate in 1952 and the presidency in 1960 and his appointment threatened to politicize the Justice Department.

During Kennedy's tenure, the White House staff assumed many of the Cabinet's advisory functions. Under the direction of McGeorge Bundy in foreign affairs and Theodore Sorenson in domestic affairs, an efficient staff was developed. Primarily academics, the Kennedy White House staff were an able group of technicians well versed in specific aspects of social, economic, and foreign policy. It included such men as Walt W. Rostow, William Bundy, Arthur Schlesinger, Jr., Jerome Wiesner, Walter Heller, and David Bell. Reliance on the White House staff strengthened Kennedy's authority. First, because these men directly advised the president, an executive privilege claim could neutralize Congress's traditional oversight role and enable Kennedy to formulate policy secretly. Unlike Cabinet members, who were confirmed by the Senate and whose authority was created by congressional statute, White House aides were not subject to interrogation by congressional committees. Second, again unlike Cabinet officials, who were appointed because of their political base or their association with powerful special interest groups (the labor and commerce posts), White House aides lacked an independent constituency. Their authority derived from their access and loyalty to the president.

The changes in the role of the White House were not simply intended to rationalize decision making, but to promote the implementation of the president's policy goals. His inaugural pledge most succinctly captured Kennedy's conception of America's role in the 1960s: "Let every nation know, whether it wishes us well or ill, that we shall pay any price, bear any burden, meet any hardship, support any friend, oppose any foe to assure the survival and success of liberty."

## THE NEW FRONTIER AND THE
## LIMITS OF DOMESTIC REFORM

A strengthened presidency did not insure congressional enactment of the president's New Frontier program of health insurance for the aged, improvements in Social Security benefits, tax reform, an increase in the minimum wage and an expanded definition of those covered, elimination of regional poverty and technological unemployment through federal financial assistance, and federal aid to education for school construction and teachers salaries. To enact such programs, the president had to circumvent conservative southern Democratic domination of the major congressional committee posts owing to the seniority principle. Relying on Vice President Johnson's inside knowledge of the Senate, the president worked closely with Democratic Speaker Sam Rayburn to neutralize the power of conservatives who controlled the crucial House Rules Committee. Rules Committee Chairman Howard Smith, a southern Democrat, had voted regularly with Republicans to create a 6–6 committee tie vote. The administration's intensive lobbying for Rayburn's plan to increase the committee's membership by three succeeded, thereby creating a new 8–7 majority.

Congress's mood remained conservative and thus the administration suffered a series of defeats. The House Rules Committee blocked bills for commuter transit assistance, construction grants and loan assistance to medical schools, and aid for migrant workers. The administration's tax reform proposal was drastically amended, its public school aid bill was killed in committee, and the House rejected its proposal to tighten production controls to reduce the size of the agriculture surplus. Congress refused to enact the administration's Social Security reforms to increase payments, broaden coverage to another 4.3 million retail, laundry, restaurant, and hotel workers, and extend the number of weeks unemployed workers could collect benefits. The Congress did modestly raise the minimum wage. More important, by a vote of 52–48, the Senate rejected the administration's most daring proposal—medical insurance for retired workers over sixty-five to be financed under Social Security.

Having failed to move Congress, the president then attempted to develop popular support for his legislative program through televised press conferences and nationwide addresses and to focus the 1962 congressional campaign on these issues. The Cuban missile crisis of October 1962 intervened, compelling an abrupt termination of the president's planned campaign. The 1962 congressional elections accordingly returned no electoral mandate for the New Frontier. The composition of Congress was not significantly altered: A number of conservative congressmen were defeated (notably Walter Judd in the House and Homer Capehart in the Senate), and the Democrats sustained their dominant position in the Congress, losing two seats in the reapportioned House (259–176) and gaining four Senate seats (68–32).

The New Frontier was never enacted into law. The Kennedy Administration, instead, won only minor legislative victories. The Congress enacted the Area Development Act of 1961 to aid rural and economically depressed areas, the Higher Education Act of 1963 to aid colleges and community colleges to construct buildings and improve libraries (similar assistance was provided to medical and dental schools), and the Manpower Retraining Act of 1962 appropriating $435 million over three years to train the unemployed in new skills. Congress also appropriated $9 billion over five years under the Apollo program to send a man to the moon before the end of the 1960s. In addition, Congress ratified the president's March 1961 executive order creating the Peace Corps. Under this program, thousands of young men and women (and some middle-aged and retired persons) went overseas to provide technical and educational assistance to underdeveloped countries. By March 1963, five thousand volunteers served overseas; this increased to about ten thousand by 1964.

Overall, Kennedy's legislative record did not contrast strikingly with Eisenhower's. This was not due to the absence of economic problems at this time. In 1961, 6.7 percent of the labor force was unemployed; in 1960 the rate of national growth was less than 3 percent; and between 1957 and 1960 the nation's balance of payments deficit increased from $1 billion to nearly $4 billion.

The administration's major priorities, however, were not liberal reform but to pursue an activist foreign policy, balance the budget, and curb inflation. Douglas Dillon's appointment as secretary of the treasury pointedly reflected the president's fear of inflation and excessive domestic spending programs.

The administration's desire to maximize U.S. international influence through higher defense spending also undermined any prospect for costly economic reforms. Between 1961 and 1963, the development of solid-fuel intercontinental missiles, an accelerated submarine-launched Polaris missile program, and strengthened conventional forces including a counterinsurgency capability added roughly $17 billion to the defense budget. Committed to controlling inflation and improving the U.S. trade position, the Kennedy administration often deferred to the budgetary demands of the fiscally conservative congressional leadership.

Rather than relying on federal spending to stimulate the domestic economy, the administration instead sought to increase business productivity and efficiency. Thus in 1962 it recommended a tax bill providing a 7 percent tax credit to business firms for investment either in new machinery or plant modernization. Similarly, in 1962 the Internal Revenue Service liberalized depreciation allowance rules, speeding up by more than one-third the rate at which machinery and equipment could be written off for tax purposes. The combination of tax credits and liberalized depreciation reduced business taxes by $2.5 billion in 1962 and amounted to an 11 percent tax cut for corporations. In 1963, Kennedy recommended a tax measure that combined modest reforms with a $10 billion cut (the latter justified as needed to stimulate the economy). Succumbing to conservative pressures, the president reduced the bill's tax reform provisions to win House approval on September 25, 1963, by a vote of 271–155. Senate action on this measure was delayed until after Kennedy's death. Fiscal policy probably contributed to a 5 percent economic growth rate—given the tax measure's provisions businessmen benefited most, contributing in the process to a 70 percent increase in corporate profits between 1960 and 1965.

At the same time, the administration tolerated the flow of American capital to Europe. A serious balance of payments problem existed and threatened to worsen. By 1960, the United States was spending and investing $4 billion more abroad than foreign states did in the United States—leading to a gold export of $2 billion in 1960 alone. This capital outflow continued and, between January 1960 and January 1969, total U.S. foreign investment increased from $29.7 billion to $64.7 billion. By 1966, U.S. firms and individuals provided slightly more than 60 percent of all foreign capital investments in the world ($54.5 billion of $89.6 billion). (In striking contrast to this level of U.S. foreign investment, the Japanese component was only 1 percent; instead Japanese earnings were reinvested at home.)

The Kennedy administration had no solution to the unfavorable balance of trade. On the one hand, the president considered, but then rejected as unfair, curbs on foreign tourism. Capital investment overseas was not controlled or discouraged through higher taxes, restrictions were not imposed on dollar convertibility, and the dollar was not devalued to improve the U.S. trade position. Instead Kennedy sought to stimulate foreign trade. In 1962, he urged another two-year extension of the Reciprocal Trade Agreements Act of 1934 and requested discretionary authority to reduce U.S. tariff rates by as much as 50 percent over a five-year period and reduce to zero tariffs on those commodities traded primarily between the United States and the European Common Market.

The administration's economic policies were nonetheless sharply challenged by the business community. On April 10, 1962, U.S. Steel president Roger Blough advised Kennedy of his firm's decision to raise steel prices by $6 dollars a ton (well beyond the administration's voluntary wage and price guidelines). Other steel companies followed suit. Concerned over the inflationary consequences of this decision, the administration acted to force a rollback. Secretary of Defense McNamara ordered defense contractors to buy steel from manufacturers who held prices while the Justice Department initiated an investigation to ascertain whether price increases were justified and further whether there was collusion among the steel companies in violation of the antitrust laws. Kennedy's strong-arm tactics succeeded: On April 12, Bethlehem announced cancellation of its price increase, followed shortly by U.S. Steel.

Not a major Kennedy priority at first, civil rights soon became his administration's most sensitive domestic problem.[1] During the 1960 campaign and the first months of his administration, the president and his attorney general had expressed sympathy for black Americans and had condemned southern segregation. Yet, in 1961 and 1962 Kennedy neither advocated civil rights legislation nor exercised bold moral leadership on the issue. Instead, he and his brother preferred the more time-consuming process of litigation.

The civil rights revolt wrecked the administration's cautious strategy. In the aftermath of the 1954 *Brown* decision, black leaders were unwilling to wait for the inevitable end of segregation. Civil rights leader Martin Luther King, Jr., captured this frustration when observing "This 'Wait' had always meant 'Never.' " The civil rights movement's decision to challenge southern segregation more aggressively insured confrontation. Black college students led this challenge, with students at North Carolina Agricultural and Technical State University, Greensboro, North Carolina, in February 1960 staging a sit-in to desegregate chain-store lunch counters. Soon sit-ins spread throughout the South (eventuating in the desegregation of lunch counters in over two thousand southern cities by 1962). The Supreme Court's unanimous decision of November 13, 1956, when affirming a lower court ruling declaring unconstitutional an Alabama statute segregating bus terminals, precipitated the famous "freedom rides."

The well-publicized freedom rides encountered bitter white resistance in the South. Outside Anniston, Alabama, the Greyhound bus carrying the CORE freedom riders was burned by a white mob; continuing on another bus, the same freedom riders were assaulted at a Trailways terminal in Birmingham, Alabama, and then arrested and jailed in Jackson, Mississippi. CORE compelled the Justice Department to act. The Justice Department pressured the ICC to issue on September 22 rules banning segregation in carriers and terminals. Thirteen of the fifteen southern airports voluntarily complied; the Justice Department then brought suit against the other two. At the same time, through quiet negotiations between civil rights leaders and the Ford Foundation and the Taconic Fund, liberal private foundations, an informal agreement was reached whereby civil rights groups shifted their energies from freedom rides to voter registration.

The voter registration drive merely opened a new chapter in the violent battle between civil rights militants and diehard southern seg-

[1]See Chapter 7.

regationists. The Kennedy administration responded cautiously to this potential confrontation and actively enforced federal laws only in the event of a major crisis.

A crisis inevitably erupted in the fall of 1962. In May 1961 James Meredith, a black war veteran, had filed suit to secure admission into the all-white University of Mississippi. One year later the court ruled in Meredith's favor. Mississippi Governor Ross Barnett then announced his intention to defy the federal court's order to admit Meredith. Hoping to avoid another Little Rock, Attorney General Kennedy opened lengthy, involved, and eventually frustrating negotiations with the Mississippi governor. Kennedy's effort to convince Barnett to comply voluntarily with the law failed; the governor refused to allow Meredith to register at the university. Threatened with a contempt of court citation, Barnett backed down on September 30: In the interim, an angry mob had converged on the campus from all over the South, precipitating a riot that resulted in the deaths of a French journalist and a townsman. Another 375 people were injured, among them federal marshalls, 29 of whom were shot and 166 injured.

A similar confrontation occurred in May 1963, when Alabama Governor George Wallace sought to defy a court order to desegregate the University of Alabama. Less conciliatory and trusting this time, Attorney General Kennedy asked Wallace for definite assurances that order would be preserved. Lacking this, Kennedy federalized the Alabama National Guard and on June 11, the University of Alabama was desegregated.

These events combined to create a compelling moral and political issue. In response to the Meredith incident, the president had gone on national television to condemn senseless violence and to commend racial equality. Then, on November 22, 1962, Kennedy issued an executive order banning segregation in new public housing. Because the ban was limited to buildings owned or directly financed by the government, 85 percent of the nation's housing was excluded. At the same time, Kennedy created the President's Committee on Equal Employment Opportunity to combat discrimination in government agencies and among private contractors.

The administration had not yet abandoned a strategy of exclusive reliance on litigation. In February 1963, however, Kennedy abruptly shifted strategy and proposed a modest civil rights bill to strengthen voting rights and extend the authority of the Civil Rights Commission. Developments that year soon compelled the administration to confront the segregation issue directly. In response, on June 19, 1963, the president recommended a stronger civil rights bill to implement desegregation in places of public accommodation, in publicly owned facilities, and in employment. The proposed bill also empowered the Department of Justice to enforce voting rights and speed school desegregation. Civil rights legislation was needed, Kennedy argued, because, "We are confronted primarily with a moral issue.

Those who do nothing are inviting shame as well as violence. Those who act boldly are recognizing right as well as reality."

Southern congressmen quickly denounced the administration's proposals. The civil rights movement had by then emerged as a powerful political force: On August 28, 1963, over 200,000 citizens converged on Washington, in a March on Washington organized by civil rights leaders, to pressure Congress to enact the administration's civil rights bill.

Concurrent with this debate over civil rights and the attendant assault on segregation, the Supreme Court in *Baker* v. *Carr* (1962) decided another contentious issue. In that decision, the Court ordered state legislatures to reapportion their lower houses on the basis of population. Until that decision, rural areas usually had greater representation than more densely populated urban areas, a system suggesting the "rotten boroughs" of nineteenth-century England. The Tennessee state constitution, the state that had been the subject of the 1962 Court decision, required reapportionment every ten years. Since 1901, however, the Tennessee legislature had rejected all bills attempting to implement this constitutionally prescribed mandate. As a result, one-third of the electorate elected two-thirds of the legislature.

In *Reynolds* v. *Sim* (1964) and *Wesberry* v. *Sanders* (1964) the Court extended the 1962 ruling to apply to both state legislative bodies and to federal congressional districts. The Court's congressional district ruling had potentially large consequences since many rural and small-town dominated state legislatures had consciously gerrymandered congressional districts. Under this system urban and suburban congressional districts sometimes had 500,000 voters, while rural ones might have fewer than 100,000. In 1954, for example, Republican candidates for the House of Representatives from New York received 51 percent of the statewide vote but collected 61 percent of the seats.

## ANTI-COMMUNIST POLITICS, McCARTHYISM, AND THE FURTHER EXPANSION OF THE FBI'S ROLE

Support for President Kennedy's New Frontier reforms was partially undercut because of the persistence of Cold War anti-Communist fears. The administration failed to dispel such fears or to curb the excesses of the loyalty security programs instituted during the Truman and Eisenhower years. It also increased the authority of the FBI. Although Kennedy believed in some restrictions on individual liberties in order to safeguard the national security, he unwittingly became involved in an accidental conflict with more conservative security bureaucrats. In contrast to Kennedy's relatively tight definition of "national security" threats, those bureaucrats who commanded the top security clearance posts defined disloyalty and subversion loosely.

Otto Otepka, the Department of State's top security official, became the Kennedy administration's first unexpected problem. In early 1961 Otepka refused to recommend security clearances for some of Kennedy's key nominees (most notably Walt Whitman Rostow), basing this refusal on these individuals' past political activities. At first, the administration sought to bypass the State Department security chief by making temporary appointments or appointing individuals to the National Security Council staff, neither of which required Otepka's clearance. Later that year, by executive order, the president reduced the State Department's security staff by twenty five. The reduction eliminated Otepka's post of deputy director of the Office of Security. Since he had civil service tenure, Otepka was promoted to head the Division of Evaluations, a post that was more honorific than substantive. Disturbed by this attempt to curb Otepka, conservative senators on the Internal Security Subcommittee initiated an investigation into the adequacy of the State Department's security procedures. Inviting Otepka to testify during its 1961 hearings, the subcommittee staff thereafter retained covert contact with the security officer. In response in 1963 the State Department summarily dismissed Otepka for providing the subcommittee staff with classified documents in violation of a long-established executive order (of 1948).

The Otepka affair ultimately produced a more liberal security program under which controversial views or past radical associations did not necessarily deny one a security clearance. Despite changes in personnel and policy, an elaborate security system continued to be based on extensive files detailing dissident political activities.

In addition, in 1961 and 1962, Attorney General Robert Kennedy advocated legalizing wiretapping in national security cases and in criminal investigations involving extortion, kidnapping, murder, and narcotics. Kennedy's legislative proposal failed. The attorney general nonetheless continued to authorize wiretaps for "intelligence" (i.e., nonprosecutive) purposes and tolerated the FBI's use of this authority, uncritically acceding to all such FBI requests including (in October 1963) a wiretap on civil rights leader Martin Luther King, Jr. And, by misrepresenting Attorney General Brownell's May 1954 memorandum concerning the FBI's power to install microphones during criminal and security investigations without the attorney general's prior approval, Hoover secured Kennedy's tacit consent to this procedure. On October 12, 1961, moreover, Hoover independently instituted another COINTELPRO to "disrupt" the Socialist Workers Party (SWP). The SWP's radical politics, "running candidates for public office and strongly directing and/or supporting Castro's Cuba and integration problems arising in the South," Hoover concluded, necessitated an "educational" program to "alert the public" to the SWP's "revolutionary principles."

There were, however, two sides to the Kennedy administration's national security policy: a cautious liberalism and yet a hesitancy to break from the anti-Communism of the 1950s. On the one hand, in July 1961 the administration recommended that Americans consider constructing family bomb shelters, authorized the Bay of Pigs invasion, recommended sharp increases in space and defense appropriations, and precipitated the Cuban missile crisis. All these actions further intensified anti-Communist fears. On the other hand, beginning in 1963 the administration sought to promote detente with the Soviets. In nationwide addresses, including a June 10, 1963, commencement speech at American University and speeches urging ratification of the Nuclear Test Ban Treaty (approved by the Senate on September 24, 1963), the president emphasized the importance of coexistence and the shared interests of the United States and Soviet Union in reducing Cold War tensions. On March 17, 1961, the Kennedy administration had rescinded restrictions (of 1951 and 1956) on mail deliveries of pamphlets published in the Soviet Union and other Communist countries. Kennedy's order prohibited the Post Office Department from "intercepting" such pamphlets, but the department could "continue screening" such mail. (Congress reestablished these restrictions in 1962 but in *Lamont* v. *Postmaster General* (1965) the Supreme Court declared this legislation unconstitutional.)

## KENNEDY FOREIGN POLICY: THE DIPLOMACY OF IMAGE AND STRENGTH AND THE POLITICS OF CONFRONTATION

During his three years in the White House, Kennedy built up the United States' nuclear and conventional weapons systems. Between 1960 and 1962 the defense budget increased from $43 billion to $56 billion and in 1961 alone the armed services grew by 300,000 men. Committed to combating revolutionary movements, the president authorized the establishment of a special counterinsurgency force (the Green Berets) to supplement the covert operation role formerly exercised exclusively by the CIA. In a special message to Congress on March 28, 1961, the president requested additional funds "to prevent the steady erosion of the free world through limited wars" and to deter "any potential aggressor." These funds would insure a U.S. capability that would be "suitable, selective, swift, and effective." Kennedy also tried to enhance U.S. influence through the use of foreign aid and the promotion of freer world trade. Despite his belief that most insurrectionary movements were merely "a planned phase in the communist timetable for world domination," Kennedy sought detente with Soviet leaders to curb the threat of nuclear war.

During his brief presidency, Kennedy oscillated between anti-Communist containment and policies aimed at easing U.S.-Soviet tensions. On the one hand, Kennedy's foreign policy brought the world to the brink of nuclear catastrophe during the Cuban missile crisis of October 1962; the increased U.S. military committment helped precipitate the Vietnam tragedy. On the other hand, aspects of Kennedy's policy indicated a preference for diplomatic accommodation.

The last years of the Eisenhower administration had witnessed great Soviet progress in space and rocket technology, leading Kennedy to conclude falsely that the Soviet Union had acquired a missile lead over the United States. Kennedy obtained congressional approval for vastly increased defense expenditures and greatly enlarged the strength of American deterrent missiles and Polaris-type submarines armed with missiles. General Maxwell Taylor's concept of military flexibility was adopted to meet any attack whether by strategic nuclear weapons, tactical A-bombs, or conventional arms. The United States should be able to fight on any scale, from a direct clash with the Soviet Union to local "hot" wars and so-called wars of "national liberation." Thus by 1963, the United States had achieved an estimated nuclear superiority over the Soviet Union of three to one in ICBM missiles and an arsenal of 33,000 nuclear bombs or rocket payloads, with 15,000 more in preparation! By 1965, the United States possessed an estimated four-to-one margin in ICBMs. Gradually, as the pace of U.S. procurement tapered and Soviet production increased, the American lead narrowed. Kennedy also launched a crash space program to recover the initiative, regain prestige from the Soviet Union in exploring space, and place the first man on the moon. The United States scored by landing the first men upon the moon's surface in July 1969, and by the deep-space probes and televised fly-bys of Venus and Mars.

President Kennedy once remarked that "Domestic policy can only defeat us; foreign policy can kill us." As Kennedy took office, the Soviet Union under Khrushchev appeared to threaten West Berlin, having announced it would sign a separate treaty with East Germany (the German Democratic Republic), thereby ending U.S. (and Western) occupation rights in Berlin. To moderate tensions, in June 1961 Kennedy journeyed to Vienna for an outwardly friendly two-power summit conference with the Soviet leader. There, Khrushchev made clear his determination, in his words, to get the "bone" of West Berlin out of his throat. The American president stood firm against Khrushchev's insistence on a German settlement within six months, even when Khrushchev blustered that "I want peace, but if you want war, that is your problem."

Vienna masked a grim confrontation that seemed to threaten nuclear war. According to one account, Khrushchev advised Kennedy that the Soviet Union was militarily stronger than the United States. Hence, upon his return to the United States, Kennedy alerted the American people to a new peril and requested an additional $3.2 billion increase in military spending and authority to expand the draft; he also activated 250,000 reservists, and mobilized two army divisions and fifty-four air squadrons. Not deterred, in August 1961 the Soviet Union built a wall to seal off the Soviet sector of Berlin from the Western-occupied sections of the city, the now-infamous Berlin Wall. U.S.-Soviet talks continued without success, although in October Khrushchev retracted his earlier threat to conclude a separate treaty with East Germany by December.

The Bay of Pigs fiasco in Cuba had set the stage for the Vienna conference and the Berlin confrontation. Even prior to breaking diplomatic relations with Castro's Cuba, at a March 17, 1960, NSC meeting President Eisenhower had authorized the secret training and arming of Cuban exiles to overthrow the Castro government. Assigned this responsibility, the CIA drafted an invasion plan based on the premise that landing a small well-armed task force in Cuba would trigger a popular uprising. Kennedy subsequently approved this plan on the understanding that the U.S. role would not be disclosed and U.S. assistance would be confined to training and economic assistance.

From the outset, however, the CIA went its own way. CIA officials did secure Kennedy's approval for a limited air strike on April 15 (immediately prior to the planned invasion date of April 17, 1961), in support of the 1500-man brigade. When the landing did not proceed as planned—there was no massive popular uprising—the CIA and military officials attempted to insure the military operation's success. The CIA recruited members of the Alabama Air National Guard (and four American pilots were shot down—the president only learned of this action two years later) and an American destroyer (contrary to the president's orders) sailed right under the guns of Castro's artillery. The CIA operation nonetheless failed abysmally and the exiles surrendered on April 19.

Adlai Stevenson, the U.S. ambassador to the UN, at the time denied that U.S. "personnel" or "government airplanes" had participated in the raid. The CIA-trained pilot who had landed in Florida after the April 15 bombing run, Stevenson claimed, had "apparently defected from Castro's tyranny" and "to the best of our knowledge" the planes involved in the bombing runs were from Castro's air force. "All we know about Cuba is what we read on the wire services," White House press secretary Pierre Salinger asserted. Secretary of State Dean Rusk affirmed the U.S. policy of nonintervention and claimed that the United States did not have "full information" about what was happening in Cuba. This denial of responsibility also failed and constituted an even more disastrous diplomatic debacle. Despite the failure of this mission, Kennedy remained committed to the overthrow of Castro. On November 30, 1961, the president ordered the secretary of state, the secretary of defense, and the CIA director "to use all available assets. . . . to help Cuba overthrow the Communist [Castro] regime." In response to these orders, the CIA not only supported attempts to overthrow Castro but launched at least eight attempts to assassinate the Cuban prime minister.

The Kennedy administration's covert use of the CIA was not confined to Cuba. In Southeast Asia, the administration found its clients in Laos losing to the Soviet-backed Pathet Lao. Kennedy first considered direct military involvement but then wisely decided to seek a diplomatic solution. Eventually, in July 1961, the United States reached an agreement with the Soviet Union to neutralize Laos. Despite this agreement, the CIA covertly assisted right-wing Laotian militarists in violation of the negotiated neutralization.

The CIA, in fact, served the Kennedy administration's Southeast Asia policy. In May 1961, the president ordered the CIA to undertake a program of covert action against the North Vietnamese government of Ho Chi Minh, including infiltrating agents into North Vietnam for sabotage and intelligence gathering. Moreover, of the formally authorized CIA covert operations conducted between 1947 and 1968, 163 were conducted during Kennedy's three-year administration (in contrast to 8 during Truman's eight years, 170 during Eisenhower's eight years, and 142 during Johnson's five years). In early 1961 the CIA also developed a special office, known as Executive Action, responsible for establishing a general capability to disable foreign leaders, including assassinations.

Activism abroad, the hallmark of the Kennedy years, culminated in the Cold War's most serious international crisis: the Cuban missile crisis of October 1962. In the aftermath of the Bay of Pigs fiasco, President Kennedy had declared that the substance of power, and not prestige, counted most in international affairs. Yet Kennedy soon practiced the politics of prestige.

The Bay of Pigs invasion prompted Soviet leaders to arm the Cubans with intermediate range nuclear missiles that could reach the American mainland and, during the summer and fall of 1962, forty-two such missile sites were established in Cuba. Sensitive to the domestic and international ramifications of Soviet military assistance to Cuba, but lacking hard intelligence about Soviet actions, in September Kennedy flatly warned Soviet leaders that the United States would act if Cuba provided "an offensive military capacity for the Soviet Union." Soviet Foreign Minister Gromyko falsely assured Kennedy one week before the crisis broke that the Soviet Union would not provide Cuba with offensive missiles. On October 14, however, U.S. reconnaissance planes discovered the camouflaged silos of Soviet missiles capable of attacking the U.S. mainland with missile weapons.

Possessing for the first time hard evidence of direct Soviet military power in the American hemisphere, on October 22, 1962, Kennedy publicly announced the discovery of the missile sites and "under the authority entrusted to me by the Constitution as endorsed by the resolution of the Congress" directed a strict naval blockade of all offensive military equipment shipped to Cuba. He also demanded withdrawal of all the missiles that had already arrived. Requesting an emergency meeting of the UN Security Council, Kennedy warned the Soviet Union that the United States would "regard any nuclear missile launched from Cuba against any nation in the Western hemisphere as an attack by the Soviet Union on the United States, requiring a full retaliatory response upon the Soviet Union."

Khrushchev found himself in a dilemma. Having challenged the United States near the center of its own power, he either had to retreat or risk a major war. He chose to retreat and on October 28 agreed to withdraw the missiles in what Secretary of State Rusk called an "eyeball-to-eyeball" confrontation. On November 20, 1962, Kennedy publicly announced the withdrawal of Soviet missiles and bombers from Cuba, U.S. respect for Cuban territorial integrity, and that U.S. forces would not invade Cuba. A potential world nuclear holocaust had been averted—even though the crisis involved less a threat to U.S. security (after all the United States had missile and bomber bases encircling the Soviet Union in Turkey and Western Europe since the early 1950s) than a reflection of changes in the existing military balance.

With the passing of the missile crisis, U.S.-Soviet relations improved appreciably as both sides, having been sobered, sought a measure of detente. As a first step, in June 1963 the United States and the Soviet Union signed a limited nuclear test ban treaty. Nuclear tests were to be limited to those areas which could be monitored without on-site inspection: the atmosphere, outerspace, and underwater. Despite conservative opposition, the Senate ratified the treaty on September 24, 1963, by an impressive majority of 80–19.

The Alliance for Progress represented Kennedy's second response to the threat Castro's Cuba raised of future revolutions throughout Latin America. President Kennedy adopted the thesis, proposed by his adviser Walt Rostow, that a long-term assistance program could spur economic development and that cumulative economic growth could avert left-wing revolutions. On March 13, 1961, Kennedy announced his new Latin American program, emphasizing as its goal the promotion of substantial economic development, social reforms, and political freedom.

Latin American leaders reacted warily to Kennedy's proposal for an "Allianza para el progreso." At a conference held in August 1961 at Punta del Este in Uruguay, the United States promised up to 55 percent of $1.1 billion each year for a ten-year, $20 billion program for rapid economic development. Of the remainder, the United States expected 15 percent each to come from private American investors, public and private sources in Western Europe and Japan, and international lending agencies. The alliance was not just another handout from Washington, but an ambitious program to transform Latin America. Latin American countries—Cuba was excluded—pledged appropriate tax and land reforms as well as housing, health, and educational programs. Steady economic growth and concomitant social reforms, the administration hoped, would eliminate any need for radical change in the Western hemisphere.

In operation, the Alliance for Progress recorded some achievements but by and large fell short of its announced goals. The average economic Latin-American growth rate rose to only 2 percent, which a rapidly growing population more than consumed; conservative ruling classes resisted yielding their entrenched privileges and condemned American pressure to do so as "Yanqui" interventionism; and radicals accused the United States of seeking to patch up a corrupt and moribund capitalism, to cure a cancer with Band-Aids. To have achieved substantial progress, Latin America would have had to undergo a political and social transformation which the Kennedy administration had never countenanced, and indeed had sought to avert.

The Peace Corps was another Kennedy innovation. During the 1960 presidential campaign, Kennedy had endorsed the sending of trained American men and women to help underdeveloped nations achieve modern skills and to demonstrate democracy at work. Until 1970, the Peace Corps received substantial support across the United States, especially from idealistic youths, and as well from most underdeveloped nations. By 1969 ten thousand corpsmen had been sent abroad to teach, to help build schools, roads, and sanitary systems, and to encourage farming reforms.

## VIETNAM:
## AN AMBIGUOUS LEGACY

In 1961, the Kennedy administration's principal interest in Indochina was Laos, not Vietnam. It simply persisted in implementing the policy of backing the Diem government in South Vietnam. With Diem's inability to suppress the Vietcong insurgency, Kennedy soon increased the U.S. military role. By January 1962, the number of U.S. military advisers to the South Vietnamese army had reached 7,600, while navy minesweepers patrolled the Vietnamese coast, and air force planes flew surveillance and reconnaissance missions.

This increased involvement did not alleviate South Vietnam's principal problem: the Diem government's failure to provide stability and order. Having dispatched General Maxwell Taylor and Walt Rostow on a special mission to South Vietnam, Kennedy acted on their advice. Taylor and Rostow perceived the situation in classic Cold War terms—"The Communists are pursuing a clear and systematic strategy in Southeast Asia"—and only secondarily as the result of the Diem government's corruptness and inefficiency. Kennedy accordingly implemented a counterinsurgency strategy. In return for promised South Vietnamese reforms, in December 1961, Kennnedy increased U.S. military assistance, particularly by providing helicopters to improve the mobility of South Vietnamese troops.

Further U.S. military aid failed to quash the revolutionary situation in South Vietnam. By the summer of 1963, Buddhist reaction to Diem's religious repression forced the administration to reassess its policy. To salvage the deteriorating situation within South Vietnam the administration encouraged South Vietnamese generals to overthrow Diem. Finally, on November 1, 1963, a group of generals stormed Diem's residence, captured the unpopular president, and immediately executed Diem and his even more unpopular brother-in-law Ngho Dinh Nhu (the South Vietnamese police chief). The military coup brought neither stability nor order—additional coups and governmental changes ensued. A persistent internal crisis constituted the ambiguous legacy Lyndon Johnson inherited following President Kennedy's assassination on November 22.

Ironically, Vietnam was a diversion from the priorities and goals of the last year of Kennedy's presidency. Having initially focused on foreign affairs, by 1963 the president had shifted his attention to domestic concerns. The administration now supported more liberal social and economic reforms and moved haltingly to confront the challenges posed by southern segregation and repressive anti-Communist politics. Whether the administration would have adopted even bolder positions cannot be known. On November 22, 1963, Kennedy was assassinated in Dallas, Texas, while on a trip to repair the deep divisions within the Texas Democratic party and to mobilize support for his reelection. In death, Kennedy became a daring young president who had called the nation to greatness and who seemed on the verge of providing magnificent bold, moral leadership. Americans preferred to remember their fallen leader as a handsome, bold, prince of Camelot rather than a cool, calculating Machiavellian fox, driven as much by opportunism as principle.

# CHAPTER NINE
# THE TRAGEDY OF LBJ:
## *Domestic Triumphs,*
## *Foreign Reverses,*
## *1963–1968*

Elevated suddenly to the presidency after John F. Kennedy's assassination, Lyndon Baines Johnson moved quickly to impose his stamp on national politics. His transition from vice president to president was eased by his having served on the NSC, chaired the National Aeronautics and Space Council and the president's Committee on Equal Employment Opportunity, and having been fully briefed by President Kennedy on all important policy matters.

In serving as Kennedy's vice president, Johnson had surrendered a powerful position, Democratic Senate majority leader, for a prestigious but largely honorific office. Compounding this personal loss of power, many Kennedy aides belittled Johnson for his folksy manner and political operator's style. Inevitably, then, personal considerations complicated his transition from functionary to policy maker. Although at first retaining most of the Kennedy Cabinet and expressing his commitment to the deceased president's general policies, Johnson intended to chart his own course and establish his own policy priorities.

### THE GREAT SOCIETY:
### ANTI-COMMUNISM AND REFORM

These priorities were symbolized in the phrase Lyndon Johnson used to describe his administration's basic purposes: the Great Society. The Great Society, the president stressed in his annual message of 1965, "asks not only how much, but how good; not only how to create wealth, but how to use it. It proposes as the first test for a nation: the quality of its people." Based on New Deal principles, the Great Society reflected Johnson's focus on domestic reform, not foreign adventures. The president's 1964 speech declaring an "unconditional war on poverty" eloquently captured his aims.

> On similar occasions in the past we have often been called upon to wage war against foreign enemies which threaten our freedom today. Now we are asked to declare war on a domestic enemy which threatens the strength of our nation and the welfare of our people. If we now move forward against this enemy . . . this Congress will have won a more secure and honorable place in the history of the nation and the enduring gratitude of generations of Americans to come.

The Great Society theme incorporated another premise which Lyndon Johnson articulated during his successful campaign for the presidency in 1964: the "quest for union." He urged Americans "come, let us reason together," implying that no differences were so fundamental they could not be reconciled and that reforms could be attained without social and economic conflict. As president, Johnson tried to be a conciliator who recognized disadvantaged groups and reconciled class divisions and competing claims. In this capacity, Johnson pointedly commended southern acceptance of civil rights. Indeed, he delivered his most eloquent speech of the 1964 campaign in New Orleans, counseling southerners to abandon the passions engendered by the Civil War and Reconstruction and accept integration. Racism, this southern president maintained, was the chief reason for the South's backwardness and the main obstacle to its advance. To emphasize this point, he quoted from a Mississippi-born Texas senator. After recounting Mississippi's poverty and degradation, the Texas legislator remarked, "Poor old state, they haven't heard a real Democratic speech in thirty years. All they ever hear at election time is nigra, nigra, nigra."

Johnson's Great Society legislative program included the promotion of civil rights, recognition of the arts as well as intellectuals' contributions to society, repeal of discriminatory immigration legislation, public assistance for the urban and rural poor, health care for the aged, federal aid to education, consumer protection, and job-training programs for those who lacked the necessary skills to secure employment in a complex industrial economy. The programs did reduce poverty and stimulate the economy. The GNP increased steadily and impressively—7.1 percent in 1964, 8.1 percent in 1965, and 8.5 percent in 1966—while the rate of unemployment declined from 5.7 percent in 1963 to 3.8 percent in 1966.[1] Despite a substantial increase in federal spending for domestic programs, the rate of inflation remained at 2 percent in 1965 and rose to only 3.7 percent in 1966. Between 1963 and 1966 while the federal budget ran only modest deficits—from a

---

[1] It is still unclear how much of the economic growth and reduced unemployment resulted from Johnson's domestic reforms and how much from higher military expenditures and manpower demands associated with the Vietnam War.

low of $1.6 to a high of $5.9 billion—not until the Vietnam War intensified after 1965 did price inflation and federal deficits soar.

Paradoxically, this president who sought to promote consensus, to establish a harmony of interests, and to concentrate on domestic reform soon became the storm center of political confrontation and domestic violence. Johnson's administration also became dominated by foreign affairs. In part, the intensification of the Vietnam War had dissolved the harmony forged in the heady days of 1964–1965. Yet, this breakdown of consensus predated the war and was the product as well of domestic racial and economic divisions. The contrast between goals and accomplishments which produced social and political conflict, marked the most crucial legacies of the Johnson presidency.

In 1963 and 1964 Lyndon Johnson hoped to extend popular respect for liberal principles, intellectual dissent, and civil liberties. In one of his first symbolic acts as president, Johnson conferred the Fermi Prize on J. Robert Oppenheimer, thereby commemorating the atomic scientist's many contributions to science and society. Johnson's decision to honor a controversial scientist symbolized the president's initial willingness to challenge Cold War conformity.

To further respect for intellectuals, the Johnson White House also scheduled a festival of the arts for June 1965. Intended as a testimony to American humanists and to commemorate the positive consequences of intellectual freedom, the festival almost immediately became embroiled in a heated public challenge to the Johnson administration's foreign policies. Of those invited to the festival, some (including the poet Robert Lowell) publicly refused to attend for reasons of principle; others (the novelists Saul Bellow and John Hersey) attended but let it be known that they considered the festival simply a commendation of the arts (a purpose they thought commendable) and not an acceptance of the administration's domestic or foreign policies; still others (notably the film critic Dwight Macdonald) attended in order to use the festival as a forum to condemn the president's foreign policy.

The passions of the unruly intellectuals paled before those of the president. Fearful of public criticism, Johnson ordered the FBI to conduct name checks on those artists who had not yet been invited. The FBI uncovered derogatory information on six (four of whom had art works on display). At first insisting that these six not be invited, Johnson eventually agreed to invite them to avoid being charged with establishing a political test: namely, honoring only those artists who supported his policies or whose ideas were noncontroversial. To avert the recurrence of such incidents in the future, the president thereafter required prior FBI name checks on prospective guests to White House social functions.

The president's use of the FBI was not confined to screening White House guests or conducting security investigations of presidential appointees.

Beginning in 1965, the Johnson White House requested the FBI to conduct name checks on anti-Vietnam war critics, including congressmen. This practice fed on itself. In time, the Johnson White House requested FBI name checks on such prominent newsmen as David Brinkley, Joseph Kraft, Peter Arnett, Ben Gilbert, and Peter Lisagor, and in 1966 it asked that the FBI monitor both the Senate Foreign Relations Committee's hearings on the administration's Vietnam policy and any contacts between congressmen and their staff and foreign embassy officials. The FBI director was further directed to "brief" conservative congressmen on the anti-Vietnam demonstrations "so that they might not only make speeches upon the floor of Congress but also publicly."

FBI officials unhesitatingly acceded to presidential requests. They helped write, and then promoted the nationwide dissemination of conservative Virginia Congressman Howard Smith's speech labeling the antiwar movement as subversive. In May 1968 FBI field offices were ordered to forward information to headquarters "on a continuing basis" for "prompt dissemination to the news media . . . to discredit the New Left movement" as part of another COINTELPRO to "neutralize" the New Left. The FBI Director had earlier independently authorized two other COINTELPROS: in 1964 against white extremist groups and in 1967 against black nationalist groups. In 1964, moreover, a special FBI squad had been sent to the Democratic National Convention in Atlantic City to monitor the activities of dissident civil rights organizations. This squad closely followed the activities of Martin Luther King, Jr., and Robert Kennedy (the latter in part because Johnson was fearful of a possible effort to draft Kennedy for the vice presidency).

If Lyndon Johnson's extreme sensitivity to criticism flawed his administration's efforts to temper Cold War hysteria, his attorneys general, Nicholas Katzenbach and Ramsey Clark, did much to protect civil rights and civil liberties. Under their leadership, the Justice Department aggressively used civil rights legislation to extend the rights of blacks in the South. Never refusing a single FBI request to wiretap or bug in national security cases, Katzenbach tightly restricted FBI electronic surveillance of domestic political activities. In 1965, the attorney general rescinded Robert Kennedy's authorization of the wiretap on civil rights leader Martin Luther King, Jr. The FBI was ordered to create a written record of all taps and bugs and prepare a special ELSUR index listing all those whose conversations had been intercepted. Katzenbach's successor, Ramsey Clark, further restricted FBI electronic surveillance to investigations "directly affecting the national security." To insure that "national security" would not provide a cover for domestic political surveillance, Clark required that FBI wiretapping and bugging authorization requests specify: the person to be tapped or bugged, the expected information, and reasons for suspecting the individual. During Clark's tenure as attorney general, accordingly, the number of "national security" wiretaps declined to 82 in 1968 from highs of 519 in 1945, 322 in 1954, and 244 in 1963, and the number of bugs from a high of 102 in 1955 to 0 in 1967 and 9 in 1968.

The heart of the attorney general's anticriminal program centered on special task forces and improving the professionalism of local and federal police forces. In contrast to his Cold War predecessors, Clark opposed legalizing electronic surveillance. The attorney general even refused to use the authority provided under Title III of the Omnibus Crime Control and Safe Streets Act of 1968, which explicitly legalized wiretapping and bugging during criminal and national security investigations.[2]

An investigation initiated in 1965 by the Senate Subcommittee on Administrative Practice and Procedure, chaired by Senator Edward Long, posed a graver threat to the FBI. Concerned that Long's investigation might uncover illegal FBI activities, FBI Director Hoover in 1965 and 1966 issued orders banning break-ins and mail opening programs and imposing stringent numerical limitations on the installation of bugs and wiretaps. Moreover, following *Ramparts* magazine's disclosure in February 1967 of CIA subsidization of the National Student Association, Hoover imposed a 21 year minimum age restriction for FBI informers.

The combined effect of the Long Committee investigations and the attorneys general's administrative reforms tempered government violations of civil liberties under the guise of national security. But the president's post-1965 responses to the antiwar movement reinvigorated the suppression of dissent. In a 1965 speech, Vice President Humphrey claimed that antiwar demonstrations were "organized and masterminded" by "the international Communist movement." In a May 18, 1966, speech in Chicago, President Johnson accused "Nervous Nellies" of undermining his administration's conduct of foreign policy. Antiwar critics, the president publicly charged, were ready to "turn on their own leaders, and on their own country, and on our fighting men." Johnson castigated prominent Senate critic J. William Fulbright as "a frustrated old woman" who "cannot understand that people with brown skins value freedom too." Implying that criticism of national policy was harmful, if not actually subversive, the president offered a standard for judging the critic: "Is he helping the cause of his country or is he advancing the cause of himself?" In private, Johnson was even less restrained when assessing his critics' motives. He urged the FBI, the CIA, and the NSA to uncover evidence of foreign direction in the antiwar and civil rights movements. In response to presidential pressures, beginning in 1967 CIA and NSA investigations were expanded to encompass domestic organizations and individuals prominent in antiwar and civil rights protests. Thus, CIA agents infiltrated domestic organizations while the NSA intercepted the

---

[2]This law contained a gaping loophole to its prior court authorization requirement: The president could order wiretaps and bugs "as he deems necessary" during "national security" investigations.

international telecommunications of targeted individuals and organizations. Recognizing the illegality of their domestic surveillance, NSA officials devised special filing procedures and CIA officials admonished recipients of the "sensitivity" of their reports.

Former White House aide Eric Goldman recounted in *The Tragedy of Lyndon Johnson* how the president commended the FBI and CIA for keeping him informed of his critics' actions. "Liberal critics! It's the Russians who are behind the whole thing," the president claimed. Antiwar senators were in close contact with the Russians "who think up things for the senators to say. I often know before they do what their speeches are going to say."

The administration's assault on its antiwar critics benefited conservative politicians like Richard Nixon more than the president and other liberal anti-Communists. Since 1965, Nixon had sought to exploit the deteriorating situation in Southeast Asia and the emerging domestic antiwar movement. Prior to the president's decisions to increase U.S. involvement in Vietnam, first bombing North Vietnam in February 1965 and then steadily increasing the number of U.S. ground troops after April 1965, Nixon assailed the Kennedy-Johnson Vietnam policy for permitting "privileged sanctuaries" in North Vietnam and a "Yalu River concept in South Vietnam." A negotiated settlement to the Vietnam War, he said, amounted to "surrender on the installment plan." Nixon decried each of Johnson's increases in military aid and action as inadequate. He also echoed the president's assault on antiwar critics, condemning their words and actions as encouraging "the Communist leaders to prolong their resistance."

Unlike the Korean War period, radical dissent was not silenced. The national mood had shifted profoundly during the early 1960s, especially among college youth.[3] The Vietnam War intensified student protest. After 1965 college campuses increasingly became centers of political and intellectual dissent. By 1968, demonstrations against the war and the Johnson administration were more belligerent, student dissent extended to a more general critique of American society, and the college unrest spilled over to the junior high and high schools. College students actively participated in the 1968 Democratic presidential primaries, supporting the candidacies of Eugene McCarthy and Robert Kennedy.

## THE POLITICS OF POVERTY
## AND OF CIVIL RIGHTS

Johnson's Vietnam War policy pushed politics in a direction in which tolerance and civility were sacrificed to the quest for order and discipline. This in turn frustrated the president's efforts to redress economic and racial in-

[3]See Chapter 7.

equities. To wage an unconditional war on poverty, Lyndon Johnson in May 1964 had recommended a variety of legislative programs to fund the development of underdeveloped regions (Appalachia), the acquisition of skills by the unemployed (the manpower development program), and redress the deficiencies of the disadvantaged ($1 billion was appropriated under the educational opportunities bill to assist primary and secondary schools to raise educational levels and improve the quality of teaching).

The programs promised a real improvement in the lot of the poor. A number of agencies were created under the Office of Economic Opportunity[4] to assist the poor, including Head Start, Upward Bound, VISTA, the Neighborhood Youth Corps, and Community Action. Their purpose was "to eliminate the paradox of poverty in the Nation by opening to everyone the opportunity to live in decency and dignity." Federal funding would remedy the technical and educational deficiencies presumably causing poverty. Thus, Head Start would improve the learning skills of preschoolers, Upward Bound motivate and assist disadvantaged students to attend college, and the Job Corps provide skills for school dropouts. Essentially a domestic Peace Corps, VISTA offered technical skills and resources to deprived, poverty-striken areas, while the Neighborhood Youth Corps and the Community Action program utilized neighborhood centers to organize community resources.

The promise of this "war on poverty" was not fully realized. In part, the appropriation of $1.6 billion for all OEO programs did not constitute a full-scale war on poverty. (The original plan OEO Director Sargent Shriver had submitted in 1965 called for appropriations of $1.4 billion in 1966, $9.2 billion in 1967, $12.1 billion in 1968, $14.3 billion in 1969, and $17 billion in 1970.) The impact of even limited funding was further reduced because local and state officials administered these programs, sometimes using funds for political purposes. A large percentage of the funds went for salaries and administrative expenses.

The gap between the promise and the reality of the war on poverty caused renewed conflict. On the one hand, many ghetto leaders assailed the antipoverty programs as irrelevant and paternalistic; on the other hand, many conservatives assailed them as inflationary and misguided. Conservatives charged that thoughtless federal spending would lead to a loss of private initiative, to disrespect for the work ethic, and to an attitude of permissiveness.

The Johnson administration's simultaneous assault on the twin evils of racial segregation and discrimination further aggravated domestic tensions. The civil rights movement had encouraged southern blacks to register and to vote as never before, often for the first time. In Selma, Alabama, for

[4]OEO, the acronym for the umbrella organization, was the centerpiece of the Johnson administration's war on poverty.

example, fully 97 percent of registered voters had been white in a county where blacks outnumbered whites (15,000 to 14,000). In Lowndes and Wilcox counties, Alabama, not one black had registered to vote even though they outnumbered whites four to one. The violent resistance of white officials to peaceful black-led registration efforts strengthened the belief that federal action was required to insure elementary voting rights.

In 1964 Congress acted. It passed a new Civil Rights Act, which outlawed racial, religious, and sex discrimination in employment and in places of public accommodation; authorized the attorney general to intercede in private suits for relief from discriminatory racial practices and sue to desegregate public facilities and schools; terminated federal funding of discriminatory local and state programs; and extended the life of and granted new powers to the Civil Rights Commission. In 1965 Congress enacted the Voting Rights Act prohibiting counties from employing literacy or other tests as a means to determine voter eligibility. The attorney general could appoint federal registrars when it could be proven that local officials discriminated against blacks and assign election observers to insure fairness in voting. The 1964 and 1965 laws constituted fundamental shifts in federal policy toward the South, significantly extending federal assistance to blacks. In 1966, moreover, Johnson nominated Thurgood Marshall to the Supreme Court (the first such black appointment, and a prominent lawyer in the NAACP assault on segregation).

The civil rights "revolution" of the Johnson years satisfied neither black nor white Americans. Many black ghetto leaders decried the Johnson programs as tokenism and as liberal white elitism. By contrast, opponents of civil rights contended that liberals had encouraged disrespect for the law, laziness, and criminality. The conservative counterattack touched a sensitive nerve, whose reaction edged national politics to the right.

## A MORE CENTRALIZED PRESIDENCY AND THE JOHNSON LANDSLIDE OF 1964

Excepting the 100 Days of Franklin Roosevelt's first term, there is no parallel to Lyndon Johnson's legislative record. Even Roosevelt's record pales in contrast: During the so-called 100 Days Congress approved fifteen Roosevelt-proposed measures while between January 4, 1965, and October 23, 1965, Congress approved eighty-five administrative-sponsored bills, many having been proposed earlier but never implemented.

To obtain his objectives, Johnson combined an inside knowledge of the congressional power system with a more centralized presidency. On the one hand, by cajolery, pressure, and congressional rules changes, he removed legislative roadblocks. He lobbied to change House rules to permit the leadership to bring bills to the floor that the Rules Committee held for over twenty-one days. In 1964, the Johnson White House also helped defeat a southern-led filibuster against civil rights legislation. The campaign was efficiently organized, with timely calls for quorums and for votes on key amendments. In addition, the president sacrificed other administration programs to enact a civil rights bill. Johnson's tactics, Republican minority leader Everett Dirksen's decision to support cloture, and the intensive lobbying by civil rights, labor union, and church groups combined to override the southern filibuster—the first time a filibuster had not succeeded during a debate over civil rights legislation. On June 10, after seventy-four days of debate and fifty-seven days of filibuster, the Senate voted cloture by a margin of 71–29. On July 2, Johnson signed into law the Civil Rights Act of 1964 (discussed earlier in this section).

Meantime, Lyndon Johnson further consolidated presidential power. He committed U.S. air power and troops to Vietnam and the Dominican Republic in 1965 without a congressional declaration of war. He continued Kennedy's diminution of the Cabinet's functions and extended the powers of the White House staff. Johnson differed from Kennedy mostly in presidential style. The domineering Texan insisted on the unquestioned loyalty of White House aides. Walt Rostow replaced McGeorge Bundy as principal adviser on foreign affairs while Marvin Watson assumed Theodore Sorenson's former role.

The president used the intelligence agencies to advance his political goals. He turned to the agencies for name checks on the Senate staff of 1964 Republican presidential candidate Barry Goldwater and any information which might discredit his critics. Johnson's ability to use the intelligence agencies for political purposes and then to preclude public and congressional scrutiny, illustrated how an obsession with internal security served to increase presidential powers.

In early 1964, moreover, Johnson exploited the emotional reaction to his predecessor's assassination to pressure Congress to enact Kennedy's proposed tax cut and civil rights bills. On February 26, 1964, Congress approved an $11.2 billion tax cut and on July 2, 1964, Johnson signed the Civil Rights Act of 1964. In addition, in August 1964 Congress created the Office of Economic Opportunity and shortly thereafter appropriated $375 million for urban mass transit, a food stamp program, and expanded the National Defense Education Act, hospital construction, and legal aid to the poor.

Johnson next capitalized on the opportunities provided by the 1964 presidential campaign. In that campaign, conservative Republicans mounted a direct challenge to New Deal policies and principles. The Republican party had lost the presidency since 1936, conservatives argued, because it refused to nominate a candidate who forthrightly challenged New Deal domestic policies. Committed to transforming national politics and realigning the Republican party toward greater conservatism, they sought an ideal candidate.

In Arizona Senator Barry Goldwater, conservative Republicans found their man. He was personable, with a rustic handsomeness, and he was an effective spokesman for an unabashedly anti-Communist foreign policy and anti-New Deal domestic policy. Republican conservatives also controlled party organizations in those states where delegates were selected at party caucuses or state conventions and could thereby elect Goldwater delegations.

When he entered the presidential primaries, Goldwater was uncertain of victory. But his candidacy, whatever its outcome, could promote conservative influence in the Republican party and strengthen the party's base in the South and Southwest. The Goldwater campaign was thus about party principles, not mass popularity, and candidate Goldwater lost every contested primary but one (California). Yet Goldwater's candidacy was enhanced by the divisions among moderate Republicans, the hesitancy of any one other than the controversial Nelson Rockefeller (then governor of New York and recently divorced and remarried) to challenge Goldwater for the nomination, and Richard Nixon's equivocation. His defeat of Rockefeller in the June California primary assured Goldwater the Republican nomination. The Arizonan won a first-ballot victory at the San Francisco convention.

Because their major goal was to reshape the Republican party, Goldwater Republicans were uncompromising. At the convention, they made no concessions to Republican moderates over the platform or the vice-presidential nominee. An obscure, right-wing congressman, William Miller, was nominated vice president, and Goldwater's acceptance speech caught the new tone of the platform: "Extremism in the defense of liberty is no vice . . . .Moderation in the pursuit of justice is no virtue." During the actual campaign, Goldwater advocated the sale of TVA, assailed agricultural subsidies, denounced social security, supported right-to-work laws, opposed civil rights, and proposed giving local military commanders control over nuclear weapons.

Appalled by the Goldwater delegates' open animosity toward "eastern Republicans" and the news media, many moderate Republicans (notably Michigan Governor George Romney and New York Senator Kenneth Keating) decided after the convention either to disavow Goldwater's candidacy or to concentrate on state and local contests. Republican party or national politics were not realigned, however. Goldwater not only lost resoundingly, but conservative candidates in the Southwest, Far West, Middle West, and East were defeated while moderate Republicans trimmed their own losses.

The Democrats' campaign strategy both commended the Johnson administration's legislative achievements and exploited the resentments and fears elicited by Goldwater's assault on New Deal programs. Consequently, the profound philosophical differences between the two candidates were not debated. The Democrats focused on Goldwater's avowed antiwelfare state conservatism and Cold War militancy. This approach was exemplified in Democratic vice-presidential nominee Hubert Humphrey's acceptance speech. Citing the extensive bipartisan support for such administration-proposed measures as the Civil Rights Act of 1964 and the Test Ban Treaty of 1963, Humphrey intoned after each citation "but not Senator Goldwater." Goldwater was depicted as an insensitive reactionary, whose policies were irresponsible, and whose election might cause a searing depression and nuclear war. One Democratic TV ad featured a little girl picking petals from a daisy that dissolved into a mushroom-shaped cloud, while another commercial showed two hands tearing up a Social Security card. In one speech, Johnson pointedly queried: "Where'd we be if the other—the philosophy of opposition and destruction—had prevailed? The wrecker can wreck in one day what it takes years for the builder to build . . . and if the only choice before us is between surrender and nuclear war, then we'll all be dead."

Their campaign strategy resulted in an overwhelming Johnsonian and Democratic victory. Johnson captured 61.1 percent of the popular vote (43,126,506) and 486 electoral votes (to Goldwater's 27,176,799 popular and 52 electoral votes) and carried all the states of the union but Louisiana, Mississippi, Alabama, South Carolina, Georgia, and Goldwater's home state of Arizona. In addition, Democratic majorities in the House increased to 295–140 and in the Senate to 68–32, and the Democrats picked up over 500 state legislative seats.

The size of his popular mandate and the composition of the new Congress (owing to the defeat of conservative Republicans and the election of liberal Democrats) increased Johnson's political leverage. The president moved quickly to secure congressional approval of his major legislative recommendations. Responding, in 1965 Congress repealed the national origins system for immigration quotas; enacted legislation on voting rights, health insurance for the aged, and pollution control; provided federal support for the arts, and appropriated $1.5 billion for education, including scholarships to the poor and aid to both public and private schools; extended Social Security coverage and benefits and federal assistance to the Appalachian region; raised and broadened minimum wage coverage; and created the Department of Housing and Urban Development and a manpower training program. In 1966, Congress approved other Johnson recommendations to aid consumers (truth-in-packaging), establish highway and safety standards, create a department of transportation, provide rent subsidies for the poor, and fund a model (or demonstration) cities program.

Thereafter, the administration's domestic reforms lost momentum. Its subsequent major legislative victories consisted of congressional enactment in 1968 of another civil rights act—barring discrimination in the selling, renting, financing, and advertising of 80 percent of the nation's housing units—and a 10 percent tax-surcharge to fight the inflation created by the

Vietnam War. But the president now had to make major concessions to obtain congressional approval of his recommendations. The administration agreed not to oppose a rider to the housing bill making it a crime to cross state lines to participate in demonstrations to incite violence. To insure that committee chairman Wilbur Mills reported his proposed tax-surcharge bill out of the House Ways and Means Committee, the president publicly agreed to slash $6 billion in federal expenditures. Moreover, in 1968 (despite administration opposition), Congress passed an anticrime bill, the Omnibus Crime Control and Safe Streets Act, that among other provisions for the first time authorized federal wiretapping.

The steady decline in Johnson's legislative influence revealed a changed congressional mood. By 1968 the administration's relations with Congress were acrimonious, contrasting sharply with 1964 and 1965 when Congress unhesitatingly enacted the president's far-reaching legislative program. The Vietnam War polarized the liberal community, warped the climate of opinion that had been basic to the enactment of Great Society legislation, and contributed to a steep decline in Johnson's popularity. According to the Gallup poll, 66 percent of respondents approved Johnson's presidency in November 1965; only 44 percent in October 1966. The Republicans were the principal beneficiaries of changing attitudes. On the one hand, the administration's call to fight Communism abroad and to silence antiwar critics at home strengthened conservative anti-Communist influences. On the other hand, the inflationary impact of increased defense spending justified restricting domestic spending. The Republicans used these issues to make striking gains in the 1966 elections, winning an additional 8 governorships, and 47 House, 3 Senate, and 540 state legislative seats. In postelection polling, Gallup concluded that the Vietnam War was "probably the prime reason why the GOP did so well."

## A NEW PHASE IN THE COLD WAR

The Vietnam War dominated the debate over the Johnson administration's foreign policy. Nonetheless, Lyndon Johnson's presidency marked a new phase in the Cold War. The Johnson administration rejected potentially provocative commitments and promoted detente with the Soviet Union while "building bridges" with Eastern Europe. Yet the administration relied on the CIA to destabilize "unfriendly" governments and political leaders. In the Dominican Republic crisis of 1965 and the Vietnam imbroglio of 1964 to 1968, the administration's policy was wholly consistent with the containment practiced by the Truman-Eisenhower administrations during the late 1940s and 1950s. These contradictory policies in turn exposed the changing nature of the U.S. international role, and concomitantly, the expanded authority of the president and the intelligence agencies.

First, despite the Vietnam War, the Cold War abated in intensity. In the immediate aftermath of the Cuban missile crisis of October 1962, the United States and the Soviet Union concluded that, regardless of shifts in the balance of nuclear weapons, each possessed more than enough to destroy the other and lacked the means to contain the other power's influence. Since then, both powers acted more cautiously and sought to achieve a degree of detente in their mutual relationship. Second, the domestic strains associated with the costly involvement in the Vietnam War eroded the Cold War consensus. The emerging "credibility" crisis affecting Johnson's leadership contributed to concerns about presidential powers and to a new cynicism about U.S. foreign policy. Some critics demanded a more humanitarian foreign policy, others called for constraints on presidential initiatives and on the intelligence agencies. In addition, the multiplying signs of divisions between the Soviet Union and Eastern Europe and the Soviet Union and the People's Republic of China dispelled belief in the Cold War dichotomy between "free" and "Communist" worlds and demonstrated the new diversity of Communism. Third, the 1960s witnessed a return to a multipower world in which emergent and revived nationalisms divided both the NATO and Soviet systems and led many states in Africa, Asia, Latin America, and the Middle East to an increasing assertiveness.

As China, Japan, and other nation-states (notably the oil producing states of OPEC) sought to influence global affairs more directly, a world dominated by two superpowers alone had clearly vanished. The United States and the Soviet Union remained far more powerful than any other nation-state; hitherto subservient nations, however, now openly challenged the superpowers.

Under Johnson, the CIA continued its covert activities, at times without the president's authorization. In the Congo, CIA pilots flew T-28 fighter bombers in support of Moise Tshombe's efforts to suppress Congolese rebels. Since 1960, U.S. policy had sought to establish a unified but pro-Western Congolese government. Initially acting to undermine Patrice Lumumba's government (including CIA plans to assassinate the unpredictable Congolese nationalist), the United States later supported a United Nations effort to establish order by suppressing Tshombe's secessionist movement in the mineral-rich Katanga province. When Tshombe reversed his policy and emerged as a leader of pro-Western forces, the United States supported him. At the insistence of the State Department, however, Cuban exiles replaced CIA pilots.

In contrast to the Congo where the CIA acted to implement administration policy, in Ghana the CIA operated independently. Thus, whereas the so-called Forty Committee (the NSC board established to review and authorize CIA-directed operations) specifically prohibited any CIA intervention in Ghanaian affairs, in 1966 the CIA assisted in the overthrow of Ghanaian president Kwame Nkrumah. Yet CIA dispatches to Washington erroneously reported that all contacts with the plotters of the coup had been undertaken only to obtain intelligence.

CIA misinformation extended to presidential briefing requests. In February 1967 the syndicated columnist Drew Pearson reported that the CIA had been involved in efforts to assassinate Cuban Premier Fidel Castro, Dominican Republic President Rafael Trujillo, and South Vietnamese President Ngo Dinh Diem. President Johnson immediately requested a briefing from CIA Director Richard Helms on the accuracy of these allegations. In his report to the president, Helms described the CIA's role in the assassinations of Diem, Trujillo, and Castro (plans had been devised but not implemented—or in the case of Castro had been unsuccessful). Helms's report implied that CIA efforts to assassinate Castro had ceased in 1962; in fact they continued until 1965. Helms also did not brief Johnson about CIA assassination plans against Lumumba.

Yet the Johnson administration's foreign policy was less bellicose than such CIA plots suggested. In 1965, the president rejected a Pentagon recommendation to establish a multilateral force (MLF) under which the United States would provide tactical nuclear weapons to her NATO allies. The proposal to grant West Germany access to nuclear weapons, in the process intensifying the nuclear arms race, had precipitated a heated debate within the administration and within the NATO alliance. At the same time, the administration sought to normalize relations and encourage trade with the Communist governments in Eastern Europe, thereby reducing their subservience to Moscow. The president similarly sought to improve relations with the Soviet Union. The Vietnam War complicated this effort but it was only the Soviet invasion of Czechoslovakia on August 20, 1968, that caused Johnson to postpone the announcement, intended for August 21, of a summit meeting with Soviet leaders.

## FOREIGN ADVENTURISM:
## THE DOMINICAN REPUBLIC
## AND THE VIETNAM QUAGMIRE

The Johnson administration's Latin America policy similarly emphasized internal order and stability, highlighted by its April 1965 responses to developments in the Dominican Republic.

Following Dominican strongman Trujillo's assassination in 1961 and the election, in early 1963, of a constitutional government under Juan Bosch, the Dominican Republic collapsed in social and economic conflicts. Bosch's inability to resolve the situation led to a military coup seven months later, and the installation of an unpopular government headed by Donald Reid Cabral.

Because the Cabral government failed to develop popular support, a group of pro-Bosch colonels, led by Colonel Francisco Camaano Deno, revolted and invited Bosch back from exile. More conservative Dominican officers, led by Air Force General Elias Wessin y Wessin and encouraged by

U.S. Ambassador W. Tapley Bennett, immediately attempted a counter-coup. Fearing that pro-Bosch elements might triumph and pursue policies hostile to U.S. interests, Bennett telegraphed Washington to urge direct U.S. military intervention. On April 28, 1965, President Johnson publicly committed U.S. troops, ostensibly "to protect American lives." When U.S. television exposed the extensive U.S. military role, the administration claimed, in the words of Secretary of State Dean Rusk, that "the Communists had captured the revolution according to plan, and the danger of a Communist takeover was established beyond any question." Rusk's statement paralleled President Johnson's May 2, 1965, charge that "Communist leaders, many of them trained in Cuba," had infiltrated the rebel movement. U.S. intervention, Johnson argued, was intended to prevent the rise of another Castro. To support this contention, the U.S. Embassy in Santo Domingo released a list of fifty-four Communists in the rebel ranks. News reports, however, revealed that many of the fifty-four alleged "Communists" had not been prominent in the revolution, some were then outside the country, and some names were counted twice.

The direct U.S. military role and subsequent American mediation brought to power a military dictatorship headed by General Antonio Imbert. The United States again intervened to arrange elections. In these elections, held in July 1966, Joaquin Balaguer won the presidency and installed a more moderate government. In addition, the Johnson administration pressured the Organization of American States (OAS) to sanction, albeit reluctantly, U.S. intervention.

Johnson's Dominican policy exemplified his conception of the proper U.S. role in international affairs. Based on his reading of the Truman administration's Asian policies, the Bay of Pigs fiasco, and the 1962 Cuban missile crisis, Johnson had concluded that diplomatic indecisiveness threatened national security and that Communist expansion could be averted by the vigorous use of military power. Johnson expressed this assessment in remarks to a newspaper columnist: "The real danger is that the other side is going to underestimate us—it's happened before. The danger is that they'll think we are fat and fifty—just the country club crowd."

Lyndon Johnson's conception of the American mission was also moralistic and patriotic. He truly believed that America's diplomatic course was morally right. This caused him to be intolerant of domestic and foreign criticism. Johnson's inflexibility eventually produced an American tragedy—the increasingly unpopular Vietnam War which tarnished the image of both the presidency and the American nation.

For Johnson, the prospect of a Communist victory in Viewnam tested American will and resolve. Unlike his predecessors, Johnson no longer had the luxury of limited, relatively uncostly options. He thus chose to authorize a direct U.S. military role. Before 1964, the United States had provided economic, technical, and military aid to the South Vietnamese government;

after 1964 the United States directly intervened militarily in the Vietnam War.

At first, President Johnson adhered firmly to Kennedy's and Eisenhower's policy of limited intervention in Southeast Asia. Opposed to deeper U.S. involvement, he and his principal advisers soon concluded that the United States must resort to military power. In February 1964, the President agreed to initiate Plan 34A, which set in motion psychological and sabotage activities intended to pressure the North Vietnamese government of Ho Chi Minh to halt its assistance to the Vietcong insurgents in South Vietnam.

The problem, however, was the inability of the successor military juntas to the Diem government to govern effectively. By March 1964, Secretary of Defense Robert McNamara described a bleak situation in South Vietnam. The Vietcong controlled 40 percent of South Vietnam, large groups of the population were apathetic, and the South Vietnamese government's position had weakened.

Convinced that the principal problem was not indigenous discontent but Communist subversion and that the United States must sustain a pro-Western government in South Vietnam, the president was partly constrained by domestic politics. If wedded to an anti-Communist foreign policy, the public was indifferent to the civil conflict in Vietnam. Moreover, in the 1964 presidential campaign, Johnson had cast himself as the "peace" candidate, challenging the messianic Cold War rhetoric of the Republican standard-bearer, Senator Barry Goldwater.

Exploiting an incident in the Gulf of Tonkin, Johnson ordered a stronger response against North Vietnam. Since the approval of Plan 34A, U.S. destroyers had been patrolling the Gulf of Tonkin area, conducting electronic eavesdropping on the North Vietnamese and assisting South Vietnamese sabotage operations. On August 2, 1964, North Vietnamese torpedo boats attacked the U.S. destroyer *Maddox*, which with its sister ship, the *C. Turner Joy*, had been on patrol. The Johnson administration protested this attack and, when it received confusing reports of another attack on August 4, ordered reprisal air raids against the torpedo boat bases and oil storage areas in North Vietnam. At the same time, the president secured congressional approval (by a unanimous vote in the House and an 88–2 vote in the Senate) of the so-called Gulf of Tonkin resolution. Under this resolution, the Congress empowered the president to "take all necessary measures to repel any armed attack against the forces of the United States and to prevent further aggression."

The Johnson administration's August 1964 response was measured and limited. It nonetheless signaled a new, and ominous development: the decision to provide direct U.S. military involvement in support of the South Vietnamese government. Johnson considered Asia as strategically important to the United States, viewed South Vietnam as a victim of Communist aggression, and believed that the People's Republic of China sought a Communist-dominated Asia. He accordingly concluded that the United States must intervene. A formal show of American strength would alone deter the North Vietnamese and encourage the South Vietnamese to resist. The Johnson administration next authorized a series of cumulative steps, each increasing the level of U.S. involvement and resulting in direct and full U.S. military participation.

Following a Vietcong raid of February 6, 1965, on military barracks in Pleiku which killed nine U.S. advisers to the South Vietnamese military, Johnson ordered air strikes on four targets in North Vietnam. After a quick review by the National Security Council, the president authorized the massive bombing of North Vietnam, code-named "Operation Rolling Thunder". U.S. troop commitments to South Vietnam were then increased, an effort to protect the air bases. In time, even this "limited" role was abandoned. U.S. troops were next authorized to engage in "search and destroy" missions. From there, it was but a natural step to full U.S. military involvement. And, whereas there had been only 33,500 American troops in South Vietnam in April 1965 by mid-1968 there were over 500,000.

With the steady increase in U.S. involvement in Vietnam after 1965, a "great debate" erupted in the United States about the morality and wisdom of the administration's foreign policy. Influential critics such as Senators Wayne Morse and J. William Fulbright expressed mounting concern that the United States had unwisely intervened in a civil war which affected no vital American interests. Senator Morse, one of only two senators to vote against the Tonkin Gulf resolution, charged that Johnson's war, as it became known, was unconstitutional because Congress had never formally declared it. Beginning in 1965, a new phenomenon occurred on American college campuses—the "teach-ins." Intended to promote a debate over the wisdom and morality of U.S. military involvement in Vietnam, the teach-in movement precipitated intense opposition to Johnson's Southeast Asia policy. As American casualties soared from 2,500 in 1965 to 33,000 in 1967, and 130,000 in 1968, as television newscasts brought home to American audiences the brutality of the Vietnamese war, domestic antiwar opposition intensified. Many Americans also began to question the morality of a war in which American officers explained that villages had to be destroyed in order to be saved, in which more shells and bombs were dropped on Vietnam than on Germany and Japan combined during World War II, and in which American military power was employed against a helpless civilian population, driving five million people into makeshift refugee camps.

Yet, until the January 30, 1968, "Tet Offensive" launched by the Vietcong and the North Vietnamese against American bases and thirty-nine of the forty-four major cities in South Vietnam, the president remained firmly committed to his policy. The Tet Offensive was beaten back with heavy losses to the North Vietnamese and the Vietcong. Even so, Johnson

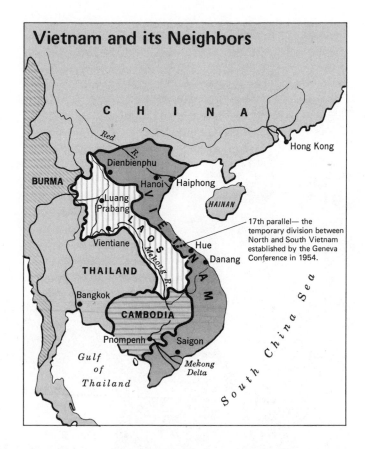

**Vietnam and its Neighbors**

C H I N A

Red R.

Dienbienphu

Hanoi  Haiphong

BURMA

Luang Prabang

HAINAN

Hong Kong

17th parallel— the temporary division between North and South Vietnam established by the Geneva Conference in 1954.

Vientiane

Hue

Danang

L A O S

V I E T N A M

Mekong R.

THAILAND

Bangkok

CAMBODIA

Pnompenh  Saigon

*Gulf of Thailand*

*Mekong Delta*

*South China Sea*

reluctantly concluded that a military victory was unattainable because of its political costs at home. The Tet Offensive had confirmed how limited was South Vietnamese and U.S. troops' control of the cities and the countryside. The impact of the North Vietnamese attack was further compounded by the request of General William Westmoreland, the U.S. commander in South Vietnam, for an additional 206,000 troops. (Such an addition would have increased the U.S. troop commitment to 750,000 and would have required mobilizing 250,000 reservists and a budget increase of $10 billion.)

Having recently suffered an embarrassing defeat in the New Hampshire primary and faced with the prospect of an even more unsettling loss in the forthcoming Wisconsin primary, President Johson suddenly accepted his advisers' recommendations to seek a negotiated settlement to the war. In a nationwide television address on March 31, 1968, he announced that he would not be a candidate for reelection and further that the United States "will confine our air and naval attacks of North Vietnam to the military targets south of the 20th parallel." Johnson simultaneously invited the North Vietnamese to peace negotiations. After considerable, often petty wran-

The war hits home (James Pickerell/Black Star)

gling, the negotiations began in Paris in May 1968. On October 31, 1968, to speed the negotiations, Johnson ordered a complete bombing halt over North Vietnam.

## THE POLITICS OF 1968

Directly and indirectly, the Vietnam War dominated the politics of 1968. A more conservative mood prevailed, impelled principally by fears of disorder. This campaign was dominated more by personality than issues—the perceived dishonesty of the president. Polls of the respected Center for Political Studies of the University of Michigan captured this popular cynicism: Whereas 62 percent of respondents had expressed a "high" degree of trust in government in 1964, that figure declined to 35 percent by 1970. "Law and order" emerged as an equally strong campaign issue, and again this debate focused on people, the Chief Justice Earl Warren and the U.S. Attorney General Ramsey Clark. The assassination in April 1968 of the civil rights leader, Martin Luther King, Jr., in Memphis had touched off deep anger in the black community, resulting in riots in over one hundred of the nation's cities. Typifying a popular attitude, Chicago's Mayor Richard Daley publicly suggested that if the police shot looters future riots might be averted. Responding to Daley's statement, Attorney General Clark sharply rebuked "loose talk of shooting looters."

Clark's statement became a prominent issue in the 1968 campaign. In his campaign for the Republican presidential nomination and later for the presidency, Richard Nixon adopted the law and order theme and assailed Clark's attorney generalship. In his August 8, 1968, acceptance speech, Nixon pledged, "If we are to restore order and respect for law in this country, there's one place we're going to begin: we're going to have a new Attorney General of the United States of America." Law and order was the "top [domestic] priority." Nixon promised to appoint conservative jurists to the Supreme Court and to curtail federal efforts at school integration. In an effective appeal to dissatisfied citizens, Nixon commended "the Forgotten Americans . . . those who do not break the law, who pay their taxes and go to work . . . people who love this country . . . cry out . . . that is enough, let's get some new leadership."

Alabama Governor George Wallace similarly, if less subtly, exploited these passions. In the aftermath of his 1963 attempt to prevent the desegregation of the University of Alabama, Wallace emerged as a symbol of southern resistance to federal integration policy. Carrying his campaign to the North in 1964, Wallace entered Democratic primaries in Wisconsin, Indiana, and Maryland, where he polled 34 percent, 30 percent, and 43 percent of the vote respectively. As the 1968 presidential candidate of the American Independent Party, Wallace exploited an aversion to the race riots and campus antiwar demonstrations of 1965 to 1968 by denouncing the elitism of liberals and the paternalism of Washington. "Liberals, intellectuals, and long hairs have run the country for too long," he charged. He would throw out "all these phonies and their briefcases," restore respect for law and order, and deal forcefully with demonstrators: "If any demonstrator ever lays down in front of my car, it'll be the last car he'll ever lay down in front of."

New Deal principles were obliquely challenged during the 1968 campaign. And the Democrats were badly divided over Lyndon Johnson's conduct of the Vietnam War. Announcing his candidacy for the Democratic presidential nomination on November 30, 1967, the relatively unknown liberal Democratic senator, Eugene McCarthy, appealed to widespread resentment over the war and the centralized presidency, as did a belated entrant (March 16, 1968) into the race for the Democratic nomination, the then New York Senator Robert Kennedy who also capitalized on antipathy to Johnson.

Insofar as Robert Kennedy's and Eugene McCarthy's campaigns had focused on resentment over Johnson's presidency, Lyndon Johnson's March 31 announcement that he would neither seek nor accept the Democratic nomination altered the resultant campaign. On April 27, Vice President Hubert Humphrey announced his candidacy in an appeal to the Democratic organizational leadership and centrist wing. Not entering the primaries, Humphrey concentrated on wooing the party's leaders. His principal strength derived from being the candidate of the Democratic middle and from tapping deep emotional and popular resentment over the life-style and antiwar dissent of college students, Senator McCarthy's principal source of support. Robert Kennedy's assassination on June 5, on the eve of his success in the California primary, removed Humphrey's real opponent for the nomination. For unlike Kennedy, McCarthy had little appeal to party professionals, labor unions, and white ethnics (traditional constituencies for liberal candidates).

Radicalized by the Vietnam War, thousands of antiwar youths converged on Chicago to demonstrate their opposition to the war and to disrupt the Democratic National Convention. To insure a minimum of disorder, convention organizers turned the convention site area into a fortress, mobilized federal troops, and devised elaborate security plans including electronic surveillance by the army's intelligence division. Under Mayor Daley's direction, the Chicago police confronted the young demonstrators with force, which produced what a subsequent commission study concluded was "a police riot."

Repression was not confined to controlling dissenters outside the convention hall. The Democratic leadership employed similar tactics to effect Humphrey's nomination. These efforts bitterly divided the party which, ironically, for many dissatisfied voters became a symbol of the danger of permissiveness and for still others the danger of repression. Starting his campaign for the presidency late, Humphrey was able to patch together the divided party. He diluted Wallace's appeal to ethnics and unionists by stressing economic issues and belatedly adopted a more moderate position on the Vietnam War. President Johnson's last-minute announcement of a bombing pause in late October 1968 further aided Humphrey's candidacy, by muting the bombing issue and offering the prospect of the imminent end to the unpopular Vietnam War. Nonetheless, Nixon eked out a narrow victory, with Wallace cutting heavily into traditional southern support and northern urban ethnic support for the Democratic ticket.

The Wallace and Nixon campaigns did not simply appeal to racial prejudice. Both exploited middle- and lower-class resentment over the consequences of the liberal reforms and social controls of the 1960s. Both Wallace and Nixon repudiated the Great Society's premises and the making of national social policy by academic experts. In the final analysis, Nixon and Wallace appealed not to common purpose but to common resentment. If Nixon's 1968 strategy sought to build a new political alignment, his essentially negative campaign meant that such an alignment could only be fragile. Not philosophical conservatism, but mass antipathy to the Johnson presidency had produced Nixon's 1968 success.

By the end of 1968, the Vietnamese War had caused tragedy for all involved. For the North and the South Vietnamese, the use of American military power spelled disaster. Countless villages had been destroyed, the land had been ravished, and millions of lives (both civilian and military) had been lost. For Americans, the Vietnamese War meant domestic discord, civic disorder, and a loss of trust in the national leadership. For many young adult male Americans, it meant the loss of life, limb, or sanity on a Vietnamese battlefield, exile abroad as "draft dodgers" or military deserters, and unease at home in a society that had become foreign to them. Even many war veterans returned not as heroes but as forgotten soldiers; for them the costs and sacrifices seemed pointless. For Lyndon Johnson, Vietnam dissolved his dreams of recognition as a great reform president, a true successor to Franklin D. Roosevelt. The war drove Lyndon Johnson from office almost in disgrace, an incumbent president fearful of attending his party's national convention lest he be physically or verbally abused. Thus the war in Vietnam had become a tragedy without end, and thus it would remain for the first four years of Richard Nixon's administration.

At the time he announced his decision not to seek reelection, Lyndon Johnson's popularity had declined to its lowest point. According to a Gallup poll, only 36 percent of Americans approved Johnson's leadership, a level of unpopularity exceeded only by Harry Truman's 1951 low of 23 percent. Leaving office a repudiated president, his politics of consensus shattered, Johnson was really no weaker a president than the even less-popular Truman. Under Lyndon Johnson, executive powers had been extended and an even more centralized presidency had been forged. But the Vietnam War had precipitated a critique of both national security appeals and presidential powers. Eugene McCarthy's 1968 presidential candidacy and the 1966 Senate Foreign Relations Committee hearings on the administration's Vietnam War policy thus foreshadowed liberal responses to the Nixon administration during the 1970s.

Johnson bequeathed to Richard Nixon an ambiguous and contradictory legacy. On the one hand, he left a strengthened presidency and a more politicized intelligence community. On the other hand, the Cold War consensus dissolved, the Congress abandoned its customary deference to presidential prerogatives, and the public mood turned cynical. This ambiguous legacy shaped the politics of the Nixon presidency.

# CHAPTER TEN
# RICHARD M. NIXON
# AND THE CRISIS
# OF AMERICAN POLITICS,
# 1968–1976

Richard Nixon first attained national prominence during the 1940s and 1950s as a member of the House Committee on Un-American Activities (HUAC) in 1948 and as Eisenhower's vice president. His rise to national prominence then, and later as a critic of Kennedy-Johnson foreign policies, to a great extent derived from his appeal as a fervent anti-Communist. As a candidate in 1968, Nixon in addition appealed to the law and order issue and projected the image of a moderate committed to the work ethic and to restoring respect for traditional values and patriotism.

Nixon television commercials flashed pictures of rioting cities and campuses, assailed the "permissiveness" of federal authorities, and condemned the Supreme Court and Lyndon Johnson's attorney general, Ramsey Clark. Nixon strategists taped a series of interviews with pro-Nixon panels in an effort to appeal to middle-class and middle-aged fears about crime (between the years 1960 and 1968, murders had increased by 36 percent, rapes by 65 percent, and assaults by 67 percent) and about youthful dissent. The Republican candidate pointedly contrasted the shouting of youthful protesters with "another voice, it is a quiet voice in the tumult and shouting. It is the voice of the great majority of Americans, the forgotten Americans, the nonshouters, the nondemonstrators." These "forgotten Americans," Nixon asserted, were the "good people" of America: "They're decent people. They work and they save and they pay their taxes and they care." "When 43 percent of the American people are afraid to walk in the streets of their cities," Nixon charged in another speech, "it's time for a housecleaning, a new attorney general, and a new policy to establish freedom from fear in this country. Let me tell you: I am an expert in this field. I pledge to you I'll take personal charge." He would restore the "first civil right of every American, the right to be free from domestic violence." Shifting to the attack, Nixon blamed the Democrats for : "the longest war in American history, the highest taxes in American history, the worst crime rate in American history, the highest increases in prices in a generation, the lowest respect for America we have ever had."

This strategy succeeded in insuring Nixon's slim electoral victory of 1968: 43.4 percent of the popular vote and 301 electoral college votes to Humphrey's 42.7 percent popular and 191 electoral votes and Wallace's 13.5 percent popular and 46 electoral votes. Nixon narrowly defeated Humphrey by 500,000 votes (31,275,165 to 31,785,480).[1]

Nixon's 1968 victory did not, however, constitute a conservative mandate. The Democrats, for one, retained control of both the Senate (57–43) and the House (244–191)—having lost 7 Senate seats but only 4 House seats. Nixon, moreover, had no specific program which he was prepared to implement in 1969—no plan to end the Vietnam War, to use tax incentives as a substitute for social welfare spending, and no specific economic, environmental, energy, or civil rights recommendations. Foreign affairs was his principal concern, to which he devoted his energies and talents throughout his presidency. In a November 1967 speech he had expressed these priorities: "All you need is a competent Cabinet to run the country at home. You need a President for foreign policy; no Secretary of State is really important, the President makes foreign policy."

Not resigned to a caretaker role, the new president intended to shape national policy. Suspicious of the federal bureaucracy and committed to streamlining decision making, Nixon favored administrative reforms to further centralize power in the White House. Thus, in March 1970 he announced a major reorganization plan creating the Office of Management and Budget. At the same time, Nixon's suspicions of the Washington press corps contributed to the infrequency of his press conferences. (Nixon held only 31 press conferences during his first term, an annual average of 7.7, in contrast to Kennedy's 64 and 21 per year average, Johnson's 126 and 25 per year average, Eisenhower's 193 and 24 per year average, and Truman's 322 and 40 per year average.)

---

[1] Nixon and Wallace, however, ran similar campaigns and together received 57 percent of the popular vote. Not that the Wallace vote would have gone entirely to Nixon; many blue-collar workers identified with Wallace's racial views and with liberal economic policies.

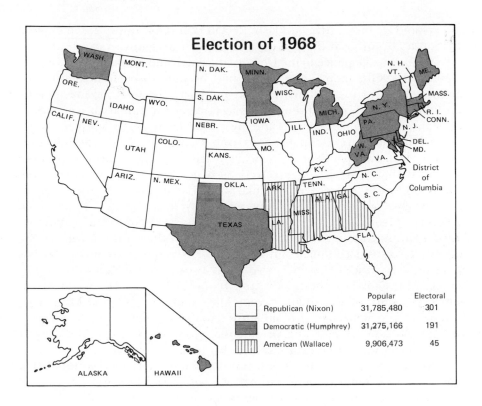

## Election of 1968

|  | | Popular | Electoral |
|---|---|---|---|
| ☐ | Republican (Nixon) | 31,785,480 | 301 |
| ■ | Democratic (Humphrey) | 31,275,166 | 191 |
| ⫴ | American (Wallace) | 9,906,473 | 45 |

ALASKA        HAWAII

## THE POLITICS OF IMAGE, RACE,
## AND REPRESSION

Nixon had won the presidency in 1968 by successfully projecting the image
of a decisive leader committed to reordering national policy. His intent to
lead further diminished the role of the Cabinet and concomitantly enhanced
the authority of the White House (National Security Adviser Henry Kissinger in the foreign policy area and White House Chief of Staff H. R.
Haldeman in the domestic policy area). Nixon's Cabinet appointees were for
the most part bland, undistinguished personalities: Melvin Laird as secretary of defense, William Rogers as secretary of state, and John Mitchell as
attorney general (although Mitchell's role as Nixon's 1968 campaign manager threatened to politicize the Department of Justice). Chief of Staff
Haldeman tightly controlled access to the president and forged a hierarchical, disciplined staff; Kissinger did the same in the foreign policy area.

A realignment of national politics seemed opportune. The Vietnam
War and the urban race riots of the 1960s had dissolved the liberal consensus

and created a conservative backlash. Recent economic and social changes in the South also offered the prospect of Republican gains.

Southern allegiance to the Democratic party had weakened during the 1950s and 1960s; many southerners had become disenchanted with the liberal policies of the national Democratic party. Democratic presidential candidates had found that their gains in northern urban areas were counterbalanced by the defection of the once-solid Democratic South.

In the 1968 presidential contest, only George Wallace's candidacy on the American Independent Party ticket averted a Republican sweep of the South. In that year, Nixon received 34.6 percent of the southern vote (carrying Florida, Tennessee, Virginia, South Carolina, and North Carolina) while Wallace polled 34.4 percent (winning the electoral votes of Louisiana, Alabama, Mississippi, Georgia, and Arkansas). Democratic candidate Hubert Humphrey, in contrast, won 31 percent of the southern vote, carrying only Texas and leading in only 237 of the 1,105 southern counties (all but 83 of these counties being in Texas). Fully two-thirds of Humphrey's percentage of the total southern vote came from blacks. By 1972, when Nixon won every state of the union except Massachusetts (and the District of Columbia), the South had virtually shifted to the national Republican party. In that election, Democratic presidential nominee George McGovern's southern vote was 10 percent less than his national average.

Republican gains in the South resulted from the related issues of civil rights, internal security, and national defense. Anti-Communist appeals extended to identifying the civil rights movement as subversive. The increase in federal defense spending, from $51 billion in 1951 to $85 billion by 1973, had altered the South's economy, given the large number of military bases located in the South and of southern firms receiving defense contracts. National security and economic advantage had combined with unabashed patriotism to move southern politics to the right. By the end of the 1960s, white southerners were more attuned to the militant anti-Communism of the Republican party's conservative wing than to the liberal policies of the national Democratic party.

The resultant Republican gains were not confined to presidential contests. Between 1955 and 1970, Republicans captured 6 of the 22 southern senators and 27 of the 109 southern representatives. In addition, southern Democratic congressmen aligned increasingly with the majority of Republicans on major foreign and domestic policy issues. Thus, whereas as recently as 1953 and 1954 not a single House Democrat had voted as often with Republican as with Democratic majorities, by 1967 and 1968 53 did (all but one coming from southern and border states).

Because he was cognizant of the slimness of his 1968 victory, Nixon almost immediately began to plan for reelection in 1972. Part of this involved a strategy to win over the Wallace constituency. Thus, Nixon replaced retiring Supreme Court Chief Justice Earl Warren, on May 21, 1969, with federal judge Warren Burger. Then, on August 18, 1969, he nominated another conservative jurist, Clement Haynsworth, Jr., a South Carolina federal judge, to replace Abe Fortas. Disturbed by Haynsworth's civil rights and labor decisions on the lower court, northern civil rights advocates and labor union officials lobbied to defeat his confirmation. They succeeded as the Senate rejected the nomination by a vote of 55–45 on November 21, 1969. Following the defeat of the Haynsworth nomination, on January 19, 1970, Nixon submitted the name of G. Harrold Carswell, a Florida Court of Appeals judge, for Senate confirmation. The Senate again rejected this nomination on April 8, 1970, by the closer vote of 51–45. Central to this decision were Carswell's undistinguished legal and judicial record, questions about his competence, and revelations of his earlier segregationist views. Lamenting that no southern federal judge could be confirmed who believed in the "strict construction of the Constitution," on April 14, 1970, Nixon nominated and the Senate later confirmed another conservative jurist, Harry Blackmun of Minnesota.

At the same time, the administration publicly opposed extending the Voting Rights Act of 1965, and delayed enforcement of a 1969 desegregation deadline. It halfheartedly implemented recently enacted civil rights legislation (leading many career lawyers in the Department of Justice and the chairman of the Equal Employment Opportunity Commission, Clifford Alexander, to resign); petitioned a federal court to postpone the scheduled date for desegregating thirty-three Mississippi school districts. The administration also publicly opposed court orders for busing pupils to integrate northern and southern public school systems, recommended reductions of $4 million in enforcement programs for fair housing, and supported "no-knock" and preventive detention legislation to curb crime in the District of Columbia.

In the 1970 congressional elections, President Nixon and Vice President Spiro Agnew had undertaken an extensive, well-publicized speaking campaign which hit hard on the themes of student protest and law and order. White House personnel funneled millions of dollars to key Republican Senate and House candidates. The Nixon White House hoped once again to exploit free-floating popular fears rather than have the campaign focus on its conservative socioeconomic policies. This is highlighted by Vice President Agnew's September 10, 1970, statement to reporters: "One of the principal issues is whether policies of the United States are going to be made by elected officials or in the streets." In a speech in Phoenix, Arizona, Nixon characterized antiwar demonstrators as a "band of violent thugs." Yet this strategy failed to elect conservatives and gain Republican control of the Senate. The Democrats responded effectively to the Nixon-Agnew strategy, which Senator Edmund Muskie, in an eloquent election-eve speech, labeled a "politics of fear." The Democrats increased their House majority by nine (255–179) and they lost only two Senate seats (55–45). Many vulnerable

Democratic senators, who had won elections in the 1958 and 1964 contests, were reelected and the Democrats gained eleven governorships, reversing the Republican margin of 32–18 to a Democratic majority of 29–21.

## DOMESTIC PRIORITIES
## AND THE ECONOMY

Throughout his presidency, the state of the economy constituted one of Nixon's more troublesome domestic problems. Between 1969 and 1973, the cumulative impact of the Johnson administration's defense expenditures, the Nixon administration's reliance on costly bombing to fight the Indochina War, and the steady rise in the nation's balance-of-payments deficit generated inflation. To reduce the federal deficit, which had increased by over $73 billion, nondefense expenditures were cut in 1970 which in turn fostered unemployment. The administration's reduced domestic expenditures, however, neither slowed inflation nor ended federal budget deficits. By 1971, the rate of unemployment had risen to 6 percent (from 3.3 percent at the end of 1968) and inflation remained high (5.5 percent in 1970, and a 14.5 percent increase between January 1969 and August 1971). An economic recession and loss of anticipated tax revenues produced a projected federal budget deficit for 1971 of $23.2 billion.

Thus, in August 1971 President Nixon announced a ninety-day freeze on wages, prices, and rents; tax cuts for business; and a 10-percent surcharge on imports. The nation's balance of payments improved, inflation temporarily eased, and the recession ended. Then, in November the president introduced a new antiinflation program. In place of the rigid freeze, the president substituted ceilings on wages (5.5 percent) and prices (2.5 percent) but no controls on profits or dividends. To improve the nation's foreign trade position, he devalued the dollar and floated U.S. currency in international markets. As a result, by the first quarter of 1972 industrial production exceeded that of the previous year by 5.3 percent and the nation's leading corporations reported profits 11.7 percent higher than the previous year. Pleased by the economic recovery, the administration shifted abruptly again and in late 1972 abandoned mandatory controls entirely for a program of recommended guidelines and supervised wages and prices.

A policy of selective controls, then abrupt reversal to a policy of voluntarism, had mixed results. The economy suffered a series of setbacks including the steady decline of the dollar on the foreign monetary market, a worsened balance-of-trade deficit wherein imports exceeded exports for the first time since 1893, a balance-of-payments deficit of $29.6 billion, an 8.8 percent rise in the Consumer Price Index, and a housewife-led consumer boycott against rising meat and food prices. By 1973 inflation was increasing at an annual rate of 9 percent, and prices for farm products and processed food and feed had reached what would have been an equivalent annual rate of 43 percent. The Nixon administration responded in June 1973 by freezing food prices for sixty days at the levels of the week of June 1–8 and announcing the possible reinstatement of wage and price controls. Inflation continued unabated, becoming an even more critical issue in 1974 when it was complicated by an economic recession.

In contrast, the president's effort to alter the direction of the Supreme Court was more successful owing to the September 1971 resignations of Supreme Court Justices John Harlan and Hugo Black. Nixon's nominees, Lewis Powell and William Rehnquist, added to his 1969 court appointees, Warren Burger and Harry Blackman, created a conservative majority which marked a decided departure from the Warren Court's controversial, activist majority.

In general, Richard Nixon's domestic and foreign policies dramatized how fundamentally American conservatism had changed during the Cold War years. Between 1969 and 1974 a conservative president resorted to secret executive agreements and summit diplomacy, imposed New Deal-type controls over exports, prices, and wages, advocated a welfare reform plan (FAP) similar to the liberal's proposal of a guaranteed annual wage, further centralized power in the presidency, and authorized illegal procedures that imposed far-reaching restrictions on individual liberties. All these actions violated once-traditional conservative principles of opposition to centralized power and affirmation of the right to privacy.

Nixon's "national security" policies required an active federal spending and interventionist role. Wage-price controls were the exception—Nixon's economic policies which were otherwise consistent with traditional conservatism. Since 1969, the president sought to phase out such Great Society programs as Model Cities, the Job Corps, and the Office of Economic Opportunity; to reduce federal welfare assistance; and to protect the existing oil depletion allowance. Unable to win congressional approval for his policy goals (Congress voted to continue the Great Society programs and to reduce the oil depletion allowance from 27.5 to 22 percent), Nixon resorted to vetos and to impounding congressionally approved funds. On January 26, 1970, he successfully vetoed a Health, Education and Welfare bill which would have increased appropriations by $1.1 billion over his request. Nixon also vetoed the Hill-Burton Hospital Construction Bill, and the Housing and Urban Development (HUD) and Education appropriation bills. Congress sustained Nixon's HUD veto but overrode vetoes of Hill-Burton and Education. The president failed to secure congressional enactment of his Family Assistance Plan (FAP) to replace the existing cumbersome welfare system with one granting each family on welfare a set payment of $1,600. In 1972 he secured congressional approval for revenue sharing, distributing $30.1 billion in federal funds over a five-year period to state, city, town, and county governments. Fresh from his resounding reelection victory of 1972, in which he had denounced congressional spending policies as irresponsible and as causing inflation, Nixon claimed the right to impound congressionally appropriated funds to reduce federal spending. Nixon's authority to do so was immediately challenged. In June 1973, one federal judge characterized the president's impoundment of $6 billion in water pollution control funds as a "flagrant abuse of executive discretion and in violation of the spirit, intent, and letter" of the congressional act providing for the funding.

The core of Nixon's policy to stimulate the economy was to increase defense expenditures. This followed from the administration's general foreign policy goals. Thus, on March 14, 1969, the president requested congressional funding for an antiballistic missile system (Safeguard), to protect U.S. "land-based retaliatory forces against a direct attack by the Soviet Union." Such a system, Nixon argued, was "vital for the security and defense of the United States." Despite intensive administration lobbying, the ABM proposal encountered spirited congressional opposition. On August 6, 1969, however, the Senate narrowly defeated, 51–49, the liberals effort to restrict ABM funding to research and development. Three months later, the House overwhelmingly approved the Safeguard system.

## A NEW PHASE IN THE COLD WAR: FROM CONTAINMENT TO BALANCE OF POWER

Despite having built his political reputation as a fervent anti-Communist, during his presidency Richard Nixon paradoxically tempered the Cold War policy of containment, launched a new era of detente with the Communist world, and proved remarkably flexible in foreign affairs. Nixon's visit to Communist Rumania in August 1969 signaled his new approach, his willingness simultaneously to reach agreement with the Soviet Union and to exploit the nationalist tendencies of Communist states as a weapon against Soviet political and economic influence. By 1968, the bipolar U.S.-Soviet world had clearly collapsed. The widening Sino-Soviet conflict and the increasing independence of France under President Charles DeGaulle, leading to French withdrawal from NATO, disclosed the new global realities. Nor could Middle Eastern, African, Latin American, and Asian developments be understood and dealt with only in terms of U.S.-Soviet relations. Vietnam poignantly demonstrated the fallacies in orthodox versions of containment. It also shattered the Cold War consensus essential to public and congressional support for an interventionist foreign policy.

Nixon's principal foreign policy adviser, the former Harvard political scientist Henry Kissinger, challenged conventional policies and prescribed an alternative, more successful scheme to advance U.S. strategic interests. With Nixon's authorization, Kissinger built up the National Security Council

Superstars of the early seventies, Joe Namath (left) and Henry Kissinger (right) (Leo de Wys, Inc.)

as the locus for making foreign policy. Thus, William Rogers, one of Nixon's closest and oldest friends, headed the State Department from 1969 to 1973, and Washington seethed with rumors concerning his lack of influence. Missouri Senator Stuart Symington dismissed Rogers as "the laughing-stock of the cocktail circuit," because Kissinger "had become secretary of state in everything but title."

Kissinger contributed to a further decline in the influence of the State Department. Since about 1944 presidents had restricted the State Department to administering foreign policy. The creation of the National Security Council and the Central Intelligence Agency in 1947 hastened this tendency as presidents increasingly relied on these agencies to gather information, assess policy options, and conduct covert operations.

Nixon only accelerated this centralizing trend. In November 1971, he created the National Security Council Intelligence Committee as part of a far-reaching reorganization of the intelligence community. The objective of this reorganization was to make the intelligence community more responsive to the needs of the White House. By giving policy guidance to the intelligence agencies, the committee could insure their responsiveness to the president's will. In February 1970, moreover, Nixon issued NSCM (National Security Council Memorandum) 40 creating the so-called 40 Committee to review and approve all major, politically sensitive CIA operations. The review procedure was made flexible to provide presidential "deniability" should a particularly sensitive operation become publicly compromised. (The CIA involvement in the Chilean military coup, discussed later in this chapter, for example, was not formally brought before the 40 Committee.)

To retain the foreign policy initiative, Nixon made annual public reports on the state of foreign affairs. His first report, in February 1970, called for a "lowered profile" for the United States in world affairs, with greater emphasis on self-help and partnership with other nations in coping with world crises. But Nixon had not renounced an active international role. Indeed, in a June 4, 1969, address at the Air Force Academy, he counseled the American public not to relapse into isolationism. Such would "be disastrous for our nation and the world . . . America has a vital interest in world stability and no other nation can uphold that interest for us." Thus at the same time that Nixon suggested curtailing overseas U.S. commitments, he remained committed to the concept of globalism.

Subsequently, in an August 1969 press conference on Guam during an Asian tour, the president proclaimed a "Nixon Doctrine" for that area, and presumably for the world. The United States stood ready to meet Communist attacks on any area deemed vital to American security. For other kinds of aggression, such as subversion or border clashes, the United States would furnish economic aid and moral support but the countries directly involved would bear the main burden: "Asian hands must shape the Asian future."

## THE GREAT TRIUMPH:
## REVERSAL OF U.S. CHINA
## POLICY AND DETENTE
## WITH THE SOVIET UNION

In 1971 and 1972 Nixon successfully pursued detente with the two great Communist powers, the People's Republic of China and the Soviet Union. The famous "ping-pong gambit" of April 1971, when the People's Republic of China invited and royally received an American table tennis team then on tour in Japan, opened the way for a Sino-U.S. rapprochement. Capitalizing on this opportunity, Henry Kissinger secretly flew to Peking, and then on July 15, 1971, President Nixon announced his own forthcoming visit to China "to seek the normalization of relations" between the United States and Communist China. Secretary of State William Rogers followed this reversal of what had since 1949 been an inflexible policy toward China by announcing on August 2, 1971, that the United States supported the admission of the

People's Republic of China to the United Nations while retaining Taiwan's right to a seat. The People's Republic, however, refused to join the United Nations unless the Chinese Nationalist government in Formosa was unseated. Over strenuous U.S. objections, in October 1971, the United Nations General Assembly voted first to expel Taiwan, 59–55, and then to seat the Peking government, 76–32.

Kissinger's balance-of-power theories underpinned the Nixon administration's rapprochement with the People's Republic of China. An improvement in Sino-American relations, he contended, would constrain Soviet influence in Asia, and throughout the world. It might also offer the prospect for a way out of the Vietnam quagmire. Similar considerations explained Peking's overtures to the United States. Fearful of the Soviet Union, whose troops were massed along the Chinese borders, Peking consciously wooed the United States. Chinese interests could be furthered by rapprochement with the United States by providing a counterbalance to the Soviet Union.

Nixon's China trip took place on February 22, 1972. For the first time since ex-President Grant had been there in 1879, an American chief executive visited China, a country with which his government had had no official relations for a quarter of a century. During his well-publicized visit, which included a tour of the Forbidden City in Peking and the Great Wall (hundreds of journalists accompanied the President and the major networks provided full television coverage), Nixon held lengthy talks with Mao Tsetung, Chou En-lai, and other Chinese leaders. The meetings produced a fifteen-hundred-word communique which, in marked contrast to the usual diplomatic procedure, frankly presented each side's views. The United States announced its desire to reduce world tensions and promote human freedom; China repledged its faith in the liberation of oppressed peoples and the "inevitable" proletarian revolution as the "irresistible trend of history." Despite such rhetorical flourishes, both powers pledged to move toward normalizing their mutual relations, reiterated their intentions to rescue the world from the dangers of international warfare, and rejected any intent to negotiate in behalf of any third party or to aid each other in any threatening moves aimed against a third party. The two governments also agreed to improve relations through exchanges of scientists, artists, journalists, and athletes. The Taiwan issue was evaded rather than resolved. The final communique acknowledged "that all Chinese on either side of the Taiwan Strait maintain there is but one China and that Taiwan is part of China." Despite this ambiguous statement, President Nixon conceded the "ultimate objective" to withdraw "all United States forces and military installation from Taiwan" without setting a specific timetable. Formal diplomatic relations were not then established. One year later, however, in the spring of 1973, the two nations announced an "informal" exchange of diplomatic missions.

In June 1972 President Nixon followed his triumphal visit to China with an equally productive visit to the Soviet Union. Both well-publicized events heralded the easing of the Cold War and continued progress toward detente among the great powers.

Since the fall of 1969, the Nixon administration had been in negotiations with the Soviet Union on limiting nuclear weapons, the so-called Strategic Arms Limitations Talks (SALT). For the next three years these talks continued, rotating between Helsinki and Vienna. Eventually Nixon and Soviet Premier Leonid Brezhnev signed a treaty in Moscow, freezing the total number of antiballistic missiles (ABM) for each nation at 200 which could be deployed in two separate systems. More substantively, Nixon and Brezhnev concluded an executive agreement, the Interim Agreement on Offensive Weapons (which was not submitted for Senate ratification) to freeze at the existing ratio each side's intercontinental ballistic missiles (ICBMs). Under this agreement, which was to last five years, both signatories agreed that compliance should be verified through telemetry measures, that these information-collection methods should not be interfered with, and

The great diplomatic turnaround, Nixon-Mao handshake (Wide World Photos)

that deliberate concealment methods should not be employed. The "limitations" on offensive weapons protected a United States advantage in the total number of warheads, 4000 at the end of 1970 compared to 1800 for the Soviets, and a Soviet lead in the size of warheads—that is, in the total megatonnage of missile warheads. Both powers retained enough nuclear weapons to destroy each other and the whole world many times over. Nixon and Brezhnev further agreed on the necessity to avoid future armed confrontations. Despite some conservative criticism, in October 1972, the Senate overwhelmingly approved the ABM treaty.

## THE VIETNAM "PEACE"

Nothing better illustrated Nixon's foreign policy aims and his independent exercise of executive power than the war in Vietnam. The president had journeyed to Peking and Moscow to establish better relations with the two major Communist powers. Yet during these same years he dispatched American bombers over Hanoi, Laos, and Cambodia, blockaded the North Vietnamese port of Haiphong, and invaded Cambodia and Laos all to contain the expansion of "international communism." Having promised Americans an era of peace and global goodwill, Nixon expanded the war in Southeast Asia and misled Congress and the American people about his administration's intentions.

The Cambodian and Laotian invasions of 1970 and 1971 implemented the administration's general policy of "Vietnamization"—a policy which sought to reduce U.S. troop commitments while the South Vietnamese assumed the military burden. On the one hand, U.S. troops were steadily withdrawn from South Vietnam beginning with the president's March 1969 announcement of a 25,000 troop withdrawal—reaching 115,000 by the end of 1969 with gradual withdrawals thereafter. On the other hand, in 1969 North Vietnamese supply lines in Cambodia were bombed and bombing raids in North Vietnam and Laos were intensified. Viewing Cambodian Premier Norodom Sihanouk's attempt to preserve Cambodian neutrality as an obstacle to the success of its policy of Vietnamization, the Nixon administration encouraged General Lon Nol's coup of March 1, 1970, at a time when Sihanouk was absent from Cambodia. When the North Vietnamese retaliated by increasing their troop levels in Cambodia, Nixon announced on April 30, 1970, a joint U.S.-South Vietnamese invasion of Cambodia. Attempting to silence domestic resistance the president argued: "If when the chips are down the United States acts like a pitiful helpless giant, the forces of totalitarianism and anarchy will threaten free nations and free institutions throughout the world."

The Cambodian invasion neither insured the success of Vietnamization nor the durability of the Lon Nol government. It precipitated a bitter domestic reaction, particularly on college campuses. Student strikes erupted on 448 college campuses in May 1970. Many even closed before the completion of the semester.

Not dissuaded by violent domestic protest or the limited benefits of an expanded military action, on February 17, 1971, Nixon authorized a South Vietnamese invasion of Laos supported by U.S. air power. No match for the better disciplined North Vietnamese, the South Vietnamese troops eventually withdrew on March 24. The Laotian operation was a complete failure.

Then, when the North Vietnamese and Vietcong undertook a major drive across the demilitarized zone and into Cambodia in May 1972, Nixon retaliated by resuming intensified bombing of the North, unleashing America's strategic B-52 bombers in devastating raids on Hanoi and the seaport of Haiphong. To reduce the steady flow of arms from China and the Soviet Union, North Vietnamese ports and waterways were mined. These bombing raids had two important diplomatic consequences: first, they helped break the stalemated Paris peace talks and, second, they exposed Soviet and Chinese intentions. Detente continued; both Soviet and Chinese leaders were concerned more over their own national interests than the cause of North Vietnamese Communists.

Following secret negotiations with North Vietnamese negotiator Le Duc Tho, Kissinger announced on October 8, 1972, a breakthrough in the peace talks. North Vietnam abandoned its demand for a coalition government, instead accepting a military cease-fire without a precise political settlement. In return, the United States agreed to withdraw its troops and to allow more than 100,000 North Vietnamese troops to remain in the South after the cease-fire. When the Paris talks subsequently bogged down because of South Vietnamese objections, Nixon personally promised continued American support of South Vietnam and again unleashed bombers over North Vietnam in the Christmas 1972 bombing raids that exceeded all previous assaults. Once again his tactics appeared to succeed—the deadlock in the Paris talks broke and a truce was signed on January 27, 1973. In effect a cease-fire, this agreement evaded all difficult political questions, guaranteeing that the political composition of Vietnam would be resolved by the Vietnamese themselves. Under the terms of the truce, Poland, Hungary, India, and Canada were to comprise a special commission to supervise a cease-fire in South Vietnam. All American troops were to be withdrawn within sixty days without a matching North Vietnamese withdrawal; both sides were to release all prisoners of war; and the International Control Commission (the four above-listed countries) would supervise the truce and the release of prisoners. Then, on August 3, 1973, Congress, having earlier repealed the Gulf of Tonkin resolution, adopted a resolution forbidding any further U.S. military activity after August 15, 1973, in, over, or off the shores of Cambodia, Laos, and North and South Vietnam.

Thus ended the longest war in American history. More than 50,000 American troops had been killed, over 300,000 had been wounded, and $150 billion had been expended in twelve years of bloody conflict. South Vietnam lost an estimated 200,000 dead and perhaps as many as 500,000 civilian casualties, and North Vietnam–Vietcong an estimated 1 million casualties. No accurate count existed of civilian casualties in the North, where American bombing had destroyed agricultural villages, industrial cities, highways, and bridges. Two peripheral areas of the Southeast Asian conflict, Laos and Cambodia, had suffered equally severe human and material losses. Indeed before peace returned, Cambodia, once the most placid and prosperous of Southeast Asian lands, had been shattered beyond recognition.

The Vietnam tragedy had not yet ended. Peace in Vietnam, Nixon and Kissinger assured the American people, satisfied U.S. objectives in Southeast Asia. American sacrifices had been worthwhile because Communist expansion had been checked, American honor had been preserved intact, and South Vietnam had survived as a free nation. To a South Vietnamese government now bereft of the American military power that for two decades had stood between it and collapse, Nixon in a secret letter of January 5, 1973, to South Vietnamese President Nguyan Van Thieu promised, "You have my assurance of continued assistance in the post-settlement period and that we will respond with full force should the settlement be violated by North Vietnam." To the North Vietnamese, the Nixon-Kissinger peace agreement vindicated the cause they had been fighting for since 1946. The removal of *all* American military forces meant that the Vietnamese could settle their own civil war. North Vietnamese leaders were certain that the collapse of the American-supported government in the South and the emergence of an independent united Vietnam under Communist control was only a matter of time. Promising all things to all people, the Nixon-Kissinger peace simply delayed a North Vietnamese–Vietcong victory.

## OTHER TROUBLED AREAS

Despite Henry Kissinger's "shuttle diplomacy," the Middle East continued to defy U.S. efforts at peace making and promoting greater stability. When Egypt's Gamal Abdel Nasser in June 1967 compelled the United Nations police force to withdraw from the region, blockading the vital Israeli port of Eilat and moving Egyptian forces closer to the Israeli frontier, he precipitated another round of war in the Middle East. On June 5, Israel struck first, before the more populous Arab nations could act. Six days later, Israeli armies had smashed both the Jordanian and Egyptian military, occupied all of the Sinai desert up to the banks of the Suez Canal, controlled the entire west bank of the Jordan River, and driven a salient force into Syrian and Lebanese territory with the seizure of the Golan Heights. The Six Days' War thus constituted an even more decisive Israeli victory and crushing humiliation for the Arabs than the 1956 war. Yet Israeli gains only increased tensions in the area and virtually ensured future military confrontation.

The Nixon administration at first pursued an "even-handed" policy in the Middle East, which effectively enabled the Israelis to enjoy the fruits of their military prowess. At the same time, the administration sought to pressure the Israelis and the Egyptians to make the concessions essential to a peace agreement. The Soviets, who ever since 1956 had been supplying the Arabs with arms and advising the Egyptian military, also reacted cautiously. The Soviets did nothing tangible to assist the Arab states to regain the territory that they had lost in 1967 on the battlefield. With Nasser's death in 1970, however, his successor, Anwar Sadat, maneuvered to reduce Egyptian reliance on the Soviet Union and in August 1972, he expelled Soviet military advisers, turning toward the United States for assistance. Syria and Iraq simultaneously made friendly overtures to the United States. A pleased Kissinger urged Israel to make concessions and thereby reduce tensions in the region. But the Israelis remained intransigent. Consequently, in October 1973, at the moment of the Jews most sacred holy day, Yom Kippur, Arab armies struck against an unprepared Israeli military. The surprise attack momentarily succeeded; but Israeli armed forces soon regrouped and halted the Arab penetration. Kissinger engaged in yet another round of shuttle diplomacy that produced yet another truce in the Arab-Israeli conflict. An enduring peace remained elusive—this time, however, the Arab states (combining economic self-interest with Arab nationalism) employed oil as a weapon in an attempt to move U.S. policy away from its commitment to Israel.

International conflict erupted in another trouble spot. In late 1971, chronic Indian-Pakistani rivalry exploded into a short war. This conflict was precipitated by mounting discontent within East Pakistan, inhabited largely by Bengalis who resented rule by the military dictatorship entrenched in West Pakistan. When the Bengali rebels proclaimed the independent state of Bangladesh and appealed to India for aid to avert defeat by West Pakistani armed forces, India responded. In the ensuing war, the Pakistani armies were decisively defeated.

Seeing a chance to outflank China, the Soviet Union provided military aid to India and also cast a veto against a United Nations motion calling for a cease-fire and mutual withdrawal. The Soviet Union thereby gained prestige and favor in India; the United States government, meanwhile, ordered the American fleet into the area as a gesture in behalf of Pakistan. The episode further strengthened Sino-American relations, since China also felt threatened by India's success and its pro-Soviet leanings.

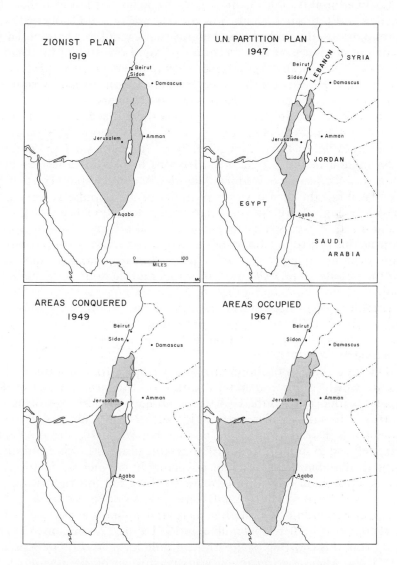

ZIONIST PLAN
1919

Beirut
Sidon
• Damascus

Jerusalem
• Amman

• Aqaba

0         100
MILES

U.N. PARTITION PLAN
1947

SYRIA
Beirut
Sidon
LEBANON
• Damascus

Jerusalem
• Amman
JORDAN

EGYPT
Aqaba

SAUDI
ARABIA

AREAS CONQUERED
1949

Beirut
Sidon
• Damascus

Jerusalem
• Amman

Aqaba

AREAS OCCUPIED
1967

Beirut
Sidon
• Damascus

Jerusalem
• Amman

• Aqaba

Israeli Expansion (Yahya Armajani, *Middle East Past and Present*, © 1970, p. 323.
Reprinted by permission of Prentice-Hall, Inc., Englewood Cliffs, N.J.)

## A NEW LATIN AMERICAN POLICY

The Nixon administration's Latin American policy was less grandiose than Kennedy's and Johnson's. In his "low profile" address of October 31, 1971, the president in effect told Latin America not to look for substantial U.S. government aid but instead to rely on increased investment by American businessmen. American corporations and financiers, in turn, preferred to invest in those Latin countries, most notably Brazil, in which repressive military governments guaranteed foreign investments.

The Nixon administration was concerned more about promoting economic gain than democracy and social reform, demonstrated poignantly by events in Chile. In 1964, the United States (through the CIA) had spent over $3 million in the presidential elections to prevent a victory by the Chilean socialist leader Salvadore Allende. A comparable effort in September 1970 failed; Allende won a plurality of the popular vote. Alarmed that Allende might fulfill his campaign pledge to nationalize foreign holdings and institute extensive economic and social reforms, Nixon approved appropriations of $10 million, either to support a military coup to prevent Allende from assuming power or to bribe Chilean political leaders not to honor the popular vote. (Allende had won a plurality but not a majority of the popular vote, necessitating that the Chilean Congress formally elect the next president.) Kissinger starkly described the rationale for this action during a July 27, 1970, 40 Committee meeting: "I don't see why we need to stand by and watch a country go Communist due to the irresponsibility of its own people."

The long Chilean tradition of military respect for constitutional government, which the commander-in-chief of the army, General Rene Schneider, supported, led the CIA to encourage a plan by right-wing Chilean officers to kidnap Schneider. This effort had unintended results. Schneider was instead assassinated on October 22, 1970, and the Chilean military refused to support a coup. The Nixon administration continued its attempt to destabilize the Allende government by increasing social and economic opposition, subsidizing, through the CIA, the right-wing press and a truckers' strike. The United States also stopped economic aid and blocked foreign credit to Chile but increased military assistance to Chile from $800,000 in 1970, to $5.7 million in 1971 and $12.3 million in 1972. In the long run, this courting of the Chilean military paid off. On September 11, 1973, the Allende government was overthrown by right-wing Chilean army officers led by General Augustin Pinochet (President Allende was murdered during the coup) and replaced with a brutal dictatorship. Promptly recognizing the new government, the United States also resumed substantial government and private economic aid.

## THE 1972 CAMPAIGN
## AND THE WATERGATE AFFAIR

The closeness of the 1968 presidential contest and the failure of the law and order strategy during the 1970 congressional elections determined the strategy behind the Nixon White House's preparations for the 1972 presidential election. What eventually became known as the Watergate Affair inadvertently loomed large in this strategy.

The Watergate Affair assumed two forms. The first involved the planning and funding by campaign and security officials of the Committee to Re-elect the President (CREEP) to bug the Democratic National Committee headquarters housed in Washington's Watergate apartment complex. The second concerned the efforts of high-level White House and CREEP officials to thwart the FBI investigation into this break-in and ensure the silence of the seven indicted men. (The seven included the chief security officer of CREEP and four Cuban-Americans, who on June 17, 1972, had been apprehended in the Democratic headquarters, and the subsequently arrested former White House aides and current CREEP officials E. Howard Hunt and G. Gordon Liddy.) As part of an elaborate cover-up, those arrested were paid large sums of money; and CREEP officials and White House aides either destroyed incriminating documents, committed perjury, suborned perjury, or made false reports to the press, the FBI, and the CIA.

At first dismissed by White House press secretary Ron Zeigler as a "third-rate burglary" (a statement Zeigler later declared "inoperative"), the Watergate break-in was much more than that. Hunt's and Liddy's involvement threatened to disclose other surveillance activities which Nixon had ordered from 1969 through 1972.

In 1969 a special White House task force had been created under the direction of a former New York City policeman, John Caulfield. Subsidized with unexpended 1968 campaign funds, this White House police force surreptitiously investigated the syndicated national columnist Joseph Kraft, the roommates of Mary Jo Kopechne (an aide to Senator Edward Kennedy who drowned when the car driven by the senator plunged off a bridge on Chappaquidick Island in July 1969), and conservative and liberal congressmen. Hunt and Liddy were members of another White House police force, the so-called Plumbers Group, which in 1971 broke into the office of Dr. Lewis Fielding (the psychiatrist to Daniel Ellsberg, who had been indicted for leaking the Pentagon Papers). For this break-in, Hunt and Liddy hired some of the same Cuban-Americans who later participated in the Watergate break-in. Hunt and Liddy were involved in still other covert activities on behalf of the Nixon White House—including doctoring State Department documents to implicate President Kennedy in the assassination of South Vietnamese President Diem. In addition, White House aide John Dean, who assumed a prominent role in the cover-up, either directly knew about or participated in other questionable White House activities.

The Watergate break-in was consistent with a general program of "dirty tricks" employed by the Nixon campaign since 1970. Senator Edmund Muskie, the acknowledged front-runner for the 1972 Democratic presidential nomination, was one target of such tricks. A February 1971 Harris poll showed Muskie leading Nixon 43–40 in a trial presidential heat; by May, Muskie's lead had widened to 47–39.

Nixon campaign officials were also worried by public opinion polls demonstrating George Wallace's political appeal. Accordingly, in 1970 over $400,000 of leftover 1968 campaign funds was secretly funneled to former Alabama governor Albert Brewer, then challenging George Wallace for the Democratic gubernatorial nomination in Alabama. A defeat would have denied Wallace a base for launching another third-party presidential campaign. Failing in this, in 1972 the Nixon strategists shifted their attention to the American Independence party, and secretly funded the American Nazi party's membership drive in California. Their purpose was to reduce the American Independence party's membership and thereby deny that party a place on the California ballot in 1972. These amateurish efforts had no significant impact on the 1972 presidential race. Arthur Bremer's attempted assassination of Wallace on May 15, 1972, during the Maryland Democratic primary, in contrast, did. The attempted assassination ended any possibility that Wallace might launch another third-party campaign.

The Nixon White House's containment of the Watergate investigation in the summer of 1972 eliminated a potentially explosive political issue and permitted a campaign strategy to depict Democratic presidential candidate George McGovern as an inconsistent, incompetent, and dangerous radical. McGovern's radicalism was seemingly confirmed by his controversial stands on the Vietnam War, welfare, and tax reform. McGovern's inconsistency was suggested by his changing positions on his vice-presidential choice (dropping Senator Thomas Eagleton from the ticket when it became known he had undergone psychiatric treatment), tax program, and his postconvention efforts to repair relations with labor leaders and urban bosses.

By creating an independent committee to promote Nixon's presidential candidacy, the Committee for the Re-election of the President, Nixon strategists appealed to independents and dissatisfied Democrats. The committee's title confirmed their sense of Nixon's vulnerabilities. Nixon's Republicanism was not mentioned and support was solicited for the officeholder, not the man. (A poll taken in sixteen states the month before the 1972 election disclosed Nixon's limited popular appeal: only 34 percent of the respondents thought Nixon the more attractive personality, 26 percent chose McGovern, and 32 percent responded "neither.")

Nixon overwhelmed McGovern in the 1972 contest, receiving

45,767,218 popular and 521 electoral votes to the Democratic candidate's 28,357,668 popular and 17 electoral votes (McGovern carried only Massachusetts and the District of Columbia). This strategy of minimizing Nixon's Republicanism and conducting a campaign wholly independent of the Republican National Committee contributed to the distinctiveness of the 1972 election results: In striking contrast to comparable presidential contests (those of 1920, 1936, and 1964) in which the victorious candidate had received over 60 percent of the popular vote, the Republicans failed to win control of the Congress in 1972. Instead, the Democrats actually increased their congressional majorities by two seats in the Senate (57–43) and one in the House (256–178).

## THE POLITICS
## OF NATIONAL SECURITY
## AND AN IMPERIAL PRESIDENCY

An atmosphere of disrespect for the law pervaded the Nixon White House, a tone set by a president who held monarchical conceptions of his powers. "It is quite obvious," Nixon declared in a 1976 deposition, "that there are certain inherently governmental actions which if undertaken by the sovereign in protection of the nation's security are lawful but which if undertaken by private persons are not." Nixon aides justified "clearly illegal" activities on "national security" grounds and were confident that secrecy would foreclose public or congressional discovery. In this respect, the Nixon years constituted both the culmination and the breakdown of the Cold War consensus.

This is particularly illustrated by wiretapping policy. Wiretapping had been prohibited by Section 605 of the Federal Communications Act of 1934. This section's prohibition, the Supreme Court had ruled in 1937 and in 1939 (*Nardone* v. *U.S.*), applied to federal agents; information gained through illegal wiretapping was inadmissible as evidence in criminal proceedings. Despite the statutory prohibition and the Court's rulings, the FBI used wiretaps and bugs during so-called national security investigations. It relied on secret executive directives of 1940, 1946, and 1954, which were never subject to a formal court test.

Obliquely in *Berger* v. *New York* (1967), however, the Supreme Court ruled that, prior to installing taps, state and local officials must establish probable cause that a specific crime had been or was being committed. *Berger* thereby implied that court-approved wiretapping was constitutional. Encouraged by this signal and reacting to the rise in domestic crime and civil unrest, Congress enacted the Omnibus Crime Control and Safe Streets Act of 1968. Title III of this act authorized court-ordered wiretapping and conceded the president's undefined constitutional "national security" powers to authorize wiretapping "as he deems necessary."

The Nixon administration immediately exploited the legislative loophole. In a brief filed during the 1969 trial of the so-called Chicago Eight (radical antiwar activists indicted for crossing state lines to incite a riot at the 1968 Democratic National Convention), Attorney General John Mitchell claimed that the president could authorize warrantless wiretaps of individuals and groups who threatened the "domestic security." In an unanimous decision of June 19, 1972, (U.S. v. U.S. District Court), the Supreme Court rejected Mitchell's claim of inherent powers. The president, it ruled, could not order warrantless wiretaps during "domestic security" investigations; the president's authority in indisputable national security cases (espionage or foreign intelligence) was tacitly conceded.

Until the 1972 Supreme Court ruling, the Nixon administration had unhesitatingly used federal agencies to curb political dissent. In 1969 the Small Business Administration issued new rules for the granting of loans: Loans were denied to members of "subversive" organizations or those taking the Fifth Amendment when declining to testify about "subversive" activities. That same year the Internal Revenue Service established a special staff to target for tax investigations individuals and organizations prominent in liberal or radical political activities. Attorney General Mitchell urged the Supreme Court to reverse its requirement, under U.S. v. Alderman (1969), that illegal wiretap information must be turned over to defense attorneys. In an unprecedented effort to influence the Court, Mitchell delivered wiretap logs to the justices, hoping to convince them that the Alderman ruling, by disclosing foreign embassy wiretaps, would thereby impair the national security. Moreover, when the Congress on September 16, 1971, repealed the emergency detention title of the Internal Security Act of 1950, Mitchell agreed with FBI Director Hoover that "repeal of the Emergency Detention Act does not prohibit or limit the FBI's authority to keep and maintain . . . an administrative index." (Mitchell's ruling meant that the sole effect of Congress's prohibition was that the formerly named Security Index became renamed Administrative Index.)

Alarmed by liberal and radical criticism of the administration's foreign policy, the Nixon administration in 1969 directed the FBI to use wiretaps to uncover the source(s) of unauthorized leaks of classified information to the press. Beginning in May 1969 and extending through February 1971, the FBI tapped the residences and offices of thirteen White House and National Security Council staff members and four Washington reporters. These taps produced valuable political intelligence and were thus continued even when the source(s) of the suspected leak were not uncovered. The phones of National Security Council aides Morton Halperin and Anthony Lake, in fact, continued to be tapped after both had left government service and had joined the campaign staff of Democratic presidential aspirant Senator Edmund Muskie.

The Nixon White House consistently red-baited its foreign policy critics. Speaking on national television on November 3, 1969, the president proclaimed that "North Vietnam cannot defeat or humiliate the United States. Only Americans can do that." Because there was no real basis for linking antiwar dissent to Communist manipulation, administration officials pressured the FBI and the CIA to document foreign funding and direction of domestic dissent. Knowingly violating provisions of the National Security Act of 1947[2]that prohibited CIA internal security investigations, the CIA investigated and compiled files on thousands of American individuals and organizations. No evidence of foreign funding was uncovered. Indeed, the CIA reported in 1969 and 1970 to the Nixon White House that student-led antiwar protests were domestic in origin and nature. Simultaneously, the National Security Agency (NSA) intercepted the international telecommunications of left-wing individuals and organizations, targeted because of their prominence in the antiwar and civil rights movements. Sensitive to the adverse political consequences should its illegal activities become publicly known, NSA officials sought "to restrict the knowledge that such information is being collected and processed by the National Security Agency."

With explicit authority from high-level White House officials, White House aides Hunt and Liddy in 1971 organized a break-in to the office of Dr. Lewis Fielding, Daniel Ellsberg's California psychiatrist. (A former Defense Department employee, Ellsberg had recently been indicted for releasing the classified multivolume Pentagon study of the origins of U.S. involvement in Vietnam.) The objective of the break-in was to uncover derogatory information about Ellsberg's character. The White House also ordered the CIA to prepare a psychological profile on Ellsberg and to provide equipment to be used in the Fielding break-in. Both requests violated the 1947 ban against CIA involvement in domestic surveillance.

Nixon nonetheless remained dissatisfied with the FBI's and CIA's failure to establish the "subversive" character of the antiwar movement. Accordingly, in June 1970, he appointed a special interagency committee to ascertain the adequacy of existing investigative procedures. On the basis of this investigation, the committee recommended presidential authorization of a number of "clearly illegal" activities (known as the Huston Plan): the extensive use of wiretaps, bugs, and mail opening; recruitment of students to infiltrate campus radical organizations; and establishment of an interdepartmental agency under White House supervision to coordinate and direct the activities of the federal intelligence agencies. Nixon formally approved this plan on July 14, 1970.

FBI Director Hoover had originally opposed the proposed new inter-

[2]In a February 18, 1969, memorandum to Henry Kissinger, CIA Director Richard Helms emphasized that an accompanying report on the dissident activities of American students encompassed "an area not within the charter of this Agency, so I need not emphasize how extremely sensitive this makes this paper. Should anyone learn of its existence it would prove most embarrassing for all concerned."

agency, fearing its impact on the bureau's independence. The FBI director's concern heightened owing to the Huston Plan's authorization procedure, which would mask the president's role. Hoover feared that this would render the FBI vulnerable should its resort to the illegal techniques become publicly compromised. Whenever resorting to these techniques, Hoover accordingly advised Attorney General Mitchell, the FBI intended to create a paper record that it was complying with presidential orders. Hoover's decision would thereby have compromised Nixon's strategy of "deniability." Sensitive to this political risk, the president on July 27 recalled Huston's authorization memo.

The Nixon administration nonetheless expanded the intelligence agencies' surveillance activities and implemented later that year at least two of the Huston Plan's recommendations. In September, the FBI began recruiting college students to spy on campus and off-campus radical organizations. In December, the Intelligence Evaluation Committee was created. Housed within the Internal Security Division of the Department of Justice, this committee was assigned the task of coordinating and evaluating all information gathered by the FBI, CIA, NSA, and military intelligence concerning domestic radicalism and foreign subversion. Ironically, and despite the president's rescission of the Huston Plan, the intelligence agencies continued many, ongoing surveillance projects which they had instituted independently, some as early as 1942, and about which the president had not even been briefed in June and July 1970 (the CIA's mail intercept program, the FBI's COINTELPROs, and the NSA's international electronic surveillance program).

When approving the Huston Plan Nixon had also intended to rationalize decision making and make the intelligence agencies more responsive to White House orders. This same objective underlay another program, Inlet, formally initiated on November 26, 1969. Since at least Franklin Roosevelt's presidency, FBI officials had periodically forwarded derogatory information about radicals to the White House. This information had been submitted episodically and the timing had been dependent on the whims of the FBI director. Inlet's more formal reporting procedure instead insured a continuous and intensive flow of information to the president. Information forwarded by the FBI to the Nixon White House under Inlet also included "items with an unusual twist or concerning prominent personalities which may be of special interest to the President or the Attorney General."

Richard Nixon's expansive conceptions of presidential powers and secretive style of operation necessitated extensive surveillance. Thus, from 1969 until the May 1970 U.S. military invasion of Cambodia, the administration secretly authorized 3,630 bombing raids over Cambodia. To preserve the secrecy of these operations, reports on the U.S. bombing missions were deliberately falsified as having occurred over South Vietnam. This falsification continued until April 1971, even after the May 1970 invasion, with the administration publicly professing respect for Cambodian neutrality. Responsible State and Defense Department officials also misled congressional committees about U.S. military activities in Cambodia.

Through extensive claims to "executive privilege," the Nixon White House sought to limit Congress's and the public's access to information held by the executive branch. The president claimed the unreviewable right to prevent any White House aide from testifying before congressional committees. On March 15, 1972, he rejected the requests of two congressional committees for documents on U.S. Information Agency programs. Attorney General Richard Kleindienst arrogantly justified Nixon's policy of noncompliance during April 1973 congressional testimony. The president could prevent the testimony of *any* employee of the federal government (including, by this standard, the custodial staff of federal agencies). Should Congress object, the attorney general observed, it could either test this authority in the courts or attempt to impeach the president.

An August 1973 lower federal court ruling soon challenged Kleindienst's assertion. The court rejected President Nixon's right to an unreviewable executive privilege to refuse to turn over specified White House communications to federal prosecutors (the Oval Office tapes, discussed later in this chapter). In an unanimous 8–0 ruling on July 24, 1974, the Supreme Court in *U.S.* v. *Nixon* upheld the lower court decision. The Court refrained from delineating the limits to presidential executive privilege claims. Rejecting Nixon's sweeping claim to an absolute presidential right to determine whether information should be made public, the Court narrowly affirmed that, because essential to ascertaining the possible involvement of White House aides in illegal activities, the subpoenaed tapes must be produced.

Publication of the Pentagon Papers in 1971 had earlier precipitated a spirited public debate over executive classification policies and the wisdom of blindly acceding to presidential "national security" claims. Over 95 percent of classified documents could be declassified without adversely affecting the national security, a former military classification expert maintained during congressional testimony that same year; classification only shielded high officials from political embarrassment.

The House Committee on Freedom of Information had already initiated a review of executive classification procedures. After a two-year study, the committee recommended revising the existing classification system. Stricter legislative guidelines, the committee argued, could alone insure the proper balance between the public's right to know and the administration's claim to secrecy on national defense grounds. This confrontation sharpened as the Nixon administration attempted in 1973 to restrict the news broadcasting and political programming of the federally funded Corporation for Public Broadcasting. The administration first recommended reducing the corporation's funding and then appointed personnel less supportive of in-depth political analysis and reporting.

In combination, the Nixon administration's actions provoked the Congress to curb presidential powers and reestablish congressional oversight. In November 1973, Congress overrode Richard Nixon's veto to enact the War Powers Act of 1973. Restricting presidential war-making powers, this act required congressional approval within sixty days of any presidential decision to commit U.S. troops overseas. Earlier, in January 1971 Congress repealed the Gulf of Tonkin resolution but Nixon had ignored this attempt to restrict his administration's commitment to South Vietnam, claiming as commander-in-chief the right to conduct foreign relations. In addition, the CIA's paramilitary effort in Southeast Asia, which had steadily expanded during the 1960s, peaked in 1970 (leveling off in 1971 only because the agency's Laotian program was transferred to the Defense Department).

## EXPOSURE AND RESIGNATION

President Nixon's unprecedented authorization of illegal activities eventually destroyed his presidency. With the combination of the Vietnam War and the relaxation of Cold War tensions, Congress and the journalists had become more assertive of their traditional prerogatives. The scope of Nixon campaign officials' involvement in the planning of the Watergate break-in had inadvertently necessitated a massive cover-up effort that could not, in this altered setting, remain secret permanently. Leaks combined with the inquisitiveness of several journalists (Carl Bernstein and Bob Woodward of the *Washington Post*), a federal judge (John Sirica), and congressmen (notably Senator Sam Ervin) to expose Nixon's involvement in the post-June 1972 attempts first to contain the investigation of the Watergate break-in and then to silence the Watergate defendants.

The Woodward and Bernstein *Washington Post* stories had raised serious questions in the summer and fall of 1972 as to whether the seven indicted men had been acting alone. But, except for the *Post* and the *New York Times*, the nation's press did not cover a potentially explosive story. The cover-up was broken only with Judge Sirica's intercession during the actual trial in 1973 and his threat to hand down severe sentences. Unwilling to be sacrificed, convicted Watergate burglar James McCord, formerly employed as CREEP's security chief, wrote to the judge on March 23, 1973, charging that witnesses had committed perjury during the trial and that he and other defendants had been subject to "political pressure . . . to plead guilty and remain silent."

The month before, the Senate had created a Special Committee on Presidential Campaign Activities (the Ervin Committee) to probe the Watergate break-in and any other improprieties connected with the 1972 presidential campaign. After careful preparations, the Ervin Committee opened nationally televised hearings which lasted from May 17 through August 7, 1973, and which transformed Watergate into political dynamite. The committee's investigation conclusively established CREEP's and the Nixon White House's involvement in the Watergate cover-up, the possibility of the president's complicity, and the president's authorization of several illegal activities (the Huston Plan and White House Plumbers). The Ervin Committee's most damning discovery was that in 1971 Nixon had had installed a secret taping system in the Oval Office, which recorded conversations which could prove the president's guilt or innocence. The Oval Office tapes proved to be Nixon's undoing. His refusal on "executive privilege" grounds to release the tapes first to the Ervin Committee and then to Special Prosecutor Archibald Cox led to the first Supreme Court test of the constitutionality of Nixon's claim. (Created in May 1973, the office of special prosecutor was empowered to investigate White House involvement in the Watergate Affair—serious questions having been raised about the independence of the Justice Department.) Cox's insistence on the production of the tapes precipitated a further political crisis in October 1973 when Nixon dramatically fired the special prosecutor. (Attorney General Elliot Richardson resigned and Deputy Attorney General William Ruckelshaus was fired for refusing the president's order to dismiss Cox.) Responding partly to the public furor created by this "Saturday Night Massacre," the House Judiciary Committee considered resolutions calling for the president's impeachment and commenced impeachment hearings in February 1974.

Attempting to be thorough and fair, the Judiciary Committee proceeded deliberately. The committee did not publicly release evidence gained from its preliminary investigation until July 9 and nationally televised hearings on articles of impeachment did not begin until July 24. Because the evidence was overwhelming, on July 30 the committee approved three articles to impeach President Nixon (for involvement in the Watergate cover-up, using federal agencies for political purposes, and defying Congress by withholding evidence).

Before the full House could debate the proposed articles of impeachment, the president admitted in a nationally televised address on August 5 having withheld relevant evidence from the Judiciary Committee and the special prosecutor's office. That same day Nixon released the subpoenaed tapes of his Oval Office conversations (on July 24, 1974, the Supreme Court in *U.S.* v. *Nixon* had rejected the president's executive privilege claim). One of the released tapes of a June 23, 1972, White House meeting confirmed the president's direct participation in the Watergate cover-up. Following this revelation (the latest in a series documenting the scope of the Nixon White House's abuses of power), even diehard Nixon supporters demanded the president's resignation or impeachment. During an August 7 meeting with the president, Republican congressional leaders advised Nixon of the certainty of his impeachment. Senator Barry Goldwater bluntly conceded that, "I can only vouch for four or five Senators who would stay with you right to the end." Protesting his innocence but claiming a desire to avert a lengthy confrontation and constitutional crisis, Richard Nixon announced on August 8, 1974, his resignation as the thirty-seventh president of the United States. On August 9, Gerald Ford was sworn in as the new president. (On October 10, 1973, Spiro Agnew had been forced to resign the vice presidency after pleading no contest to an income tax evasion charge. To fill this vacancy, Ford had been confirmed vice president in November 1973.)

Ford's accession to the presidency in August 1974 ended the second[3] most serious constitutional crisis in the nation's history. Nixon's dramatic resignation had ended a steady stream of revelations dating from April 1973 about his administration's seamier activities. Nixon's resignation resolved the immediate constitutional crisis. The equally important issue of the limits to presidential powers and prerogatives had not yet been addressed—namely, whether a president had "inherent" powers to involve the nation in war, to authorize covert operations and domestic surveillance, and to withhold information from the public and the Congress. These broader questions underpinned congressional efforts during 1973 to 1976, first to curb presidential powers and then, during 1975 and 1976, to investigate federal intelligence agencies (FBI, CIA, IRS, NSA), events which dominated the brief but accidental presidency of Gerald R. Ford.

## THE FORD INTERLUDE

Having acceded to the presidency with Richard Nixon's forced resignation, Gerald R. Ford had inherited unprecedented political problems. The revelations of 1973 and 1974 had shattered public confidence in Richard Nixon's integrity and in the institution of the presidency, had increased public cynicism, and had contributed to a sharp decline in public optimism about the future (only 10 percent expressed such optimism when responding to a survey in 1975 whereas 75 percent had in 1965). At the same time, the nation experienced an economic crisis marked by high unemployment (8 percent), declining industrial productivity, and raging inflation (12 percent).

The newly inaugurated president's most pressing task was to restore public confidence in the national leadership. Yet, it appeared unlikely that Gerald Ford could do this. Consistently since 1973 he had defended Nixon's innocence and had condemned the congressional investigation of the Watergate affair as motivated by partisanship. When they confirmed him as vice president in November 1973, moreover, most congressmen believed that Ford lacked the ability and the ambition to seek the presidency. Ford's

[3]Civil War would certainly be the first!

personality and pledge to the Washington press corps on August 9, 1974, that he would conduct an "open, candid administration" initially won praise. This promise was then broken by his decision of September 8, 1974, to grant Nixon a full pardon—justified as essential "to heal the wounds throughout the United States." Bitterly denounced, Ford's pardon of a still unrepentant Nixon before completion of judicial proceedings raised question of yet another cover-up.

The combination of a declining economy and the Republicans' identification with Richard Nixon's discredited presidency produced a sweeping Democratic victory in the 1974 congressional elections. The Democrats won an additional 43 seats in the House and 3 seats in the Senate to command virtually a two-thirds majority—61–38 in the Senate and 290–145 in the House. An increasingly more cynical public insured the lowest voter turnout in more than thirty years: 38 percent of the eligible voters.

The Watergate revelations had soured the public against the "imperial presidency" and had simultaneously diminished public deference to "national security" claims. Thus, a *New York Times* story of December 22, 1974, filed by reporter Seymour Hersh, that the CIA had compiled dossiers on thousands of American citizens and organizations suspected of radical activities (in direct violation of the 1947 National Security Act's specific ban against a CIA "internal security" role) had a profound impact. Culminating a series of subsequent revelations about the intelligence agencies' activities, in February 1975 Attorney General Edward Levi admitted that former FBI Director J. Edgar Hoover had secretly retained in his private office dossiers on prominent individuals (including presidents and members of the Congress).

Ford attempted to control the furor precipitated by these revelations; on January 4, 1975, by Executive Order 11828, he appointed a presidential commission to investigate the CIA. Headed by Vice President Nelson Rockefeller and dominated by conservatives, the so-called Rockefeller Commission confined its investigation to the CIA's domestic surveillance activities. The agency's abuses, the Rockefeller Commission's June 6, 1975 report to the president emphasized, were either exceptions or the product of inadequate executive oversight. Limited reforms were needed, the commission concluded, and should be instituted by executive order.

Revelations of the scope of the intelligence agencies' abuses, however, negated Ford's attempt to restore public confidence in the intelligence community by the creation of a presidential commission. On January 21, 1975, Democratic Senator John Pastore introduced Senate Resolution 21 to create a special Senate committee empowered to investigate the CIA, the FBI, the NSA, and the Internal Revenue Service. Pastore's resolution was approved on January 27, 1975.

The newly created Senate Select Committee on Intelligence Activities (known as the Church Committee) secured access to the intelligence agencies' heretofore-closed files and began the first serious investigation ever of these agencies. A multitude of abuses were uncovered, including the CIA's planned assassinations of foreign leaders and extensive resort to covert operations; widespread FBI surveillance of radical political activities; extensive presidential use since Franklin Roosevelt of the FBI for political purposes; and the ineffectiveness of presidential oversight of the intelligence community.

The Church Committee's revelations about the scope of the intelligence agencies' abuses numbed the public and the Congress. Ironically, by the end of 1975 the Church Committee's investigation, and that of its counterpart committee in the House (created in February 1975 and headed by Otis Pike), raised a far different concern: Should the activities of the nation's "national security" agencies be publicized. This reversal in concerns was first raised by the assassination of CIA official Richard Welch in Athens, Greece, on December 23, 1975.

The White House quickly exploited this growing concern over the harmful effects of releasing sensitive intelligence data. In conjunction with congressional conservatives, the president lobbied for an end to this "self-flagellation" and for curbing the exposure of the nation's intelligence secrets. Responding to these pressures, on January 29, 1976, the House of Representatives voted, 246-124, not to release the Pike Committee's report—a vote which Senator Church aptly characterized as reflecting a greater concern for secrecy than for exposing abuses of power. Following quickly upon this vote, on February 18, 1976, by Executive Order 11905, President Ford announced a series of limited reforms of the intelligence community.

Ford's effort to limit congressional restriction on the intelligence agencies did not succeed. In April 1976 the Church Committee publicly released a series of reports detailing its findings and recommendations. These reports raised anew the abuse of power issue and, as well, whether the executive branch should be exclusively relied upon for needed reforms. Renewing their challenge to the "national security" concept, liberal senators on May 19, 1976, secured Senate approval of a resolution to establish a permanent committee with oversight and legislative authority over the intelligence community. The 1976 presidential election campaign, however, precluded congressional action on the Church Committee's specific legislative recommendations.

In November 1974, even before this reaction had set in, Congress overrode Gerald Ford's veto, of October 17, 1974, and passed a series of amendments to the Freedom of Information Act of 1966. Rejecting "national security" claims and affirming the principle of the public's right-to-know, these seventeen amendments narrowed the 1966 act's exceptions which had allowed federal agencies to withhold classified information from public release. Federal judges instead were authorized to review in camera and rule whether "national security" classified information was properly classified. The next month, to limit presidential use of the CIA to conduct covert operations, Congress approved the Hughes-Ryan Amendment to the Foreign Assistance Act of 1961. Before covert operations could be conducted, the president would first have to certify that they were in the national interest and then report all such activities to the appropriate congressional committees. In 1974, moreover, Senator Charles Mathias introduced legislation to regulate presidential powers in future national emergencies. Enacted in September 1976 after extensive hearings, the National Emergencies Act repealed many of the powers earlier granted under legislation dating from World War I, established guidelines for future use of presidential powers in emergencies, and required regular congressional review. Congress must concur within six months after the proclamation of a national emergency and the president was obligated to inform the Congress of all executive orders pertaining to presidentially proclaimed emergencies and submit semiannual reports on all incurred expenditures.

A legislative-executive confrontation also affected economic policy. Committed to reducing inflation by cutting federal spending, the Ford administration's fiscal conservatism conflicted with the goals of the liberal Democratic Congress. In his January 1975 budget message, Ford had warned that, unless limited to "sustainable levels," the "tremendous growth in our domestic assistance programs" would require "insupportably heavy" individual and corporate taxes over the next twenty years. Subsequently, Ford vetoed sixty-six different congressional bills. Because he commanded bipartisan conservative support, the president's vetoes were generally sustained.

Gerald Ford did not, moreover, depart from the main contours of Nixon's foreign policy. Kissinger remained secretary of state and sought detente with the Soviet Union and China. In November 1974, during a trip to Vladivostok, Ford and Soviet Premier Leonid Brezhnev pledged to negotiate a new ten-year strategic arms limitation agreement. Under its terms, Soviet leaders agreed in principle to limit the total number of warheads, 2400, and missiles with multiple warheads, 1320. The negotiations then stalemated over conflicting U.S. and Soviet demands for limitations on the Soviet backfire bomber and on the U.S. cruise missiles. (A formal agreement, the so-called SALT II, was not concluded until 1979.) In August 1975, Ford and Brezhnev met in Helsinki to sign a declaration on European security. Delineating existing territorial boundaries, this declaration in effect constituted U.S. ratification of postwar Soviet annexations in Eastern Europe. Later that year, in December, Ford traveled to China to meet Vice Premier Teng Hsiao Ping. No substantive issues were resolved and the trip amounted to no more than a public relations gambit to promote Ford's stature as a world statesman. The officials did not even issue a joint communique.

Because of the impact of the Watergate affair, Ford could no longer commit the United States to support the collapsing Lon Nol and Thieu governments in Cambodia and South Vietnam. In March 1975 Congress overwhelmingly rejected Ford's demands for a $222 million authorization of economic and military assistance to Cambodia. Unable to stem a Communist-led offensive, Lon Nol fled the capital city of Pnompenh on April 1, 1975, and the Communist Khmer Rouge quickly established control. Later that month, on April 10, 1975, in the midst of a North Vietnamese offensive initiated in March 1975, Ford requested $422 million in military aid to Thieu's government. Congress rebuffed this request as well. The Thieu government soon collapsed as South Vietnamese troops surrendered en masse or frantically sought to escape Saigon on helicopters sent to evacuate the remaining American personnel. On May 1 Saigon fell to the enemy. The war had ended in a victory for North Vietnam.

Congress may have limited the president's foreign policy options but room remained for unilateral presidential action.

On May 12, 1975, the new Communist Cambodian government captured the American merchant ship *Mayaguez* off its shores. Ford responded with a show of American power. He demanded the immediate release of the *Mayaguez*, warning that failure to do so "would have the most serious consequences." Rather than waiting for a negotiated solution, complicated because the United States had no diplomatic relations with the Cambodian government, on May 15 Ford authorized a marine attack on the Cambodian island of Koh Tang, where American intelligence mistakenly assumed the captured crewmen to be, and the bombing of the Cambodian mainland. The United States lost fifteen dead, three missing, and fifty wounded to rescue a smaller number of merchant sailors whom the Cambodians were already in the process of returning together with their ship. The president's decisive action was nonetheless applauded by the Congress, the nation's press, and most of the public.

The disintegration of European colonial empires in Africa and the rise of nationalism in the post–World War II years provided the immediate setting for another crisis, involving Angola. Since 1945 thirty newly independent African states had been created, the vast majority having achieved their independence without violent struggle.

Because the United States had rarely in the past acted as the imperialist in Africa, relations between the United States and these new African states were at first peaceful and friendly. The United States had provided minimal aid to the new African governments, and private U.S. economic investments in black Africa were also minimal, reducing the possibility for friction. But as part of the policy of containment, U.S. presidents had tacitly supported the former European colonial powers' efforts to uphold Western interests in Africa.

Although American interests in Africa had been limited, the Nixon administration had resisted the rising tide of militant black nationalism in southern Africa. Thus, on December 9, 1969, the president approved National Security Memorandum 39 calling for the "preservation of the American economic, scientific and strategic interests in the White states [of South Africa] and expanded opportunities for profitable trade and investment there." Having abandoned containment for a balance-of-power model in dealing with the Soviet Union and China, the Nixon administration's (and, as well, Ford's) African policy remained mired in the Cold War.

Viewing a strong Portugal as essential to its containment policy in Europe, American policy makers since the 1960s had supported Portuguese efforts to suppress anticolonial liberation movements in her Angolan colony. The Soviet Union thus had an uncontested opportunity to support Angolan anticolonialism. U.S. African policy was thrown into shambles by the unexpected overthrow of the Salazar government in Portugal on April 24, 1974, owing in part to internal opposition to the military and economic costs of sustaining Portuguese colonial holdings in Angola and Mozambique. Responding to the new Portuguese government's decision to grant independence to Angola and Mozambique, the Ford administration moved quickly to support the moderate Angolan nationalist movements led by Jonas Savimbi and Holden Roberto. This support was intended to avert a victory by the Soviet-backed MPLA under the leadership of Agostino Neto. Because of the deteriorating situation in Angola, in early 1975 Ford directed the CIA to formulate plans for paramilitary intervention, including introducing U.S. military advisers and expending the remaining $7 million in the CIA's Contingency Reserve Funds. Even this assistance proved insufficient and so in July 1975 Ford authorized another $14 million expenditure and later another $32 million.

Because the Hughes-Ryan Amendment of December 1974 required that the president report all covert operations to the Congress, CIA paramilitary operations could not be conducted without congressional concurrence. The president had to brief key congressional leaders, notably Senator Dick Clark, the chairman of the Senate Foreign Relations Subcommittee on Africa.

These briefings were vague and implied that the United States was not directly involved in Angola—military aid had alone been provided to pro-Western Angolans. Returning from an independent fact-finding trip to Africa, on December 4, 1975, Clark introduced a Senate resolution to terminate U.S. involvement in Angola. Partly to avert the possibility of another Vietnam and partly to respond to the Ford administration's misleading briefing, on December 10, 1975, the Senate approved Clark's resolution, 54–22; The House followed suit on January 22, 1976, 323–99. By February 1976, Neto's MPLA had decisively defeated the combined Roberto-Savimbi forces owing to the ban against CIA involvement, the Cuban commitment of 10,000 troops in support of the MPLA, and the MPLA's superior organization and popularity.

## THE 1976 PRESIDENTIAL CAMPAIGN

During his 1973 confirmation hearings, Ford had specifically disavowed any intention either of "seeking any public office in 1976 or accepting a draft." Despite this pledge, Ford decided to seek the Republican presidential nomination. An unelected, accidental president, he had to fight to win his party's nomination. His brief tenure as president had already raised questions about his competence (satirized by Chevy Chase in the weekly comedy program, "Saturday Night") and encouraged the conservative former California governor, Ronald Reagan, to seek the Republican presidential nomination.

In view of Ford's and Reagan's common conservatism, the resultant Republican contest did not center on ideology. Ford also responded to Reagan's challenge by moving to the right. The president dropped Nelson Rockefeller as his vice-presidential running mate (Rockefeller had been confirmed as vice president on December 19, 1974) and then by understating his commitment to detente with the Soviet Union. Despite the advantage of incumbency, Ford barely defeated Reagan, 1187–1070, to win a first-ballot victory at the August 1976 Republican National Convention.

The Reagan-Ford contest demonstrated the persistence of Cold War values. If more cynical about politicians and about Richard Nixon's integrity (a 1975 poll disclosed that 75 percent believed that the government "consistently lies to the people"), the public nonetheless remained committed to strong presidential leadership—viewing the crisis of Nixon's abusive presidency as requiring restrained, principled, and trustworthy leadership.

The Democratic primaries illuminated this facet of popular discontent. The most popular Democratic national figure, Senator Edward Kennedy, had in September 1974 removed himself from the race—citing family obligations (his son had recently lost a leg to cancer and his wife's emotional difficulties were widely known). There were numerous candidates for the Democratic presidential nomination (ranging from liberals such as Congressman Morris Udall, former Senator Fred Harris, Senators Birch Bayh and Frank Church, and California Governor Jerry Brown to conservatives such as Senator Henry Jackson and Alabama Governor George Wallace). Nonetheless, a relatively unknown, one-term governor of Georgia, James Earl (Jimmy) Carter, emerged from the primaries to capture the nomination.

Carter's appeal stemmed from his projected image of a principled, deeply religious leader having no ties to special interest groups or to the

Washington "establishment." In effect, Carter ran against Nixon's discredited presidency—and Nixon's post-Watergate image of a calculating, unprincipled politician. Carter's campaign slogans—"Why not the best?" and "I will not lie"—and pledges to provide a government that would be "decent and honest and trustworthy, a source of pride instead of shame," trim the federal bureaucracy, and make the government more responsive to the people appealed to the swelling public antipathy to "big government." At the Democratic National Convention the Carter forces avoided party conflicts, appealed to a broad range of groups but nonetheless supported a liberal platform, and chose a liberal from Minnesota, Senator Walter Mondale, as the Democratic nominee's running mate.

The 1976 election confirmed both the distinct advantages of incumbency and Carter's vulnerability. Carter had won the Democratic nomination in the early primaries when he was an unknown candidate who could both appeal as an outsider and yet avoid specific positions on contentious issues. His loss in nine of the final primaries (including New Jersey and California) suggested his weakness. Carter's commanding thirty-point lead over Ford at the end of the Democratic Convention almost evaporated as Republican strategists successfully focused the final campaign on the Democratic nominee's lack of political experience. Ford himself disdained active

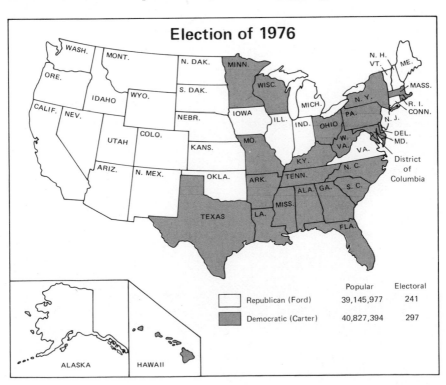

Election of 1976

| | Popular | Electoral |
|---|---|---|
| Republican (Ford) | 39,145,977 | 241 |
| Democratic (Carter) | 40,827,394 | 297 |

campaigning. Indeed, comedian Johnny Carson described the choice facing the electorate as between fear of the known (Ford) and fear of the unknown (Carter).

The result was a tight presidential race and Carter narrowly outpolled Ford in the popular (40,827,394 to 39,145,097, 49.98 percent to 47.92 percent) and electoral (297–241) votes and carried fewer total states (23–27). Carter's victory was based on his having won all the southern states except Virginia, (thereby temporarily reversing what had been a southern trend toward the Republicans), most of the liberal Northeast, a smattering of midwestern states, plus Hawaii. More specifically, Carter's principal base was the South; he captured over 90 percent of the black vote and the ten southern states plus the border states of Missouri, Kentucky, and Maryland provided 149 of his total 297 electoral votes. In contrast to the close presidential contest, the Democrats won overwhelmingly in gubernatorial and congressional races. Building upon their gains in the 1974 congressional elections, the Democrats won an additional two House seats (292–143) and retained their Senate majority (61–38). Liberal Democrats who sympathized with Carter's campaign promise to provide leadership to resolve the problems confronting American society, moreover, would dominate the new Congress.

# CHAPTER ELEVEN
# POLITICS AND DIPLOMACY IN AN ALTERED UNIVERSE, 1977 AND BEYOND

The one-term presidency of James Earl "Jimmy" Carter proved a mass of contradictions. Having reconstituted parts of the old New Deal coalition in his election victory, Carter presided over the devastation of the Democratic party. Initially committed to ending Cold War patterns of foreign policy and pursuing detente with the two major Communist nations (the Soviet Union and the People's Republic of China), Carter ended his term moving toward a new Cold War. Tolerating, at first, the United States' diminished place in the world arena, Carter left office calling for a reassertion of American power. Seeking to make the presidency a less imperial and more homely office, Carter left the American people hungering for a more commanding and decisive chief executive. Promising to curb the intelligence agencies and avert the recurrence of abuses, Carter soon called for legislation to "unleash" these agencies.

Let us see if we can decipher how and why Carter's presidency ended in dashed dreams, Republican revival, and the landslide election of Ronald Reagan.

## CARTER AND THE PRESIDENCY

Jimmy Carter entered the White House still a relative unknown to the world of Washington and most Americans. Prior to his entry into the 1976 presidential sweepstakes, he had had minimal national exposure. Never a leader within the Democratic party, Carter's sole electoral offices had been as a Georgia governor and state legislator. There he appealed to a new, postracist brand of Democratic politics in contrast to such white supremacist politicians as Lester Maddox, the former Atlanta restauranteur. Carter, the young state legislator and then governor (1971-1975), seemed to combine the vitures of old and new Souths. A self-proclaimed "born-again Christian," he personified the heritage of an evangelical, white Protestant South. An advocate of amicable and progressive race relations, he wooed the black vote. A south Georgia peanut farmer born to a family of local notables, Carter evoked images of old South rural traditions. An Annapolis graduate and nuclear engineer, he represented an emerging urban-industrial South. In short, he seemed the ideal person to restore the South to its central place in national politics.

As a presidential candidate, Carter's policies and preferences seemed much less clear than his social origins and religious beliefs. He spent much of the 1976 campaign criticizing the "politicians" in Washington, pledging to reorganize the federal bureaucracy to make it more efficient and responsive, and calling for a government "as good as the American people." In fact, he asked Americans to expect less from their leaders and to lower their expectations.

How, one might ask, would a stranger to Washington who repudiated the concept of an imperial presidency actually govern? How would a president who denigrated the "old guard" in Congress maneuver his program through the legislature?

At his inauguration Carter introduced a new-style presidency. Instead of appearing in formal attire, he wore a plain business suit. Instead of riding back down Pennsylvania Avenue to the White House in a regal limousine, he strolled casually with his family. He made a point of removing Nixon-style Praetorian Marine guards from the White House, eliminating the musical ruffles and flourishes associated with a presidential appearance, and he sold the presidential yacht. Carter also appeared in a cardigan and open-necked sport shirt for a major television address and was frequently photographed in jeans and other informal attire. The president joined in softball games with press corp and White House aides and enrolled his youngest child, Amy, in a neighborhood Washington public school. Thus did Carter engage in the symbolism of restoring the presidency to the people.

Carter's reforms were not merely symbolic. The new president pledged to restore the Cabinet to its once-traditional advisory role, in the process reducing the independence and isolation of the White House staff. In striking contrast to his immediate predecessors, Carter abandoned the claim to "inherent" presidential powers to authorize warrantless "national security" wiretaps. This decision removed the principal stumbling block to the enactment of legislation, the Foreign Intelligence Surveillance Act of 1978, requiring court approval for "foreign intelligence and counterintelligence" electronic surveillance.

Carter also used presidential power to recruit many heretofore excluded groups. No previous president appointed as many women, Afro-Americans, and Hispanic-Americans to federal office, especially the judiciary.

Yet at the administration's highest levels Carter's appointments remained quite conventional. His secretary of the treasury, W. Michael Blumenthal, was quite acceptable to Wall Street and the banking establishment; his secretary of labor, Ray Marshall, pleased the AFL-CIO hierarchs; his secretary of health, education, and welfare, Joseph Califano, gratified the social service bureaucracy; his secretary of agriculture, Robert Bergland, was satisfactory for farm interests; and his secretary of state, Cyrus R. Vance, was a key member of the post–World War II foreign-policy establishment. Even his national security adviser, Zbigniew Brzezinski, was an insider to the circles of geopolitical intellectuals and basically a Democratic party Henry Kissinger. These men, moreover, were old hands at the game of Washington politics and experienced in dealing with Congress.

But Carter himself remained a relative outsider to Washington. His White House staff appointments did little to close the distance between Carter and traditional Washington. The Georgia gang—Hamilton Jordan, Jody Powell, and Bert Lance (the Atlanta banker who was to cause Carter so much political embarrassment)—were themselves outsiders and not especially adept at congressional politics.

Thus, how the new man in the White House, lacking a clear program or a solid working relationship with Democratic party leaders, would implement his policies remained to be seen.

## THE POLITICS
## OF LOWERED EXPECTATIONS
## AND RISING RESENTMENTS

It soon became clear that, as president, Jimmy Carter did not intend to practice New Deal or New Frontier-style politics. Instead, he called for wise, efficient government management, the elimination of waste, and a balanced budget by 1980. He proposed no substantial new spending programs or major federal reform initiatives, but promised to streamline existing programs and make the "welfare state" function more smoothly. Executive departments were expected to justify their expenditures each year through a process known as "zero-based" budgeting. Carter, moreover, stressed that government could not solve all society's problems (the predominant theme of so-called neoconservative spokespeople) and hence counseled the American people to expect less from Washington.

Promising few new domestic initiatives, Carter delivered less. Not only did he lack good working relations with Democratic leaders in Congress he also had to deal with a legislature especially assertive of its rights in the wake of Vietnam and Watergate. Consequently, the administration's primary proposals to Congress for changes in federal policy either died or were emasculated. In two policy areas in particular—tax/energy and labor law reform—the president suffered bitter defeats.

During the 1976 election the AFL-CIO had supported Carter generously and strenuously. Labor expected the new president and the Democratic majority in Congress to deliver on several campaign promises. Most important to organized labor was amending federal labor law to eliminate corporate delaying tactics in National Labor Relations Board cases and to simplify NLRB union representation elections. When Carter proved unable in 1978 to quell Republican-southern Democratic resistance to labor law reform, the AFL-CIO bill went down to defeat. And, from organized labor's perspective, the president's commitment to a balanced budget and reduced inflation implied higher interest rates and greater unemployment.

Yet Carter's desire to reduce the costs of government and lower inflation conflicted with the economy's dependence on ever higher-priced imports of foreign oil. As OPEC steadily raised the price of the oil its member nations produced, the United States concurrently came to rely on the cartel for more than 50 percent of its oil. Such reliance on imported oil not only fueled inflation; it also affected the American balance of payments and placed foreign policy at the peril of OPEC.

In response, as early as 1977, Carter declared that citizens should treat the "energy crisis" as the moral equivalent of war. The president sought to encourage conservation in two ways. First, he issued an executive order setting maximum winter and minimum summer thermostat settings for all non-health-related public facilities, including restaurants and theaters. Second, in April 1977 he sent to Congress an energy plan which stressed a substantial tax on crude oil. By raising the price of petroleum products, especially gas and heating oil, the tax would compel conservation among cost-conscious consumers. The income produced by the tax could in turn be used to subsidize mass public transit (itself an energy-saving scheme) and defray partially the added energy-related expenditures of poorer consumers.

The Senate emasculated Carter's energy program. Indeed the bill, which emerged from Congress in October 1978, offered little more than symbolic concessions to the president. Congress would not take the onus for enacting a crude oil tax which would raise prices for the consumer at the fuel pump.

Carter suffered an equally embarrassing defeat in his proposals for tax reform. His initial proposal of January 1978 called for lower income taxes for the poor and the elimination of "loopholes" for the rich. The bill actually passed by the Republican-conservative Democratic coalition, however, increased Social Security taxes more than it reduced income taxes and reduced the capital gains tax, thus providing inordinate gains for the wealthy. When Democratic liberals and organized labor demanded that Carter veto the tax bill, he remained deaf to their appeals.

On the domestic front, then, Carter stumbled from defeat to defeat. His policies did nothing to restrain price rises or to allay consumer anxieties. As combating inflation became his number one priority, the president encouraged the Federal Reserve authorities to raise interest rates and he looked more benignly at rising unemployment rolls. Neither tighter money nor higher unemployment abated inflation. By the summer of 1979, gas prices were exceeding one dollar a gallon and prices for winter fuel oil threatened to do the same. When the core of Carter's energy program was finally enacted by the Congress in the spring 1980, it intensified inflation. By gradually deregulating prices on domestic oil, Carter's program pushed domestic prices up to OPEC, or world market, levels.

By 1980 Carter's economic policies had produced two twentieth-century firsts. The peacetime inflation rate reached a peak at 18 percent, as did the prime interest rate at 20 percent. The combination of record-setting price and interest rises crippled the residential construction and auto industries. In some local areas 50 percent and more of construction workers were jobless. Even the employed suffered, as higher prices and Social Security taxes reduced real income.

Although many voices began to call loudly for mandatory price and wage controls, Carter remained deaf. Instead, in the summer of 1979, he retreated to Camp David for twelve days to ponder why he had failed. Upon his return to Washington in July, he announced in a nationwide address that he had spent too little time leading the nation. To prove his new credentials as a leader, Carter summarily discharged his secretaries of treasury, HEW, commerce, and transportation, reassigned several others, and centralized more power in the White House staff. The president's precipitous dismissal of so many cabinet officers only further tarnished his reputation as a leader.

Consumer Price Indexes: 1967 to 1979 (*U.S. Statistical Abstracts,* 1979, p. 475)

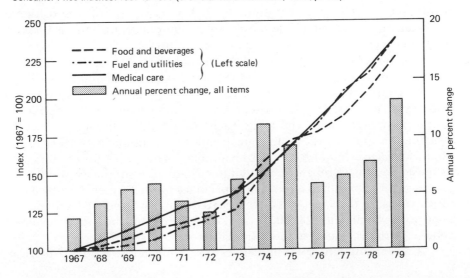

## CARTER AND THE WORLD:
## FRESH BEGINNINGS

As a candidate and then newly elected president, Carter and his advisers promised to chart a new and more enlightened course in foreign affairs. His presidency seemed to accept America's diminished power in the world and the nation's inability to shape events overseas totally to its own liking. Moreover, the administration proposed a more multilateral foreign policy based on better working relations with our European allies and Japan (the concept of trilateralism). The principles of human rights would be defended, and not just in the socialist bloc but among such American allies as South Korea, Chile, and Argentina. Finally, in a commencement address at Notre Dame University in 1978, the president declared the Cold War over and suggested that Americans no longer need have an inordinate fear of Communism.

Carter's new-look foreign policy brought several immediate triumphs. In September 1977 he completed negotiations on two Panama Canal treaties. One vested continued operation and defense of the canal in the United States until the year 2000, after which time full possession would return to Panama. The other guaranteed the canal's neutrality in peace and war. In the spring 1978, the Senate ratified the treaties by a one-vote margin and only after adding a "clarifying" amendment, which reserved to the United States the right to protect the canal, by force if necessary. Such Senate reservations notwithstanding, the treaties did improve the image of the United States in Latin America.

A year later, in December 1979, Carter established formal diplomatic relations with the People's Republic of China through an exchange of ambassadors. Leonard Woodcock, ex-president of the United Auto Workers, became the first American ambassador to mainland China since the revolution. Carter also withdrew formal recognition of the Chinese Nationalist government on Taiwan as well as renouncing the mutual defense treaty between the United States and that country.

Relations between the United States and black Africa also improved. Carter's ambassador to the United Nations, Andrew Young, a black reformer from Atlanta, developed excellent relations with delegates from third-world nations. And the Carter administration no longer tilted policy in southern Africa toward the white racist South African regime. Instead Washington joined with its European allies in a diplomatic effort to get South Africa to relinquish control of Namibia (formerly Southwest Africa) to its indigenous black majority. The United States also supported the British government's attempt to end white supremacy in the former British colony of Rhodesia. In that case Anglo-American diplomacy produced a new black majority government in 1980, headed by Robert Mugabe, which assumed control of the renamed state of Zimbabwe.

Carter's human rights initiatives also won gains. Under American pressure, the authoritarian Brazilian government lessened repression and the Argentine military rulers released some of their political prisoners, notably Jacobo Timerman, however much they continued to torture detainees. Carter even appeared to be moving toward normalizing relations with Cuba, as Castro negotiated with the United States about the freer movement of people between the two countries. Most notably in the case of Nicaragua, the administration refused to assist the dictatorial and corrupt Somoza government against the Sandinista guerillas. And when the Sandinistas triumphed in 1979 and Somoza and his followers fled the country, Carter looked benignly upon the victorious rebels whom the United States tried to encourage to pursue a middle way between Latin authoritarianism and Communist transformation.

But Carter's most important early diplomatic triumphs occurred in relations with the Soviet Union and in the Middle East. While Soviet leaders were disconcerted by the United States' evolving relationship with the People's Republic of China and Carter's allusions to Soviet repression of human rights, U.S.-Soviet nuclear arms control negotiations continued. Secretary of State Vance proved a firm advocate of detente and SALT II. At Vance's urging, SALT negotiations proceeded amicably throughout 1978. Then, on June 18, 1979, Carter and Brezhnev signed the SALT II treaty at a summit meeting in Vienna. The treaty limited the number of long-range (intercontinental) missiles in each nation's arsenal and called for an actual decrease in such weapons by 1981. The Senate never even voted to ratify the treaty, however, as the diplomatic climate chilled and the politics of 1980 intruded.

More startling and substantial was Carter's role in pressuring Egypt and Israel into a Middle East treaty. Anwar el-Sadat, the Egyptian leader, and Menachem Begin, the Israeli Prime Minister, had begun negotiations in November 1977 at Sadat's initiative. But what was referred to in Israel as the "peace process" had lost momentum by the summer of 1978. At that point, Carter invited Sadat and Begin to Camp David in September, where the president midwived the birth of peace between two formerly bitter adversaries. On March 26, 1979, in a formal ceremony in the Rose Garden at the White House, Sadat and Begin signed a treaty of peace. Israel was to withdraw from the Sinai peninsula in gradual stages until Egypt regained full possession of its former territory. In return, Egypt promised Israel the establishment of full diplomatic and trade relations. For its part, the United States pledged to assist Israel in moving strategic air bases from Sinai to Negev and to provide Egypt with advanced weapons.

Though the Israeli-Egyptian treaty reduced the threat of war between the two most efficient military machines in the Middle East, it left unresolved the sorest points in the region. Most important, the Palestinian Arabs in Gaza and the West Bank remained under Israeli control, a festering sore to the cause of Palestinian nationalism and a stimulus to PLO actions. The treaty also isolated Egypt from other Arab nations, some of which now cast warmer

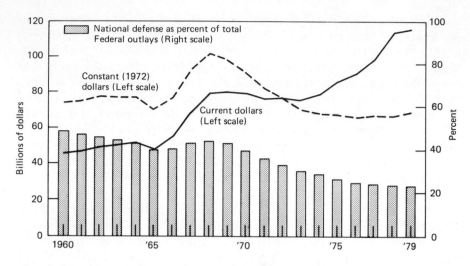

Federal Budget Outlays for National Defense: 1960 to 1979 (*U.S. Statistical Abstract,* 1979, p. 365)

glances at the Soviet Union, a possible ally in their struggle for a Palestinian state.

Even at the moment of Carter's diplomatic triumphs, however, popular doubts about American's proper role in the world emerged. Some thought that the president was too soft with the Soviet Union and too hard on America's right-wing allies. Others believed that Carter too readily tolerated a diminished world role for the United States. This dissent even surfaced within the administration. Secretary of State Vance favored detente and a lower profile overseas. National security adviser Brzezinski preferred a harder line toward the Soviets and a more assertive global role. In the last year and a half of the Carter presidency these two foreign-policy advisers fought for primacy in the White House.

## CARTER AND THE WORLD:
## CRISES, A NEW COLD WAR,
## AND PRESIDENTIAL POLITICS

The bright hopes for world peace and stability with which Carter had begun his foreign policy dissolved before he left office. Two factors undermined the initial diplomatic successes. First, the world proved as unmanageable to a noninterventionist as to an interventionist America. Second, Carter's desire to be reelected in time led him to pursue foreign policies which were calculated to prove his qualities as a decisive leader.

The first foreign crisis erupted in Teheran on November 4, 1979. Several hundred Iranian students, stirred largely by a reawakened Islamic nationalism and incensed over the shah's admission to the United States, occupied the American Embassy and held 100 people as hostages, mostly members of the American diplomatic mission. Two weeks later the students released 13 American women and blacks as a result of an initiative by PLO leader Yasir Arafat. But they continued to hold over 50 other Americans, and refused to release them for over a year.

Relations between the United States and Iran had been strained ever since the fall of the Pahlavi regime earlier in February 1979. On a visit to Iran in 1978, Carter had applauded the shah as our finest and firmest friend in the Middle East, the leader of the region's most stable government. But when a coalition of moderates, radicals, and Islamic fundamentalists toppled the shah, the United States did nothing to support its erstwhile friend and ally. Instead the Carter administration preferred quietly to encourage Western-oriented moderates among the revolutionaries, finally recognizing that the shah was despised by masses of Iranians. The United States, however, was unable to influence the dynamics of the Iranian revolution. Power flowed irresistably to the Islamic fundamentalists, whose symbolic leader was the Ayatollah Khomeini, a man who held the United States responsible for the shah's abuses and for all that was immoral in Iran. When Carter admitted an ailing shah to the United States for emergency medical care in October 1979, Iranian students seized the American Embassy. The Iranians refused to negotiate the hostages' release unless the shah was extradited to Iran to stand trial for his crimes. Neither the shah's subsequent departure first for Panama and then Egypt, nor United Nations resolutions, nor the shah's death in a Cairo hospital in June 1980 altered the captivity of the hostages.

Only a month after the seizure of the embassy in Teheran, Soviet troops invaded and occupied Afghanistan. Carter promptly labeled the Soviet invasion of that southwest Asian land the gravest threat to world peace since World War II. Some of Carter's advisers began to talk publicly about a Soviet threat to the Persian Gulf and to the vital energy resources of the Western world. Brzezinski and other administration officials referred to that part of the globe from Afghanistan on the east to the horn of Africa on the west as the "arc of crisis" in which the West would have to confront and contain a new Soviet imperialist challenge.

The Soviet invasion of Afghanistan precipitated a reversal in the administration's commitment to reforming the intelligence agencies. In his State of the Union address of January 1980 and in intensive lobbying the succeeding months, the president called for legislation to "unleash" the intelligence agencies. His recommendations included exempting intelligence agency files from the Freedom of Information Act (FOIA), repealing the Hughes-Ryan Act (requiring that all covert operations be reported to eight congressional committees), and abandoning the effort, dating from 1977, to draft legislative charters for the intelligence agencies. Although the FOIA recommendations were not voted upon, in October 1980 Congress approved the Intelligence Oversight Act of 1980. The act limited presidential reporting requirements to the House and Senate intelligence committees and required, subject to the president's constitutional powers and the need to safeguard intelligence sources and methods, that the Congress be kept "fully and currently informed of all intelligence activities."

The combination Iranian-Afghanistan crises also offered Carter an opportunity to reestablish his presidential credentials. By late 1979 Carter's political stock had fallen so low that he seemed easy prey for the Republicans in 1980. Not only that, but public opinion polls disclosed that within the Democratic party more voters preferred Senator Edward Kennedy, now a declared candidate, than Carter. Unable to reduce inflation and unemployment at home, Carter became more aggressive overseas.

In response to the Soviet invasion of Afghanistan, the president embargoed grain shipments to the Soviet Union, encouraged a boycott by the United States and its allies of the 1980 summer Olympics to be held in Moscow, and offered more arms aid to American allies in the third world. At home, he proposed substantially higher defense expenditures and the registration of American youths with the Selective Service System as a prelude to possible reinstitution of military conscription. The Soviet Union had to be shown that the United States meant business, that the Cold War climate could be refrozen as easily as it had been thawed.

Carter's firmness toward the Russians, if not the Iranians, produced temporary political gains. The president's popularity with the public rose, and he defeated Kennedy soundly in most of the early 1980 Democratic primaries. But as the Iranian hostage crisis dragged on and domestic economic news remained grim, Carter's popularity again fell. In the closing weeks of the campaign, Kennedy carried primaries in New York, New Jersey, California, and Pennsylvania, challenging anew Carter's claim to renomination.

Frustrated by his inability to secure the release of the hostages or to foreclose Kennedy's challenge, Carter acted precipitously. On April 24, 1980, he ordered a daring commando raid to rescue the hostages in Teheran. The raiders never reached their destination. Owing to mechanical and command failures, the mission had to be terminated at an isolated site in the Iranian desert—but only after the loss of eight American lives.

The abortive rescue mission had a second impact. Secretary of State Vance, who had opposed the rescue concept and who was not consulted about the mission, resigned. Vance was replaced by the popular Maine senator, Edmund Muskie. National security adviser Brzezinski, who had favored the mission, now had the dominant voice in foreign policy. This portended a harder line toward the Soviets and the real likelihood of a resumption of the Cold War.

When a domestic crisis erupted in Poland in the summer of 1980, precipitated by a workers strike in Gdansk, anxieties about a possible Soviet invasion spread. Washington delivered several stern warnings to the Russians against interference in Poland's internal affairs.

With the SALT II treaty languishing in the Senate for want of support, Soviet troops in Afghanistan, Poland driven by domestic crisis, and the Iranian hostage situation unresolved, the diplomatic scene seemed worse than at any time since the peak of the Vietnam war.

All this may have worked momentarily to Carter's advantage within the Democratic party—you don't change horses in midstream, nor a general or president in the midst of a battle. Carter did capture the Democratic nomination on the first ballot, as Kennedy's convention strategy of changing the rules to allow delegates to vote their "conscience" failed. Nonetheless, the president's leadership ability remained suspect among vast numbers of potential voters.

## THE ELECTION OF 1980

An unparalleled opportunity to gain the presidency and control of the Senate was offered to the Republicans in 1980, which they did not squander. With Carter's domestic policies a failure and his foreign policies suspect, the Republicans had good reason to expect victory in November. Carter's Gallup poll approval rating plummetted to an all-time low of 21% in July 1980—lower than Truman's 23% and Nixon's 24%. All the Republicans had to do was find the right candidate. They found him in the person of Ronald Reagan, ex-movie star, ex-liberal Democrat, ex-union president (Screen Actors Guild), General Electric Company spokesman, former governor of California (1967–1975), and from 1964 to 1980 idol of the Republican right wing and much of the party's grass roots.

Reagan had no trouble defeating his Republican primary challengers, George Bush, an ex-congressman and CIA director, and John Anderson, a Congressman from northern Illinois. The candidate effectively exploited the conservative mood of the country: opposition to federal spending as insuring inflation and support for measures to insure morality, order, and a militant foreign policy. Reagan's nomination at the Republican convention in July in Detroit was tantamount to a coronation, as idolatrous delegates enthusiastically endorsed their new leader. The Reagan forces totally dominated the convention, and the party's right wing had its way with the platform. For the first time since the Equal Rights Amendment had been placed on the political agenda, for example, the Republicans in 1980 deleted endorsement of ERA from their platform. They also adopted planks opposing abortion, advocating tax cuts, increasing defense spending and the role of the intelligence agencies, and demanding tougher policies with the Soviet Union.

Had Reagan been seen merely as an agent of the Republican right and its "Moral Majority" allies (fundamentalist Protestants committed to prayer in the public schools, antiabortion and antipornography statutes, higher defense expenditures, and a renewed Cold War), his candidacy would have been more vulnerable. But he was a more complex candidate than that. Despite an earlier career of mouthing simplistic, antigovernment platitudes either as a spokesman for General Electric or supporter of Senator Goldwater in 1964, Reagan had proved quite pragmatic as governor of California, the nation's most populous state. As governor he had signed a bill providing state funds for voluntary abortions, approved tax increases, and watched state social services expand, certainly not the actions of a right-wing ideologue.

Reagan was also a perfect candidate for the age of television. His long professional training as an actor and platform speaker prepared him to deliver his lines, however repetitious or simple, with the appearance of sincerity and originality. His ready smile and often quick wit disarmed critics of his frequently outlandish campaign pronouncements. Moreover, his vigor on the campaign trail and his Hollywood manner belied his age, 68 years old in 1980. In every sense, Reagan appeared presidential.

More important, he appealed effectively to two of Carter's basic constituencies: the white South and the blue-collar, urban ethnic worker. In the South, he could better appeal to conservative moral values and Cold War militarism and at the same time stirred memories of the good old days when the federal government did not intrude on white folks' ways and the region was free to define its own way of life. In the North, he appeared to blue-collar workers, threatened by unemployment and inflation, as someone who understood their needs, especially their traditional cultural values.

Most important, the dynamics of both domestic and foreign developments worked to Reagan's political advantage. He benefited from Carter's failures. As long as inflation raged, high unemployment persisted, Americans remained hostage in Iran, and Soviet armies threatened independent nations, Reagan's election prospects waxed. Rhetorically, he asked voters whether their standing had improved or worsened since 1976.

During the summer and fall most commentators forecast a close election. The polls confirmed impressionistic observations. Despite Carter's weaknesses, incumbency, it was thought, carried substantial political benefits. Many also believed that crises abroad worked to an incumbent's advantage. Organized labor was totally committed to Carter's reelection. Most political analysts expected the president to run well in his native South.

Two other factors imperiled Reagan's candidacy. No one knew whether the independent presidential candidate, John Anderson, who had entered the race after his defeat in the Republican primaries, would take more votes from Reagan or Carter. The other factor was Reagan's inexperience in foreign affairs; his simplistic pronouncements on foreign policy only heightened fears of having his finger on the nuclear trigger. Could an ex-actor ignorant of the world overseas and given to making dangerous statements about foreign affairs be trusted with the future of the human race? Carter and the Democrats harped on this last question.

To the benefit of Reagan, Anderson's candidacy lost momentum. Then, in a nationally televised debate with Carter only a week before the election, Reagan's smooth performance and charming manner allayed fears of his being a "Dr. Strangelove" in the White House.

Election day elated the Republicans and confirmed the Democrats' worst fears about the Carter candidacy. Reagan won 489 electoral votes to Carter's 49, 43.5 million popular votes (51%) to Carter's 34.9 million (41%). Anderson won only 5.6 million popular votes (7%). Ominously 48 percent of eligible voters did not cast ballots, the lowest voter turn-out since 1948. Though Reagan won a seeming landslide, he had gained the votes of only about 25 percent of the eligible voters.

Nevertheless the Reagan Republican victory decimated the New Deal coalition which had dominated national politics since the 1930s. Only Carter's home state, Georgia, remained in the Democratic column in the once "solid South." Reagan's triumph thus capped a Republican trend which had been building in the South since 1948. Outside the South, Carter lost blue-collar votes, Catholic votes, and more Jewish votes than any Democratic candidate since 1932. Although Anderson took away votes from Carter in many closely contested states, enabling Reagan to win with a plurality, Carter captured only the states of Minnesota, Hawaii, Maryland, Rhode Island, West Virginia, and the District of Columbia. Reagan carried every major northern industrial state. In 1980 only black Americans remained loyal to Democrats.

The Democrats, moreover, lost control of the Senate 47–53 as the Republicans gained twelve seats and lost 34 House seats and their resultant 243–192 majority in the House was imperiled by a large group of conservative Democrats who sympathized with Republican policies. Among the Democratic liberal senators who went down to defeat were George McGovern of South Dakota, Frank Church of Idaho, Birch Bayh of Indiana, Gaylord Nelson of Wisconsin, and John Culver of Iowa, losing to undistinguished right-wing Republicans.

The National Conservative Political Action Committee (NCPAC) took credit for the defeat of these liberal senators and the Democrats' other losses. NCPAC had targeted specific liberal congresspeople for defeat and circulated through papers, radio, and TV scurrilous and sometimes inaccurate charges which the victims were unable to rebut effectively. Not directly linked to the Republican party, NCPAC was not bound by federal party campaign expenditure rules and could spend money as it pleased.

The 1980 election results raised several interesting questions. Did Reagan's victory and the Republican gains mean a "critical realignment" in the two-party system as had occurred previously in the 1850s, 1890s, and

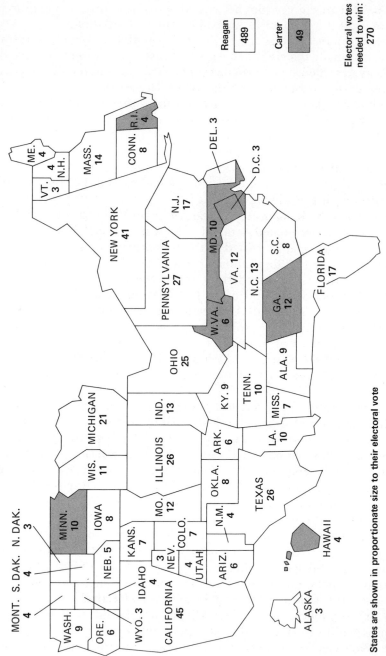

Reagan 489

Carter 49

Electoral votes
needed to win:
270

States are shown in proportionate size to their electoral vote

The Election of 1980

1930s? Did it mean that a conservative majority had succeeded the New Deal liberals? Or that the Reagan Republicans and their allies would reverse a half century of rising federal power and expanding social services? Would the new president scrap the limited reforms of the late 1970s intended to curb the intelligence agencies? The answers, to be sure, would only be revealed in the practices of the Reagan administration.

## THE REAGAN PRESIDENCY

Although only tentative conclusions can be drawn about the character and goals of a new administration after only a few months in office, certain aspects of the Reagan presidency began to take clear shape with the inauguration. For one thing, wealth, display, and pomp were no longer to be scorned. Formal attire and punctilious protocol marked the inauguration. Lavish evening wear, ostentatious displays of wealth, and a modish Hollywood style characterized the several postinaugural balls. For another, Reagan proclaimed in his inaugural address that he would be a strong president, a leader who would restore United States power at home and abroad. If his speech suggested neither New Deals nor New Frontiers, Reagan's rhetoric was reminiscent of Franklin D. Roosevelt's and John F. Kennedy's challenges to the American people.

It soon became clear how Reagan intended to reassert American power. Domestically, the administration promised to stimulate the economy by releasing the energies of private enterprise. Taxes would be cut across the board (but benefiting the wealthy the most), federal regulations would be eliminated, and federal spending would be substantially cut. The roles of the presidency and the intelligence agencies would also be strengthened. Internationally, the president called for an enormous long-term increase in defense spending ($1.5 trillion by 1986), similar contributions from American allies, and a much tougher line with the Soviets.

Reagan's cabinet appointments symbolized the new priorities. His secretary of the interior, James Watt, was a Wyoming attorney who had represented private interests eager to exploit the public domain. His secretary of energy, James Edwards, a dentist and an ex-governor of South Carolina who disputed the reality of an energy crisis, favored unregulated development of nuclear power, and looked toward elimination of his own department. His secretary of labor, Raymond Donovan, was a private construction contractor without real links to organized labor and an advocate of the elimination of several of the labor movement's most cherished federal work-safety and welfare regulations. Of such appointees, the president's critics said, Reagan had put the foxes in charge of the chicken coop. And the secretary of state, General Alexander M. Haig, former Nixon right-hand man and NATO commander, was a well-known supporter of increased military spending and a hard-line approach toward the Soviets.

From the moment he took office Reagan seemed blessed by circumstances. Even in adversity, fortune shined on the new president. On inauguration day, the Iranians released all the hostages. Although the lame-duck Carter administration had completed the negotiations which led to the release, the Reagan people could claim credit for the result. As the new administration hinted, Iran had preferred to deal with a weak Carter to a strong Reagan.

A similar good fortune blessed Reagan's energy policy. Having suggested that there was no energy shortage and the best approach was to liberate the oil companies from federal restraints, Reagan almost immediately deregulated domestic oil price controls. After an initial sharp, substantial rise in oil prices, the situation stabilized. By spring 1981, an international oil glut had developed, as production outran demand, and for the first time since 1973 prices began to fall. The Reagan administration

From the moment he took office, fortune shined on Ronald Reagan. (Bill Fitz-Patrick, The White House)

could again assume credit for the results of Carter's energy conservation program, the impact of which was finally showing.

Most of all, the administration moved quickly to implement its new economic policies. The president demanded that Republicans in Congress shelve the divisive so-called social issues championed by the Moral Majority—antiabortion, reinstituting school prayer, curbing school busing—until budget and tax bills had been enacted. For a time, the Reagan administration even abated its campaign against Soviet Communism.

During the early weeks of the Reagan presidency, it seemed that the crusade against Communism would overwhelm all other concerns. With Soviet troops still in Afghanistan, the Soviet Union threatening to invade Poland, and a civil war raging in El Salvador, Secretary of State Haig ascribed all international unrest to Soviet aggressiveness. "International terrorism," which he claimed was aided and abetted by the Soviets, and not human rights, was the world's primary problem. The administration publicly defined the conflict in El Salvador as a Cuban-Soviet intrusion into hemispheric affairs. Military aid to the ruling Salvadoran junta was increased and over fifty United States advisers were sent to train the junta's military. As this stirred congressional and popular anxieties about another Vietnam, the administration lowered its voice about El Salvador while maintaining its firm support of the junta.

Elsewhere around the globe, the administration portrayed events in terms of a bipolar U.S.-Soviet confrontation. In the Middle East, it encouraged an Israeli-Arab common front against the Soviet Union by supplying advanced arms to Saudi Arabia (including the sophisticated air defense system, AWACS) as well as to Israel and Egypt. In Africa, Reagan sought improved relations with the South African government in order to "quarantine" the southern half of that continent against Soviet penetration. The Reagan administration simultaneously moved toward closer diplomatic-military relations with two of South America's most repressive regimes, Argentina and Chile, which, according to Haig, shared a basic value with the United States, "a belief in God." As for our European allies, the administration decried tendencies toward neutrality and an overeagerness to negotiate with the Russians—signaled by the outpouring of hundreds of thousands of Europeans in antinuclear demonstrations in London, Rome, Bonn, Paris, and Amsterdam.

Reagan, however, never allowed reflexive anti-Communism to overwhelm political necessity. While decrying Soviet perfidy and immorality, in April Reagan lifted the Soviet grain embargo as he had promised farmers during the presidential campaign. While still criticizing the SALT II treaty and demanding a stronger defense, Reagan assured our European allies of his intention to pursue arms limitation negotiations with the Soviet Union.

Concomitantly, the new administration attempted to reverse the limited reforms instituted during the 1970s in the internal security area. In

December 1980, the Republican majority on the Senate Judiciary Committee revived the Internal Security Subcommittee (renaming it "Security and
Terrorism") and House Republicans lobbied for the reestablishment of the
House Committee on Un-American Activities. The president endorsed
legislation to exempt intelligence agency files from the Freedom of Information Act and to criminalize the publication and disclosure of the names of
intelligence agents, and instituted a review of existing regulations governing
intelligence activities in order ostensibly to improve antiterrorist capabilities.

Nevertheless, until the summer of 1981 the president's focus remained
on the domestic economy. It soon became clear that Reagan and his advisers,
especially the young director of the Office of Management and Budget
(OMB), David Stockman, planned to reverse fifty years of federal social
policy. The proposed Reagan budget called for sharp reductions—between
20 and 30 percent—in most discretionary welfare expenditures. It also
proposed to reduce federal influence over the spending of remaining welfare programs by combining them into block grants to the states which could
then spend the money as they preferred (the so-called new federalism).
Generally, in the first phase of the president's proposed budget costs, Social
Security and veteran's benefits were left relatively unscathed. But appropriations for the food stamp, CETA, legal aid, and other general welfare
programs were drastically cut. At the same time that the Reagan budget cut
welfare spending, it increased defense expenditures enormously, proposing
by 1984 a rise of one-third in real dollars for defense, the largest peacetime
increase in American history.

How Reagan could increase defense spending so radically, cut taxes,
and still balance the budget remained in dispute. The president said that the
solution could be found in the concept known as "supply-side economics."
What was the concept and how would its application accomplish Reagan's
economic goals?

In simplest terms supply-side economics was a reversion to the Republican policies of the 1920s. (In what proved to be an embarrassing, and
inadvertent, admission, Budget Director Stockman conceded as much in an
extended interview with a *Washington Post* reporter published in the
November 1981 *Atlantic Monthly*.) It meant that if taxes were cut for the rich
and government stimulated rather than regulated private business, the
economy would expand. As the rich lost less of their earnings to the federal
treasury, they would work longer and harder, save more, invest their surplus
productively, and hence provide employment and income for the mass of
workers. As business enterprises spent less to satisfy federal safety and
environmental regulations, they would invest more capital in productive
capacity, thus also increasing the number of jobs. The "trickle-down" theory
of economic growth (as supply-side economics was called in the 1920s) had
apparently worked well from 1921 to 1929, why not also in the 1980s? To test
the theory, Reagan at first proposed a three-year, 30 percent across the

board cut in federal income taxes and special tax benefits to spur capital investment. In the Reagan-Republican metaphor, all boats would sail on a rising economic tide.

But before Reagan could implement his economic program, in late March an attempted assassin's bullets seriously wounded the elderly president. Reagan's behavior in adversity magnified his popularity and leadership quality. As he was wheeled into the operating room, he quipped to his wife, Nancy, "I forgot to duck." That night from his hospital bed, he told aides, "On the whole, I'd rather be in Philadelphia"[1] (where the NCAA basketball championship final was being played). Reagan's recovery from the serious wounds was little short of astounding and served to confirm his good health and vigor at age 69.

Reagan left the hospital more popular than ever and committed to implementing his economic program. In May, his proposed budget sailed through the Republican-controlled Senate and in June easily passed the House when a bloc of conservative southern Democrats joined with the Republicans. Next Reagan moved to enact his tax-cut bill. Here, he had to overcome greater resistance from the Democratic majority in the House and skeptics in Wall Street who feared that substantial tax cuts combined with higher military spending would unbalance the budget and intensify inflation. Reducing the proposed tax cut to 25 percent, Reagan also responded by belittling Wall Street in populistic rhetoric and seeking, through other

Federal Budget Receipts and Outlays: 1960 to 1979 (*U.S. Statistical Abstracts,* 1979, p. 253)

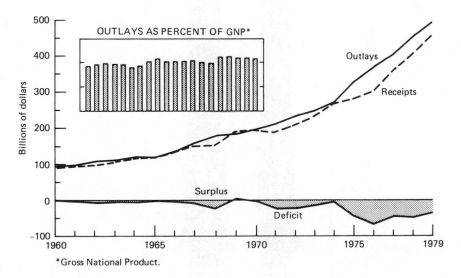

*Gross National Product.

[1]The epitaph the comedian W.C. Fields suggested for his headstone.

marginal concessions, to maintain the Republican-conservative Democratic majority in the House.

That neither the American people nor Congress were prepared to dismantle the welfare state became clear in the reaction to an administration effort to cut a variety of Social Security benefits, especially early retirement and disability income protection. The public outcry led the Senate at the end of May to defeat the Reagan proposals by a 96 to 0 vote.

Reagan's defeat on the Social Security issue suggested that the so-called

U.S. vs. Soviet Union Arsenals (*The New York Times,* June 19, 1979. © 1979 The New York Times Company. Reprinted by permission.)

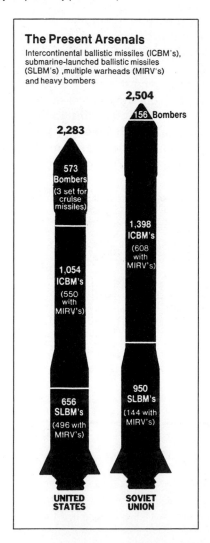

**The Present Arsenals**
Intercontinental ballistic missiles (ICBM's), submarine-launched ballistic missiles (SLBM's) ,multiple warheads (MIRV's) and heavy bombers

2,504
156 Bombers

2,283

573 Bombers
(3 set for cruise missiles)

1,398 ICBM's
(608 with MIRV's)

1,054 ICBM's
(550 with MIRV's)

950 SLBM's
(144 with MIRV's)

656 SLBM's
(496 with MIRV's)

UNITED STATES          SOVIET UNION

popular shift to the political right was as much myth as reality. The same citizens who responded to rhetorical calls to get government off their backs demanded more federal aid for health care, public transit, highways, cities, and the environment. The same people who demanded reduced government spending desired tax credits for private education and improved Social Security benefits. If the New Deal-Fair Deal-Great Society synthesis and the corporate liberal welfare state had run its course, what would replace liberal corporatism in the last two decades of the twentieth century was not yet clear. Apparently not supply-side conservatism—by the end of 1981 interest rates remained high. Wall Street stock market prices had plummeted, and the national economy was in a recession marked by an unemployment rate of 9 percent.

If America's domestic future might seem cloudy, its global prospects were yet more perilous. European leaders were unwilling to embark on a costly arms race and to renew the Cold War. In France, in June 1981 the socialist Francois Mitterand captured the presidency, the Socialist party won a majority in Parliament, and Mitterand included Communists in his Cabinet. Antinuclear and neutralist sentiment threatened to complicate European relations with the Reagan administration. Perhaps it was time for a president and a nation committed to greater military expenditures as the best means to peace to heed the warning about the nuclear arms race delivered by the great and wise diplomat-historian George Kennan in May 1981. "We have gone on piling weapon upon weapon, missile upon missile, new levels of destructiveness upon old ones. We have done this hopelessly, almost involuntarily: like the victims of some sort of hypnotism, like men in a dream, like lemmings heading for the sea."

# CHAPTER TWELVE
# WHITHER
# THE UNITED STATES:
## *American Society and the Future*

In the 1970s the United States no longer remained the world's wealthiest society. Moreover, the factors and resources that in the past had accounted for America's exceptional material wealth threatened now to undermine the United States global economic dominance. Indeed, only a quarter of a century after Henry Luce had proclaimed "The American Century," a developing international scarcity of raw materials, especially energy resources, and intensified international economic competition had dealt severe blows to the United States economy. By the mid-1970s a period of global economic contraction had set the preconditions for a domestic American crisis.

For twenty-five years after World War II the Western nations plus Japan had enjoyed a wave of economic expansion and prosperity unequalled in the history of capitalism. While Americans applauded their own "affluent society," Germans, Japanese, and Italians rebuilt their war-torn countries into productive, prosperous, and technologically advanced economies. France, too, became a "modern" industrial society, as peasant agriculture gave way to capitalist farming and small family enterprises to large corporations. Scandinavians enjoyed the highest per capita incomes and generous state welfare benefits, while the British, cursed with the slowest economic growth in the advanced industrial world, experienced enough prosperity to give rise to the slogan, "I'm all right, Jack." Even socialist states and such heretofore less-developed nations as Brazil, Mexico, Taiwan, South Korea, and Singapore shared in the global economic growth.

This wave of seemingly limitless economic expansion and prosperity ended in the 1970s. Throughout the advanced industrial world, supply outran demand, inflation replaced price stability, and mass unemployment again became a reality for millions of people. By 1980 and 1981 only Japan, among these nations, seemed able to maintain productivity and employment levels. In contrast, by the late 1970s the United States suffered from double-digit inflation, declining industrial productivity, the highest peacetime interest rates in history, and the worst unemployment since the Great Depression of the 1930s.

A society that from its founding had flourished on the unfettered exploitation of nature's bounty, in the last quarter of the twentieth century had to come to grips with limits imposed by nature on the availability of vital raw materials. A nation that customarily met the problems posed by social inequality through territorial expansion and economic growth rather than the redistribution of wealth and commodities no longer had land frontiers at home or abroad to exploit or the easy prospect of an economic pie that would be endlessly enlarged. Whether or not Americans could adjust to a new international economy in which other industrial nations competed aggressively for ever scarcer resources and in which less-developed societies used their natural resources to combat big-power domination remained problematic. Future decades would tell whether or not the United States could build a decent society for all its citizens as well as a productive economy. Yet the prospects for the American future would flow ineluctably from the heritage of the past.

## THE PERSISTENCE OF CLASS

As the nation prepared to cope with the problems of the eighties, the persistence of social class and the tensions it caused could not be evaded. Indeed, class divisions were revealed with a renewed tenacity.

The unequalled economic growth of the post–World War II decades had failed to ameliorate two faults of United States society: enormous disparities in the possession of income and wealth; and the persistence of mass poverty. The prosperity of the mid-1960s that had pulled millions of Americans above the poverty line at the end of the decade gave way to a more erratic pattern of economic growth. In 1973 the Census Bureau estimated that 24.5 million Americans lived below the officially designated poverty level, which it set at $4725 for a nonfarm family of four. More citizens now escaped poverty as a result of congressional action increasing Social Security benefits 10 percent for the elderly after January 1, 1972, than because of any basic improvement in economic conditions or in the distribution of earned income. And the payroll taxes required to finance increased Social Security payments reduced the disposable income available to the needy. Moreover, many of the fiscal and monetary policies implemented by federal, state, and local governments benefited the wealthy at the expense of the poor. A variety of tax advantages—such as capital gains write-offs, depreciation allowances, and tax and interest payment deductions—gave well-to-do citizens a government bounty that dwarfed the sums expended on welfare for the poor. The combination of a private market economy and government economic policies that favored the affluent created a system in which the rich grew richer more rapidly than the poor advanced and in which disparities in wealth widened instead of narrowing. Such a system contained within itself the seeds of discontent.

Ironically, the economic factors that had played the largest role in reducing poverty during the mid-1960s in the 1970s further strained the United States economy. The economic boom and prosperity fueled by the war in Vietnam set in motion a wave of uncheckable price inflation. Because, among other reasons, the federal government refused to raise taxes yet continued to spend beyond its income, the value of the dollar crumbled at home and abroad. By the early 1970s, despite a variety of Nixonian economic "game plans" (which included direct price and wage controls), price rises, especially for foodstuffs, outran wage increases for millions of citizens. In 1972 and 1973, as prices soared and Social Security payroll taxes climbed, workers had to cover increased family expenses with reduced take-home wages.

To restrain inflation and protect the dollar's value in the international economy, the federal government during the 1970s pursued monetary policies designed to tighten the supply of money, raise interest rates, and cool off the economy. The effect of such policies made the poor shoulder the burden of fighting inflation, a battle that brought more defeats than triumphs. As federal officials struggled to curb inflation by accepting a high level of unemployment and by keeping minimum wages from rising too high, the poor, especially if they were nonwhite or female, found themselves neglected—and not benignly. More significantly, by 1975 as "stagflation" took its toll through price inflation and unemployment that exceeded 8 percent of the labor force, for the first time since the Johnson years the number of families the Census Bureau classified as living in poverty actually increased statistically. And more surprisingly, the bulk of the increase came among white families with two-parent households whose principal breadwinner, usually the husband, had been victimized by long-term unemployment.

Between 1976 and 1980 most families' economic situation worsened. From 1967 to 1976 median family income had slightly outpaced price increases. Over the next five years, however, prices outran wages and the real purchasing power of family incomes declined. Indeed, in the summer of 1979, the Joint Economic Committee of Congress warned that the average American was likely to experience a drastically reduced standard of living during the 1980s if current economic trends persisted.

Just as poverty persisted in the 1970s, so too did racial and sexual discrimination. While the number of poor whites defined as poverty-stricken continued to decline, the number of poor blacks in the year 1972 alone increased from 7.4 to 7.7 million. In 1972, the Census Bureau estimated only 9 percent of all white people lived in poverty compared to 33 percent of all blacks. Poverty also hit hardest among female-headed households, which in 1972 formed 43 percent of all poor families compared to 23 percent in 1959. Indeed, the entire increase in nonwhite poverty occurred in families headed by women who were unemployed or restricted to the lowest paying jobs in the economy. Millions of women who worked fulltime could not earn wages sufficient to support a family. At all levels of the economy, from managerial to menial work, compensation for females lagged far behind that for men. White or black, college educated or not, talented or unskilled, women consistently earned considerably less than comparable men doing the same job.

This situation worsened later in the 1970s as the economy stagnated. The number of Americans living in poverty, which had decreased considerably during the prosperous 1960s, remained stable in the 1970s. Between 1972 and 1979 the total number of poor people rose by approximately one million and their proportion of the total population scarcely changed. Moreover, nonwhites continued to suffer more than whites from poverty.[1] In 1979, 31 percent of all blacks fell into the poverty category as did nearly 22 percent of all Hispanics.

Thus beginning in 1971 nonwhite Americans, who had made substan-

**DISTRIBUTION OF FAMILY INCOME, 1970–1977**

|  | SHARES (%) | | |
|---|---|---|---|
|  | 1970 | 1975 | 1977 |
| Lowest Quintile | 5.4 | 5.4 | 5.2 |
| 2nd Quintile | 12.2 | 11.8 | 11.6 |
| 3rd Quintile | 17.6 | 17.6 | 17.5 |
| 4th Quintile | 23.8 | 24.1 | 24.2 |
| Highest Quintile | 40.9 | 41.1 | 41.5 |
| Top 5% | 15.6 | 15.5 | 15.7 |

Source: U.S. Bureau of the Census, *Current Population Reports, Consumer Income,* Series P-60, No. 118, 1977, p. 45.

---

[1] It must be stressed that in absolute numbers for every poor nonwhite there were almost two whites.

tial economic progress from 1964 to 1969, began once again to slip down the economic ladder. The gap in median income between whites and blacks, which had diminished in the 1960s, widened again in the seventies. In 1972 black median income stood at $6,864 compared to $11,549 for whites, a cash difference of $4,685 contrasted to the differential of $3,577 that had existed in 1968. Black unemployment rose to 10 percent, or double the 5 percent rate of white unemployment, and in 1972 black teen-age unemployment soared to 33 percent and more. One-quarter of all black families, contrasted to 5 percent of white families, received public assistance. The nonwhite infant mortality rate was still at least twice that of whites. An old American story repeated itself: Blacks shared in the general economic growth, as did poorer whites, but at a consistently slower pace than whites. Neither a decade of civil rights protest and legislation nor half a decade of unequaled prosperity could alter persistent black-white economic disparities and the legacy of racialism.

Reflecting this persistence, the racial confrontations that had formerly plagued the South in the aftermath of the Supreme Court's 1954 *Brown* decision spread to the North during the 1970s. By 1974, southern schools were considerably more integrated than many northern institutions. Segregation persisted in the North in cities where racially restricted neighborhoods and carefully drawn school attendance zones created all-black and all-white classrooms and in suburbs in which the cost of housing and restrictive real estate practices excluded most nonwhites. When in the late 1960s, federal courts began to require northern urban school districts to integrate their classrooms, white resistance mounted. Candidates ran for public office

Median Annual Money Income of Families, by Race, in Constant 1977 Dollars, 1960 to 1977 (*U.S. Statistical Abstracts,* 1979, p. 436)

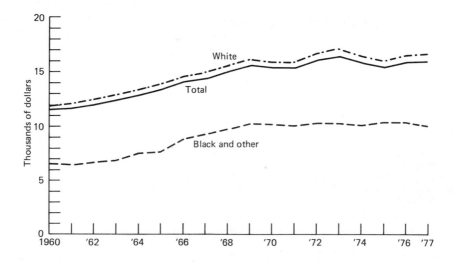

in northern cities (Boston and Los Angeles) on platforms that stressed the neighborhood school and opposed the busing of children for the purpose of integration. Many northern congressmen endorsed legislation including in some cases a constitutional amendment to outlaw "forced busing," and their proposals won the endorsements of Presidents Nixon and Ford. In Pontiac, Michigan, where a court order compelled the local school board to integrate classrooms, white parents kept their children home and some traveled to Washington to demonstrate against busing. A few among them even dynamited the city's school buses. And in Boston in the fall of 1974 white parents and their children also resisted a court-ordered school integration plan that necessitated busing. When whites and blacks subsequently fought violently in South Boston, Mayor Kevin White dispatched riot police, asked for federal marshals, and received from Massachusetts Governor Francis Sargeant unwanted state troops. Passions became so inflamed that Senator Edward Kennedy, a political idol among the state's Irish, was booed and pelted with tomatoes by a white, antibusing crowd in Boston.

Ironically, as the South integrated with "all deliberate speed" after 1955, segregation in northern school systems hastened. By 1977, two decades after the *Brown* decision, northern urban schools had become increasingly nonwhite in most large cities, while the suburbs with practically all-white schools rejected suggestions that to foster integration attendance zones cross juridical boundaries. The 1980 election results seemed to confirm nonsouthern distaste for integrated schools and the busing required to achieve it.

## ECOLOGY AND SOCIAL CLASS

Questions about the quality of life came to the forefront in the 1970s. Ecology became a new watchword. Some citizens with inherited wealth anxiously observed the new middle class invade once reserved domains. Hitherto private baronial estates were subdivided into vacation and year-round resorts where middle-class neighborliness replaced upper-class solitude. Isolated stretches of ocean beach, secluded mountain lakes, and forest wilderness areas crumbled before the real-estate developer's bulldozers. As the "recreational vehicle" industry expanded, national parks and forests became as crowded in midsummer as Coney Island had once been. Some citizens began to wonder how much longer the United States could preserve its wilderness areas when hundreds of thousands of weekly visitors camped in those parks and forests amidst sanitary bathroom facilities, electric appliances, TV antennas, and overflowing garbage cans.

Consequently, during the 1970s the traditionally wealthy and the newly affluent, combined with environmentalists to preserve and restore the quality of American life. In order to enjoy their large boats, costly fishing gear, and lakeside cottages, many affluent Americans now demanded cleaner water. Having purchased annually the millions of oversized automobiles that guzzled gas and poisoned the atmosphere, Americans from all classes called for cleaner air. Secure in their professions, wealth, and status, increasing numbers of citizens insisted that industry cease polluting streams, lakes, and the atmosphere, that the quality of life take precedence over economic growth.

The ecology movement, in short, beckoned Americans to look at the world around them in a new way. They were cautioned to think in terms of conservation, not exploitation; existence in harmony, not in conflict, with nature. Land was to be regulated and preserved by public authorities for posterity and not carelessly developed for the profit of real-estate speculators and building contractors. People were counseled to walk or bicycle, not to spew car fumes into the air. Ecology advocates suggested that industries that caused pollution should be shut down or compelled to invest in costly antipollution devices. It suddenly came to be realized that clean air and pure water, resources that had customarily been considered cost-free, came at a considerable social cost. In fact, the whole program of the ecologists carried a high price tag, in some cases so high that sharp conflict ensued concerning who should pay the price for a purified environment.

Among those who already owned suburban or exurban homes on large lots, land control and zoning codes were attractive means to restrain future real-estate development. And those who already possessed summer homes in the wilderness, mountains, or oceanfront might well struggle to preserve what remained of nature's original domain. Two- and three-car families might easily resort to the bicycle for exercise, and doctors, lawyers, and dentists might struggle to close industrial plants that polluted their communities.

But individuals who had struggled and scrimped to buy a home, as well as conservative opponents of federal regulation, had substantial reservations about zoning regulations that put the cost of land beyond their means. Those workers, who in the past had been forced to rely on mass public transit or walk to work, did not believe that they should now be denied the private cars their labor and improved wages made possible. And those citizens who for the first time could afford summer vacations away from home preferred not to vacation at Coney Island for the sake of nature and posterity. Industrial workers as well as corporate executives looked unkindly on suggestions that businesses be closed in order to clean the air and water for other citizens. Even if factory owners chose to invest in pollution-control devices rather than close down, many workers wondered about who would ultimately pay the costs.

If many high-paid workers saw in the ecology movement an effort to deny them the pleasures hitherto tasted by the wealthy, the poor perceived an even greater threat. If economic growth were restrained, resource exploitation limited, the prices of scarce items raised to conserve them, how would the poor escape their poverty? The crusade to improve the quality of American society, as personified by the suburban middle and upper classes, implied the creation of a good life for those able to purchase it. For many poor Americans, ecology suggested persistent unemployment and the pricing of many commodities, necessities as well as luxuries, beyond their pocketbooks.

*Ecology* was, then, as much a movement of, by, and for the affluent in which the economically less fortunate would receive only incidental benefits as a movement to regulate business abuse. Unless the United States redistributed income and wealth, ecological considerations could have the further effect to price the material aspects of the "American Dream" beyond the reach of millions of citizens.

And it was precisely this gap between the illusion and the reality of the "good life" which the ecologists promised that led to a political and economic counterattack at the end of the 1970s. The costs of environmental regulation, industrialists and their political allies argued, had made American business noncompetitive globally. Many workers in less competitive industries and those without jobs also questioned the costs of clean air and water. Many other Americans wondered whether ecological concerns aggravated inflationary tendencies in the economy. All these people responded in 1980 to Ronald Reagan's suggestions that conservationists not be allowed to retard economic growth and the creation of new jobs. Because of rapidly rising fuel oil and gas prices, many other Americans reacted favorably to the Republican candidate's pledge to unleash energy companies.

## THE "ENERGY CRISIS" AND A SOCIETY OF SCARCITY

Not only the poor, the nonwhite, and the female suffered economically from the inflation of the seventies. What came to be known as the "energy crisis" threatened the material comforts of even affluent citizens. In the winter of 1973–1974 the declining international value of the dollar and domestic ecological pressures precipitated a shortage of the fuels needed to run the economy, heat homes, and propel automobiles. As Western Europe and Japan prospered, international demand for oil and natural gas expanded. The United States could no longer meet its energy needs from domestic production (over 30 percent of all fuel oil had to be imported) and had to compete against stronger currencies in the international market—an economic reality that by 1973 caused shortages in heating oil, natural gas, and motor fuel, steeply rising domestic prices for the scarce resources, and the prospect of a more serious, permanent long-term fuel shortage. The outbreak of a fourth Arab-Israeli war in the Mideast in the fall of 1973 and a subsequent reduction in the amounts of oil the Arab nations supplied to the Western world exacerbated the "energy crisis."

In the aftermath of the 1973 war, the major Mideast producers, and their associates in the Organization of Petroleum Exporting Countries (OPEC), more than quadrupled the price of crude oil. And again in 1975 and in December 1976 OPEC nations increased oil prices; these price increases continued until the "glut" of 1980 when fissures began to appear in the hitherto solid bloc of oil-producing nations.

In other times coal might have provided an economical, feasible alternative source of energy. But in the 1970s the United States' superabundant domestic supply of coal (three to four centuries' amount of reserves) conflicted with national concern about ecology. The cheapest, most productive means of obtaining coal—strip mining—was also ecologically the most destructive, turning parts of the country where it was used extensively into a lunar landscape. (Furthermore, only about 3 percent of the nation's coal reserves were located in areas that could be stripped.) Not only did increased coal mining threaten to damage the landscape but the type of coal most readily available, high in sulphur content, polluted the atmosphere when burned. By 1977 the United States had fallen decades behind England, West Germany, and other European nations in the application of efficient coal-mining and coal-burning technology.

The energy crisis, whether real or imagined, permanent or temporary, produced substantial changes in the American way of life. Some were symbolic, such as President Carter's appearance on television wearing a heavy cardigan in a minimally heated White House. Other changes were much more real. As the price of gas and heating oil skyrocketed (rising about 500 percent from 1975 to 1980), many citizens had no choice but to keep their houses cooler in winter and warmer in summer. Others replaced large gas guzzlers with smaller four-cylinder cars, much to the delight of Japanese automakers and the dismay of their American competitors. Still others could no longer even afford a new car, and in 1980 and 1981, new car sales, especially of American models, fell to their lowest level in two decades.

President Carter's declared moral war against the energy crisis did not address the substantive issues ensuring this crisis. Since the end of World War II government policy, by subsidizing superhighways, suburbanization, and a geographical separation between home and work, had made the nation dependent on the private automobile and oil. Meantime, mass transit decayed and central cities deteriorated. Even after half a decade's experience with energy shortages, a presidential commission on the future of the nation recommended in 1980 that Americans be encouraged to move from the Northeast to the South and West, that, in short, the American people become even more spread out in their settlement patterns. President Reagan's budget for 1982 in effect endorsed such proposals by cutting mass transit funds and penalizing the troubled frostbelt to the advantage of the flourishing sunbelt. Reagan's answer to the energy dilemma was the discipline of the marketplace: Rising fuel prices would induce individual conservation and promote greater supply from firms earning higher profits. In short, government would favor policies intensifying reliance on oil while calling on individuals to solve the energy crisis. Or as the political scientist Walter Dean Burnham put it in 1979: "Socialize costs, privately appropriate the profits—that is the whole story."

In almost all aspects American life in the 1970s raised the specter of abundance giving way to scarcity. Just as Americans faced the ultimate prospect of fewer, smaller cars, they had to consider the possibility of less commodious and fewer private homes. By 1980 the high cost of land, the impact of inflation, and unprecedently high home-mortgage rates had placed the single-family home and even the condominium apartment beyond the reach of increasing numbers of Americans.

Most unexpectedly in the 1970s, foodstuffs, whose abundance and cheapness were long taken for granted by Americans, became temporarily a scarce and costly commodity. Again, prosperity in other nations (as well as global population growth) had increased the international demand for foodstuffs, and stronger currencies enabled foreign buyers to outbid Americans for our own farm produce. As well, the sharp rise in oil prices had increased the costs of farming and marketing. As Russians purchased American wheat, Japanese consumed American soybeans, and all industrial societies demanded more American beef, supermarket prices in the United States soared, and many people, especially the elderly and the poor, could no longer afford beef in their regular diets. If, as the United States entered the 1980s, its farms produced more than enough for domestic consumption and much for the world market, prices appeared unlikely to drop and future scarcity remained a real possibility.

Here, too, concern for ecology conflicted potentially with the production of an adequate supply of foodstuffs. Chemical fertilizers, which were responsible for a considerable share of the post–World War II growth in agricultural productivity, in many cases polluted water supplies, threatening the health of wildlife and human life. If the use of fertilizers and pesticides were restricted for ecological reasons, agricultural productivity might be cut back at precisely the moment that global demand for foodstuffs reached unprecedented levels. In that case the result could be a food shortage as perilous as the fuel shortage—and the prospect of hungry stomachs was much more serious than empty oil furnaces and gas tanks. Moreover, inflated fuel prices burdened American agriculture, which was an energy-intensive enterprise dependent on gas and oil to run its cultivating and processing machines as well as on fertilizers that were petroleum-based products. Such were the unexpected interrelationships of a complex modern economy.

## THE METROPOLITAN PARADOX

Paradox enveloped all aspects of society in the 1970s. As dissatisfaction with cities and industrial life grew apace, the United States became more urbanized and industrialized than ever. Over 75 percent of Americans resided in metropolitan areas, and despite considerable rhetoric extolling the advantages of nature, rural society continued its inexorable decline. That last stronghold of American agrarianism—the Old South—collapsed before the inroads of industry. Between 1950 and 1972, agricultural employment in the eleven former Confederate states declined from 3.8 million to 2.4 million while factory employment rose from 1.5 million to 4.4 million. Factories invaded a once totally rural landscape, as industrialists sought cheaper labor, less expensive land, and lower taxes. The Old South raced to catch up with the remainder of the nation and voluntarily sacrificed its slower, more natural rural pace of life to the insistent time pressures of modern industrial technology. Southerners, much as other Americans in the past, chose money before leisure, factory discipline over rural rhythms.

Although the Census Bureau reported at the start of the 1980s that nonurban population was growing more rapidly than city or suburban population, this in no way altered the nation's overwhelmingly metropolitan urban character. Poorer rural people still sought opportunity in metropolitan areas, and poor city residents did not move to the country. Instead wealthy city folk bought big rural homes (demonstrating the persistent appeal of the country squire or gentleman farmer image) and the continued decentralization of industry, shopping, and population made such life-styles possible. In other words, most new rural residents earned their livelihoods from a profession, a factory, an office, a shopping mall, or even inherited wealth, and not from farming.

During the 1970s, after more than a decade of controversy about the urban crisis and many experiments in urban renewal, American cities were less habitable than ever. The white middle class kept up its headlong flight to suburbia, and in the 1970s "swinging singles" joined the more respectable family-style suburbanites. Some New York City neighborhoods, once culturally rich and vital ethnic communities, resembled targets of a saturation air raid. The desolated South Bronx had become a required stop on presidential campaign swings; Carter stopped there in 1976 and Reagan in 1980. It also served as the subject of a 1981 Paul Newman-Hollywood film, "Fort Apache, The Bronx."[2]

Worse than the physical decay that infected poorer neighborhoods was the contagious fear that stalked city streets. The poor, and the nonwhite among them in particular, had always lived with the reality of random

---

[2]"Fort Apache," the name local police had sarcastically given to their precinct house in the 1960s—an outpost in hostile territory—was renamed in the 1970s "The Little House on the Prairie," because of its presence in a devastated neighborhood.

violence—whiskey-induced Saturday night brawls, teen-age gang fights, and endemic crime traditionally had figured prominently in working-class ethnic neighborhoods. In this respect black ghettoes scarcely differed from the white immigrant communities that preceded them. By the 1970s, however, past customs of lower-class crime paled in comparison to the new techniques of violence. Modern technology rendered criminals more mobile and violence more deadly. The ready availability of weapons—from the crudest handgun to the most complex automatic rifle—produced a surfeit of potential killers. In a single year more homicides occurred in New York City than in all of Great Britain, and New York, in proportion to its total population, was scarcely the most homicidal community in the United States (Detroit, the leader for a time until displaced by the booming Texas cities of Houston and Dallas, had a homicide rate more than double that of New York in a population less than one-third the size of New York City's). By the opening of the 1980s, as homicide rates declined in Detroit and stabilized in New York, they increased in the rapidly growing cities of the South and West, especially Houston, Miami, Las Vegas, and Los Angeles.

Life in the American city became a real as well as a metaphorical war for many citizens. Television news programs brought domestic and foreign violence into the living room; the most popular weekly video series featured private eyes and public cops chasing criminals and themselves causing mayhem; and movies offered superscreen images of the most technologically advanced and brutal forms of murder. At night, in many an urban resident's mind, if not in statistical fact, city streets seemed safer for muggers than for ordinary pedestrians, and criminals lurked in apartment house vestibules, stairways, and elevators. "I'm not exaggerating when I say that tenants are living under conditions of virtual house arrest," commented one resident of a New York City luxury apartment complex. "We are afraid to walk around after daylight has dimmed. No one feels completely safe."

Fear refused to abate as violent crime worsened and senseless murders occurred with shocking regularity. No single murder caused as great a reaction or as much publicity as the slaying of former Beatle John Lennon in front of his New York apartment building in late 1980. A few months later in February 1981, Supreme Court Chief Justice Warren Burger, in a speech to the American Bar Association, called violent crime America's gravest domestic peril.

Those who felt least safe in the cities or lacked intrinsic economic and cultural links to urban life fled to the suburbs. Still others moved to sunbelt urban areas. The 1980 census found that almost all the central cities in the Northeast and North Central states had lost substantial population since 1970, as had such metropolitan regions as New York, Philadelphia, and Chicago. In turn, major cities and metropolitan districts in Florida, Texas, New Mexico, Nevada, Colorado, and California grew rapidly. By 1980 the majority of Americans lived in the states of the South and West.

## WORK AND ITS DISCONTENTS

By the 1970s Americans had grown increasingly dissatisfied with the metropolitan existence the vast majority of them had chosen; as well larger numbers of citizens began to question the traditional work ethic. Sociologists discovered what they labeled the "blue-collar blues," a mental condition that flowed directly from work and its discontents. Especially among younger workers, absenteeism, drugs, alcohol, and disobedience to rules became commonplace. For the first time since the labor upheaval of the 1930s, industrial workers openly rebelled against the pace and structure of work. In Lordstown, Ohio, young workers at the General Motors Vega assembly plant struck in 1972 to slow down the pace of the assembly line and to win more autonomy for workers within the factory. Union-management negotiations throughout the economy began to focus more on work rules, safety standards, and early retirement than on higher hourly wages. For those too young for even early retirement and unable to endure the insistent pressures of mass-production labor, drugs and alcohol provided an easy escape. On many an auto assembly line "stoned" workers seemed best able to confront the day's work.

White-collar workers and lesser professionals sang their own version of the work blues. They, too, felt discontented with vocations that offered little intrinsic satisfaction and that infringed on their personal autonomy. Like industrial workers, they rebelled against rules set by their superiors and demanded more freedom and variety in their work. So-called professionals—teachers, nurses, interns, residents, and a variety of public servants—acted like traditional trade union members, and in many cases transformed hitherto ineffective professional associations into potent labor unions. Indeed, in the 1960s and 1970s white-collar workers and public employees became the most rapidly expanding sector of the labor movement. In 1980 the two largest unions in the AFL-CIO—the United Food and Commercial Workers (UFCW)[3] and the American Federation of State, County, and Municipal Employees (AFSCME)—represented white-collar workers, as did the American Federation of Teachers, one of the more powerful unions in New York City and state. As retail clerks, teachers, nurses and civil servants unions (including police and firefighters) won higher wages and improved fringe benefits, they, too, moved on to demand more effective job control.

By the late 1970s, however, three developments had combined to alter workers' attitudes and the condition of the labor movement. First, the onslaught of double-digit inflation and high unemployment, especially in the basic industries, made workers more concerned with jobs and income

[3] Formed that year by a merger of the Retail Clerks' Union and the Amalgamated Meat Cutters and Butcher Workmen.

than with leisure and shop-floor control. Second, a series of urban fiscal crises, particularly the New York City financial collapse of 1975–1977, triggered a taxpayers' rebellion against high local and state property levies. In response, state and municipal governments reduced public employment and resisted union demands. Third, employment grew primarily in non-union, low-wage sectors of the economy and nation. By 1980 the most thoroughly unionized sector of the economy—manufacturing, mining, transport, and the skilled crafts—included only 34 percent of all employees, the smallest proportion in more than half a century.

These developments constituted the travails of the labor movement. At their merger in 1955 the AFL and CIO numbered some 16 million members or 21 percent of the labor force. In 1979 the AFL-CIO had 13.6 million members, or 13 percent of the labor force.[4] The rate of union success in NLRB representation elections also declined steadily, from a peak of 80 percent in 1946 to a low of 47 percent in 1977. As *Business Week* noted in December 1978: "American business has by and large never really accepted unionism." This reality caused top labor leaders to be enveloped, in the words of an eminent labor reporter, by "a sense of insecurity."

Political trends compounded organized labor's anxiety. At one time the AFL-CIO could count on its influence within the Democratic party to advance welfare legislation and to protect labor's interests. During the 1970s this became much less true. After using all its political resources in 1976 to help elect Jimmy Carter and a Democratic Congress, the labor movement found itself at a loss. Congress refused to pass labor's most sought-after legislation. In anger, Douglas Fraser, president of the UAW, charged in 1978 that corporate business and its congressional allies were waging a "one-sided class war against working people, the unemployed, the poor, the minorities, the very young, and the very old. . . ."

The year 1980 intensified organized labor's dismay. Again the labor movement, however unenthusiastically, marshalled its resources behind Jimmy Carter. This time to no avail. Ronald Reagan not only swept the nation but gained the votes of almost half of all union members and their families. And when the newly elected president revealed his economic program three months later (February 1981), the new president of the AFL-CIO, Lane Kirkland, could only charge, "It fails every test of justice and equity."

But the labor movement scarcely seemed likely to reverse the tide. "Mr. Labor," George Meany, the president of the AFL-CIO ever since the 1955 merger, died in 1980. His successor, Lane Kirkland, a lawyer by training and a bureaucrat by inclination, was hardly the sort of leader to revitalize an

---

[4]The nation's two largest unions—the Teamsters and Auto Workers—respectively were expelled and seceded from the AFL-CIO. Even so, the AFL-CIO declined in size compared to the growth of the total labor force.

increasingly moribund movement. All this led one union president to observe that "the American labor movement is having less and less impact on society," and one of the foremost labor reporters to note that "trade unionism appears today to be a largely spent force in the national life."

## THE GLOBAL MILIEU

Labor's future and changes in the structure of the American society and economy in the 1980s were necessarily constrained by the realities of international economic competition. In the 1980s, unlike in the 1950s, the United States economy no longer reigned supreme within the nonsocialist world. While the dollar might still speak loudly at home, it only whispered abroad. As the Germans, Japanese, French, and even some socialist economies proved more productive than that of the United States, American workers could not choose leisure in preference to higher wages. The American worker now had to work harder and longer to compete with foreign workers for bread, beef, poultry, fuel, and clothing. Indeed, a real possibility existed that the stringency of global economic competition would bring about an intensification of work discipline in America, not the widening of workers' control or individual job autonomy.

By the late 1970s the direction that the American society and economy would choose for the future, then, was inextricably linked to changes in the global economic environment. Our largest corporations were already an integral part of multinational industrial empires whose domains transcended the authority of national states and national trade unions. In the 1970s corporation executives acted on an international economic stage, meeting and dealing regularly with their managerial counterparts in socialist and nonsocialist states.

Meantime, foreign competition was exacting a heavy toll on the American economy and its workers. By the middle of 1980, over 50 percent of all shoes sold in the United States were imported, as were almost 30 percent of all autos, over 15 percent of steel, and more than 10 percent of textiles. Most stereo equipment, cameras, and many color televisions were assembled in East Asia under Japanese company trademarks. In late 1979, U.S. Steel, suffering from foreign competition and declining domestic demand, closed fifteen plants in eight states, in the process idling 13,000 workers. The following year Japanese automakers for the first time in history out-produced their American competitors. As a result, in 1980, Ford and General Motors suffered the largest corporate losses in American history and Chrysler had to be rescued by a multimillion-dollar federal loan.

Foreign goods had not only invaded the domestic market, but foreign capital established its own plants in the United States or acquired American companies. Michelin made tires in South Carolina, Volkswagen cars in

Pennsylvania, and more than 200 Japanese companies in a variety of states produced everything from steel to soy sauce. More pointedly, by the early 1980s, American politicians and labor leaders demanded more, not less, direct foreign investment. It was better to use foreign capital to employ American workers than to lose American jobs to foreign laborers.

As capital and its managers operated ever more effectively on a global scale, one had to ask whether American workers would learn to do the same with their foreign counterparts. Only the future would tell.

## A CRACKED CONSENSUS
## AND THE CRISIS
## OF LEGITIMATION

Ever since President Eisenhower in the mid-1950s had legitimated the basic welfare reforms of the New Deal and curbed McCarthyism, a basic consensus had dominated American politics and thought. Both major political parties and most intellectuals were ruled by what the historian Arthur Schlesinger, Jr., called the "vital center." Voices and protests from either the so-called extreme right or far left were muted and usually unheard. When political parties chose their presidential candidates from outside the "vital center," as the Republicans did with Goldwater in 1964 and the Democrats with McGovern in 1972, the result was a landslide victory for the opposition. The consensus seemed to survive the counterculture of the 1960s as well as the curse of Watergate. Indeed, many commentators cited the resolution of the Watergate affair and Nixon's resignation from the presidency as proof of the solidity of the American political system and the shared values which bound the American people together.

But the global economic crisis of the mid- and late 1970s shattered the domestic consensus. First, increasing numbers of intellectuals and academics (the so-called neoconservatives) began to question the whole drift of federal welfare policies from Roosevelt's New Deal to Johnson's Great Society. Now, however, they challenged the "vital center" from the right, not the left. Enacting new federal welfare legislation and showering federal dollars on the poor, neoconservatives argued, was the problem, not the solution. These new critics of New Deal liberalism, many of whom earlier had been social democrats or left-wing Democrats, occupied prominent professorships in such elite private universities as Harvard, Chicago, and Stanford. Their writings were printed in the *New York Times*, *Harper's*, and *Atlantic Monthly*, whose columns were gospel for many educated middle-class Americans. They even had their own journal, *The Public Interest*, which was edited by neoconservatism's most strident voice, Irving Kristol. Neoconservatism, moreover, captured the official organ of the traditional liberal-left constituency, the American Jewish community. In the 1970s Norman Podhoretz, the editor of *Commentary* (the journal of the American Jewish Congress), opened its pages to the most vocal critics of detente abroad and social reform at home. The columns of *Commentary* decried affirmative action, federal aid for the poor, agreements with the Soviets, and even efforts to protect human rights among America's right-wing authoritarian allies. What had happened among such academics and intellectuals was aptly caught in the title of the second installment of Podhoretz's autobiography, *Breaking Ranks.* The summer soldiers of the left had deserted their old comrades during the 1970s to march with new corporate executives and Pentagon brass.

Neoconservatives not only challenged a half century of federal reform; they also questioned the whole process of opening up American society and politics to voices from below. Bemoaning what the Harvard political scientist Samuel P. Huntington called an "excess of democracy," they wanted political parties to exert more control over their constituents, professionals to manage their clients, teachers to lead their students, and the state to govern the people.

The same forces which had pushed these intellectuals to the right also acted on politicians and ordinary people. In the late 1970s politicians invariably criticized the institutions to which they sought election and people everywhere demanded release from unspecified government controls. On the one hand, a cry arose to turn federal power back to the separate states where it rightfully belonged, and, on the other hand, to transfer most decisions from the state, which had usurped power, to the private marketplace, which acted more efficiently and equitably.

The new conservatism was nonetheless filled with contradictions. If, with one voice, it demanded surcease from government controls, with another voice it urged that the state impinge on the most private, personal realms of behavior. A whole array of widely based and astutely managed "popular" movements fought to use state power to outlaw abortion, limit the availability of contraceptive information or devices, censor pornographic literature, and require prayers in the public schools. Whether calling themselves the "moral majority," the "Eagle Forum," or the National Conservative Political Action Committee (NCPAC), these groups sought to alter the political balance of power on the so-called social issues.

The cement that held this new right movement together was a shared need to reassert traditional values and methods of social control. Both the advocates of reduced government and those who desired state regulation of personal behavior wanted to resurrect the "traditional family" in which women stayed at home and deferred to men and in which children obeyed parents. They also sought a society in which workers obeyed bosses and citizens rallied behind presidentially defined national interests, whether in the streets of Chicago or the hills of El Salvador.

The 1980 election confirmed that neoconservatism resonated among voters and that the consensus around the "vital center" had cracked. Ronald

Reagan, a candidate of the conservative wing of the Republican party, won his party's nomination and then swept the nation. And, in victory, he promised to restore traditional values, revitalize federalism and state rights, liberate the marketplace, increase defense spending, and reignite the Cold War.

If what had happened politically, intellectually, and culturally in response to the crisis of the late 1970s was not yet entirely clear, certain aspects could be discerned vaguely. The right, which had languished on the fringes of American society and politics since the New Deal, had successfully regrouped its forces, had recruited a host of new intellectual allies, and, for the first time, had built a mass popular base.

The left, to be sure, had neither disappeared nor become silent. But it lacked the popular base of the right and the mass circulation and TV-radio stations which spread the message of neoconservatism and the gospel of evangelical Christian morality. Leftists still published their small journals, most of which lived a hand-to-mouth existence, and many taught in colleges and universities, though few held prestigious chairs and many, in a time of academic retrenchment, dreaded the tenure ax.

If the left remained active on the fringes, the "vital center" also lacked leadership and direction. It seemed split between "cold warriors" and detenters, prolabor and antilabor wings, family traditionalists and the products of the 1960s sexual revolution.

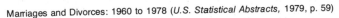

Marriages and Divorces: 1960 to 1978 (*U.S. Statistical Abstracts*, 1979, p. 59)

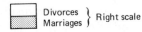

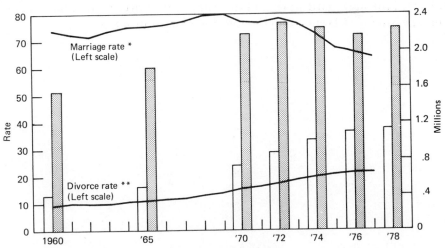

\* Rate per 1,000 unmarried women, 15 years old and over.
\*\* Rate per 1,000 married women, 15 years old and over.

In the America of the 1980s no common ground beckoned antiabortionists and proabortionists, traditional family proponents and feminists, free-market disciples and AFL-CIOers, cold warriors and peace advocates. The great American consensus had, for the time, cracked.

As Americans looked ahead from the 1970s to the future, one had to wonder if the words of social commentator Herbert Von Borch—"American society possesses virtually inexhaustible capacities for self-redress"—still rang true. In the past, Americans had proved heedless about exhausting land and natural resources. Now living on a globe in which land, water, fuel, and the air itself had become quite exhaustible, could the American spirit remain inexhaustible? Perhaps! Some might argue, as did California governor Jerry Brown, only if the national spirit became less materialistic and more egalitarian. And, on that score, the 1980 election result offered reason for disquiet.

The American spirit, as personified by Henry Luce's "American Century," proved less than prophetic and an enormous burden as well. Compared to the British century, which stretched from 1815 to 1914, the "American Century" had a half life. By the late 1970s, the United States' global dominance was a relic of the past and Americans had yet to show that a continental society could adjust as smoothly to loss of empire as an island-nation could—that improving the quality of life at home for all citizens could become as important as maintaining overseas hegemony. For some Americans the time required the renunciation of empire and the distribution of the fruits of labor more equally; perhaps, then, their society might indeed possess "virtually inexhaustible capacities for self-redress." An alternative vision, and one commanding greater popular support, was that suggested by Ronald Reagan's success in 1980: The United States remained a "City on the Hill" and through hard work and discipline could overcome inflation and unemployment at home and circumscribe Communism abroad.

# SUGGESTED SUPPLEMENTARY READING

**DOMESTIC POLITICS
AND FOREIGN POLICY**

### General

The best studies on the Presidency since FDR are Arthur Schlesinger, Jr., *The Imperial Presidency* (1973)\*; Richard Neustadt, *Presidential Power* (1980); Richard Pious, *The American Presidency* (1979); see also Raoul Berger, *Executive Privilege* (1974).\* Herbert S. Parmet, *The Democrats* (1976)\*; Arthur M. Schlesinger, Jr., Fred L. Israel, and William P. Hassen (eds.), *History of American Presidential Elections*, Vol. 4 (1971); Everett Ladd, Jr. and Charles D. Hadley, *Transformations of the American Party System* (1975); Richard Polenberg, *One Nation Divisible* (1980)\*; Walter Goodman, *The Committee* (1968); Alonzo Hamby, *The Imperial Years* (1976); and Lawrence Wittner, *Cold War America* (1974)\* survey domestic politics and elections since 1940. For a good general overview of U.S. foreign policy, see Walter LaFeber, *America, Russia, and the Cold War, 1945-1980* (1980)\*; Adam B. Ulam, *The Rivals* (1971)\*; Paul Hammond, *The American Foreign Policy Process Since 1945* (1975); Seyom Brown, *The Faces of Power* (1968); Gabriel Kolko, *Main Currents in Modern*

\*Denotes paperback.

*American History* (1976)\*; and William A. Williams, *The Tragedy of American Diplomacy* (1962).\* Surveillance and intelligence policy are surveyed in Athan Theoharis, *Spying on Americans* (1978); Frank Donner, *The Age of Surveillance* (1980)\*; Morton Halperin *et al.*, *The Lawless State* (1976)\*; Thomas Powers, *The Man Who Kept the Secrets* (1979); and William Corson, *The Armies of Ignorance* (1977).

### The Roosevelt Presidency

Domestic politics are surveyed in John M. Blum, *V Was for Victory* (1976); Geoffrey Parrett, *Days of Sadness, Years of Triumph* (1973); Roger Daniels, *The Decision to Relocate the Japanese Americans* (1975)\*; Louis Ruchames, *Race, Jobs and Politics* (1953); Richard Dalfiume, *Desegregation of the U.S. Armed Forces* (1969); and Richard Polenberg, *War and Society* (1972).\* Foreign policy is surveyed in Robert Dallek, *Franklin D. Roosevelt and American Foreign Policy, 1932-1945* (1979)\*; Robert Divine, *The Reluctant Belligerent* (1965) and *Second Chance* (1967); Herbert Feis, *Churchill, Roosevelt, Stalin* (1957); James M. Burns, *Roosevelt: The Soldier of Freedom* (1970); Gaddis Smith, *American Diplomacy During World War II* (1965); William Neumann, *After Victory* (1969); Gabriel Kolko, *The Politics of War* (1969)\*; Diane Shaver Clemens, *Yalta* (1970)\*; John Gaddis, *The United States and the Origins of the Cold War,* (1972)\*; Lloyd Gardner, *Economic Aspects of New Deal Diplomacy* (1964)\*; Richard G. Hewlett and Oscar E. Anderson, Jr., *A History of the United States Atomic Energy Commission, Vol. I, 1939/1946* (1962); and Martin Sherwin, *A World Destroyed* (1975).

### The Truman Presidency

Domestic politics are surveyed in Alonzo Hamby, *Beyond the New Deal* (1973); Robert J. Donovan, *Conflict and Crisis* (1977); Harold Gosnell, *Truman's Crises* (1980); Athan Theoharis, *The Truman Presidency* (1979); David Caute, *The Great Fear* (1978)\*; Michal Belknap, *Cold War Political Justice* (1977); Robert Griffith, *The Politics of Fear* (1970)\*; and with Athan Theoharis (eds.), *The Specter* (1974)\*; Donald R. McCoy and Richard Ruetten, *Quest and Response* (1973); William Berman, *The Politics of Civil Rights in the Truman Administration;* and Maeva Marcus, *Truman and the Steel Seizure Case* (1977). Foreign policy is surveyed in Barton Bernstein (ed.), *Politics and Policies of the Truman Administration* (1970)\*; Lloyd Gardner, *Architects of Illusion* (1970)\*; Gabriel and Joyce Kolko, *The Limits of Power* (1972)\*; George S. Herring, Jr., *Aid to Russia, 1941-1946* (1973); Daniel Yergin, *Shattered Peace* (1977); Thomas Paterson, *Soviet-American Confrontation* (1974) and *On Every Front* (1979)\*; Richard G. Hewlett and Francis Duncan, *Atomic Shield, 1947-1957* (1972); David Rees, *Korea* (1964); John Gimbel, *The Origins of the Marshall Plan* (1976); Lynn Davis, *The Cold War Begins* (1974); Lisle Rose,

*Roots of Tragedy* (1976); and John Gaddis, *The United States and the Origins of the Cold War* (1972).*

### The Eisenhower Presidency

Domestic politics are surveyed in Charles C. Alexander, *Holding the Line* (1975); Herbert S. Parmet, *Eisenhower and the American Crusades* (1972); Gary Reichard, *The Reaffirmation of Republicanism* (1975); Numan Bartley, *The Rise of Massive Resistance* (1969); Neil R. McMillen, *The Citizens' Council* (1971); James L. Sundquist, *Politics and Policy* (1968); Samuel Lubell, *Revolt of the Moderates* (1956)*; Douglas Kinnard, *President Eisenhower and Strategy Management* (1977); Archibald Cox, *The Warren Court* (1968); Walter Murphy, *Congress and the Court* (1962); and H.L. Nieberg, *In the Name of Science* (1966). Foreign policy is surveyed in Townsend Hoopes, *The Devil and John Foster Dulles* (1973)*; Melvin Gurtov, *The First Vietnam Crisis* (1967)*; Robert Divine, *Eisenhower and the Cold War* (1981);* Blanche Cook, *The Declassified Eisenhower* (1981) and Stephen Ambrose, *Ike's Spies* (1981).

### The Kennedy-Johnson Presidencies

Domestic politics are surveyed in William O'Neill, *Coming Apart* (1971)*; Arthur M. Schlesinger, Jr., *A Thousand Days* (1965) and *Robert Kennedy and His Times* (1978); Victor Navasky, *Kennedy Justice* (1970); Jim Heath, *Decade of Disillusionment* (1975)*; Carl M. Brauer, *John F. Kennedy and the Second Reconstruction* (1977); Doris Kearns, *Lyndon Johnson and the American Dream* (1976); Eric Goldman, *The Tragedy of Lyndon Johnson* (1969); Hugh Sidey, *A Very Personal Presidency* (1968); August Meier and Elliot Rudwick, *CORE* (1973)*; Kirkpatrick Sale, *SDS* (1973)*; David L. Lewis, *King* (1970); and Benjamin Muse, *The American Negro Revolution* (1969).* Foreign policy is surveyed in Herbert Dinnerstein, *The Making of a Missile Crisis* (1976); David Halberstam, *The Best and the Brightest* (1972)*; Abraham F. Lowenthal, *The Dominican Intervention* (1972); Harland B. Moulton, *From Superiority to Parity* (1973); Richard J. Walton, *Cold War and Counter-Revolution* (1972); Stephen Weismann, *American Foreign Policy in the Congo, 1960-1964* (1974); Peter Wyden, *Bay of the Pigs* (1979); Jerome Slater, *Intervention and Negotiation* (1970); Francis Fitzgerald, *Fire in the Lake* (1972)*; Townsend Hoopes, *The Limits of Intervention* (1969)*; Warren I. Cohen, *Dean Rusk* (1980); and George Herring, Jr., *America's Longest War* (1979).*

### The Nixon-Ford Presidencies

Domestic politics are surveyed journalistically in Jonathan Schell, *The Time of Illusion* (1976); David Wise, *The American Police State* (1976); Carl Bernstein and Bob Woodward, *All the President's Men* (1974)*; Emma Rothchild, *Paradise Lost* (1973); Charles P. Roland, *The Improbable Era* (1975);

J. Anthony Lukas, *Nightmare* (1976); Garry Wills, *Nixon Agonists* (1971)*; Godfrey Hogdson, *America in Our Times* (1977)*; and Jules Witcover, *Marathon* (1977). See also, the admittedly partisan Richard Nixon, *RN* (1978) and Gerald Ford, *A Time to Heal* (1979). Foreign policy is similarly surveyed in Lloyd Gardner, *The Great Nixon Turnaround* (1973); John G. Stoessinger, *Henry Kissinger* (1976); Stephen R. Graubard, *Kissinger* (1974); Roger Morris, *Uncertain Greatness* (1977); Henry Brandon, *The Retreat of American Power* (1974); Michael Tanzer, *The Energy Crisis* (1974); John Newhouse, *Cold Dawn* (1973); William Shawcross, *Sideshow* (1979)*; Leslie R. Gelb and R.K. Betts, *The Irony of Vietnam* (1979); and Gareth Porter, *Vietnam* (1979).*

## ECONOMIC, SOCIAL, AND CULTURAL HISTORY

The best synthetic and general treatments of the modern corporate, managed economy may be found in John K. Galbraith, *The New Industrial State* (1967)*, Herbert Stein, *The Fiscal Revolution in America* (1969)*, Robert L. Heilbroner, *The Limits of American Capitalism* (1966)*, Lester Thurow, *The Zero-Sum Society* (1980)*, and Richard J. Barnet and Ronald Muller, *Global Reach: The Power of the Multinational Corporations* (1974)*. For a view of the American economy more consonant with the ideas of Ronald Reagan and many conservatives see George Gilder, *Wealth and Poverty* (1981).

The following books illuminate the persistence of disparities in wealth and income as well as the extent and significance of poverty in America: Robert Lampman, *The Share of Top Wealth Holders* (1962)*; Gabriel Kolko, *Wealth and Power in America* (1962)*; Herman Miller, *Rich Man, Poor Man* (1964)*; Richard Parker, *The Myth of the Middle Class* (1972)*; Michael Harrington, *The Other America* (1981 ed.)*; and Richard Cloward and Frances Fox Piven, *Poor People's Movements* (1979)*. For somewhat different perspectives on the meaning and impact of poverty see Daniel Patrick Moynihan, *Maximum Feasible Misunderstanding* (1968)* and James T. Patterson, *America's Struggle Against Poverty, 1900-1980* (1981).

On American labor and working people's lives, the best general analysis available can be found in the last two chapters of David Brody, *Workers in Industrial America* (1982)*. Other illuminating studies are Studs Terkel, *Working* (1972)*; Stanley Aronowitz, *False Promises* (1973)*; Joseph C. Goulden, *Meany* (1972); John J. Hutchinson, *The Imperfect Union: A History of Corruption in American Trade Unions* (1970)*; and for conflicting views of the Reuther brothers and the United Auto Workers, William Serrin, *The Company and the Union* (1972) and Victor Reuther, *The Brothers Reuther and the Story of the UAW* (1979)*. Dick Meister and Anne Loftis, *A Long Time Coming*

(1977) is a fine history of Cesar Chavez and the struggle to organize farm workers.

The 1950s culture of consensus and its suburban manifestations are captured best in David Rieseman, *et. al., The Lonely Crowd* (1973 ed.)*; Daniel Bell, *The End of Ideology* (1961); William H. Whyte, Jr., *The Organization Man* (1956)*; Scott Donaldson, *The Suburban Myth* (1969); and Herbert Gans, *Levittowners* (1969)*. For marginality and confusion among leftist critics of consensus see Peter Clecak, *Radical Paradoxes* (1974)*.

Three general histories best reveal the upheaval of the turbulent sixties: William L. O'Neil, *Coming Apart* (1969)*; Milton Viorst, *Fire in the Streets* (1981)*; and Morris Dickstein, *Gates of Eden: American Culture in the Sixties* (1978)*.

Two truly fine books analyze the Afro-American struggle for freedom: Richard Kluger, *Simple Justice* (1977)* and Harvard Sitkoff, *The Struggle for Black Equality* (1981)*. Martin Luther King, Jr., *Why We Can't Wait* (1964)* must not be neglected. For the shift from civil rights to black power and the contradictions and conflicts it caused, the following books are most revealing: Clayborne Carson, *In Struggle: SNCC and the Black Awakening of the 1960s* (1981); Harold Cruse, *The Crisis of the Negro Intellectual* (1967)*; David L. Lewis, *King: A Critical Biography* (1970); Alex Haley, ed., *The Autobiography of Malcolm X* (1964)*; Eldridge Cleaver, *Soul on Ice* (1968)*; and August Meier and Elliot Rudwick, *Core* (1973)*. For a study that argues that by the 1970s class had become a more dominant factor among Afro-Americans than race see William J. Wilson, *The Declining Significance of Race* (1980 ed.)*.

For general studies of other nonwhite minority groups turn to Stan Steiner, *The New Indians* (1968)* and *La Raza: The Mexican-Americans* (1970)* as well as Matt S. Meier and Feliciano Rivera, *The Chicanos* (1972)*. On the alleged rise of a new consciousness among white ethnics, Michael Novak, *The Rise of the Unmeltable Ethnics* (1972)* and for a more conventional and sociological portrait of ethnic life, Nathan Glazer and Daniel Patrick Moynihan, *Beyond the Melting Pot* (1970)*.

A variety of books explore the revolt of the young. Among the best are Milton Viorst, *Fire in the Streets* (cited above); two perceptive studies by the psychologist Kenneth Keniston, *The Uncommitted* (1965) and *Young Radicals* (1968)*; Theodore Roszak, *The Making of a Counterculture* (1968)*; Jack Newfield, *A Prophetic Minority* (1966)*; Irwin Unger, *The Movement: A History of the American New Left* (1972)*; and Kirkpatrick Sale, *SDS* (1973)*.

The exploration of women's history and place in contemporary America has become a rapidly growing field of scholarship. A good place to begin to study the history of women are the following four books: Lois Banner, *Women in Modern America* (1974)*; Carl Degler, *At Odds* (1981)*; and William Chafe, *The American Woman* (1972)* and *Women and Equality* (1978)*. For more specialized subjects or themes consult Betty Friedan, *The Feminine*

*Mystique* (1975 ed.)\*; Caroline Bird, *Born Female* (1974)\*; and Sara Evans, *Personal Politics* (1980)\*.

For the crisis of the 1970s and the doubts it spawned among many concerning the future well-being and stability of American society see Daniel Bell, *The Cultural Contradictions of Capitalism* (1976)\*; Christopher Lasch, *The Culture of Narcissism* (1979)\*; Samuel P. Huntington, *American Politics: The Promise of Disharmony* (1981); Alvin Toffler, *Future Shock* (1971)\*; and Robert L. Heilbroner, *An Inquiry into the Human Prospect* (1975)\*. On fears of ecological crisis and the damage wrought to nature by human actions read Frank Graham, Jr., *Since Silent Spring* (1970)\*; Barry Commoner, *The Closing Circle* (1971)\*; and Emma Rothschild, *Paradise Lost* (1973)\*. How conservatives and the New Right have exploited the crisis of the 1970s can be followed in George Nash, *The Conservative Intellectual Movement in America* (1979)\* and Alan Crawford, *Thunder on the Right* (1981)\*.

# APPENDIX TABLES

**POPULATION: WHITE, NONWHITE, URBAN, AND RURAL**
(*in thousands*)

|  | 1900 | 1940 | 1960* | 1970* | JAN. 1, 1979** |
|---|---|---|---|---|---|
| Total Population | 76,094 | 132,122 | 180,671 | 204,879 | 219,044 |
| White Population | 66,900 | 118,629 | 160,023 | 179,491 | 189,204 |
| Percent of Total | 88 | 90 | 89 | 88 | 86 |
| Nonwhite Population | 9,194 | 13,494 | 20,648 | 25,387 | 29,840 |
| Percent of Total | 12 | 10 | 11 | 12 | 14 |
| Urban Population | 30,160 | 74,424 | 125,269 | 149,325 | 157,968† |
| Percent of Total | 40 | 57 | 70 | 74 | 73 |
| Rural Population | 45,835 | 57,246 | 54,054 | 53,887 | 58,570† |
| Percent of Total | 60 | 43 | 30 | 26 | 27 |

*Includes Alaska and Hawaii. All statistics are from: *Bicentennial Edition, Historical Statistics of the United States, Colonial Times to 1970* (Washington, D.C.: Government Printing Office, 1975).
**Figures compiled from *U.S. Statistical Abstracts*, 1979.
†Categories were changed from urban-rural to metropolitan (SMSAs) and non-metropolitan.

## HIGH SCHOOL GRADUATES BY SEX
*(in thousands, except % column)*

|  | 1900 | 1940 | 1960 | 1970 | 1978* |
|---|---|---|---|---|---|
| Total Number | 95 | 1,222 | 1,864 | 2,906 | 3,154 |
| Percent of Persons 17 Years Old | 6.3 | 49.0 | 63.4 | 75.6 | N.A. |
| Male | 38 | 579 | 898 | 1,439 | 1,548 |
| Female | 57 | 643 | 966 | 1,467 | 1,606 |

*Figures compiled from *U.S. Statistical Abstracts*, 1979.

## BIRTH RATE: Total for Women 15–44 Years Old By Race
*(based on live births per 1000 population)*

|  | 1900 | 1940 | 1960 | 1970 | 1977* |
|---|---|---|---|---|---|
| Total | NA | 79.9 | 118.0 | 87.9 | 67.8 |
| White | 130.0 | 77.1 | 113.2 | 84.1 | 64.0 |
| Nonwhite | NA | 102.4 | 153.6 | 113.0 | 89.9 |

*Figures compiled from *U.S. Statistical Abstracts*, 1979.

## FEDERAL GOVERNMENT EXPENDITURES FOR NATIONAL DEFENSE AND INTERNATIONAL RELATIONS
*(in millions of dollars)*

|  | 1902 | 1940 | 1960 | 1970 | 1979* |
|---|---|---|---|---|---|
| Total | 165 | 1,590 | 48,922 | 84,253 | 114,500 |
| Military Services only | 162 | 1,567 | 41,340 | 76,550 | 111,900 |

*Figure compiled from *U.S. Statistical Abstracts*, 1979.

## TRADE UNION MEMBERSHIP
*(in thousands)*

|  | 1900 | 1940 | 1960* | 1970* | 1976** |
|---|---|---|---|---|---|
| Union Membership | 868 | 8,717 | 17,049 | 19,381 | 19,634 |
| Percent of Total Labor Force | 3 | 15.5 | 23.6 | 22.6 | 20.3 |
| Union Membership as Percent of Total Nonagri-cultural Employment | 5 | 26.9 | 31.4 | 27.4 | 24.5 |

*Includes Alaska and Hawaii.
**Figures compiled from *U.S. Statistical Abstracts*, 1979.

## MOTOR VEHICLE REGISTRATION
*(in thousands; includes military vehicles)*

|            | 1900 | 1940     | 1960     | 1970      | 1978*     |
|------------|------|----------|----------|-----------|-----------|
| Total      | 8.0  | 32,453.2 | 73,868.6 | 108,407.3 | 149,100   |
| Automobiles| 8.0  | 27,465.8 | 61,682.3 | 89,279.8  | 117,100   |
| Buses      | NA   | 101.1    | 272.1    | 379.0     | 31,900**  |
| Trucks     | NA   | 4,886.2  | 11,914.2 | 18,748.4  |           |

*Figures compiled from U.S. Statistical Abstracts, 1979.
**Bus and truck registration combined.

## GROSS NATIONAL PRODUCT (GNP) IN CURRENT DOLLARS

|                      | 1900 | 1940 | 1960* | 1970* | 1978** |
|----------------------|------|------|-------|-------|--------|
| Total (Bil. Dol.)    | 18.7 | 99.7 | 503.7 | 977.1 | 2,108  |
| Per Capita (Dollars) | 246  | 754  | 2,788 | 4,808 | 9,644  |

*1960 includes Alaska and Hawaii.
**Figures compiled from U.S. Statistical Abstract, 1979.

## LIFE EXPECTANCY (in Years) for White and Nonwhite
*(prior to 1929, for death-registration area only)*

|                  | 1900 | 1940 | 1960 | 1970 | 1977* |
|------------------|------|------|------|------|-------|
| Total: Both Sexes| 47.3 | 62.9 | 69.7 | 70.9 | 73.2  |
| White            | 47.6 | 64.2 | 70.6 | 71.7 | 73.8  |
| Nonwhite         | 33.0 | 53.1 | 63.6 | 65.3 | 68.8  |

*Figures compiled from U.S. Statistical Abstracts, 1979.

## TOTAL DEGREES CONFERRED

|                                        | 1900   | 1940    | 1960*   | 1970*   | 1977**  |
|----------------------------------------|--------|---------|---------|---------|---------|
| Total Bachelor's or First Professional Degree | 27,410 | 186,500 | 389,183 | 827,234 | 993,000 |

*Includes Alaska and Hawaii.
**Figures compiled from U.S. Statistical Abstract, 1979.

# INDEX